Andreas Lorenz

The Separated User Interface in Ambient Computing Environments

Andreas Lorenz

The Separated User Interface in Ambient Computing Environments

Design, Infrastructure and Tools for the Development of Remote User Interfaces in Interactive Environments

Südwestdeutscher Verlag für Hochschulschriften

Impressum/Imprint (nur für Deutschland/ only for Germany)
Bibliografische Information der Deutschen Nationalbibliothek: Die Deutsche Nationalbibliothek verzeichnet diese Publikation in der Deutschen Nationalbibliografie; detaillierte bibliografische Daten sind im Internet über http://dnb.d-nb.de abrufbar.

Verlag: Südwestdeutscher Verlag für Hochschulschriften Aktiengesellschaft & Co. KG
Dudweiler Landstr. 99, 66123 Saarbrücken, Deutschland
Telefon +49 681 37 20 271-1, Telefax +49 681 37 20 271-0
Email: info@svh-verlag.de
Zugl.: Aachen, RWTH, Diss., 2009

Herstellung in Deutschland:
Schaltungsdienst Lange o.H.G., Berlin
Books on Demand GmbH, Norderstedt
Reha GmbH, Saarbrücken
Amazon Distribution GmbH, Leipzig
ISBN: 978-3-8381-1683-9

Imprint (only for USA, GB)
Bibliographic information published by the Deutsche Nationalbibliothek: The Deutsche Nationalbibliothek lists this publication in the Deutsche Nationalbibliografie; detailed bibliographic data are available in the Internet at http://dnb.d-nb.de.

Publisher: Südwestdeutscher Verlag für Hochschulschriften Aktiengesellschaft & Co. KG
Dudweiler Landstr. 99, 66123 Saarbrücken, Germany
Phone +49 681 37 20 271-1, Fax +49 681 37 20 271-0
Email: info@svh-verlag.de

Printed in the U.S.A.
Printed in the U.K. by (see last page)
ISBN: 978-3-8381-1683-9

Abstract

In a world of ambient services, the technology disappears into the surroundings until only the user interface remains perceivable by users. In highly computerised environments, the application of mouse or keyboard is not feasible for interacting with complex services. Powerful mobile computers and high speed wireless networking enable enhanced interaction with services from a distance, e.g. by employing a mobile phone, using gestures, or observing body movements.

The arising heterogeneity of the user interface and the service to control prevents from enhanced interaction methods. The heterogeneity of interaction styles, technology and developer teams narrows interoperability and complicates the development process. A common understanding of a solution and a detailed description of the components and their relationships are necessary. Available patterns for software architectures are rather unspecific, in particular with respect to addressing physical distribution of components.

This thesis facilitates interoperability and describes the design of a general solution to enable input devices to control environmental computing services. The approach extends the idea of separating the user interface from the application logic by defining virtual or logical input devices physically separated from the services to control. The achievement of uniformity of the design and development processes supports a common understanding, and builds a solid ground to deliver tools and auto-generation of source code.

The development process, the architectural design, and the usefulness of the tools were verified in two technical reviews. The complexity of development and the required programming effort were reduced by applying the software artefacts developed in the thesis. An application example was implemented and evaluated with 42 users. The analysis of the source code using software measures confirmed improvements in efficiency of development.

Kurzfassung

Die fortschreitende Integration von Anwendungen in die Umgebung des Anwenders verbirgt die Technologie im Hintergrund bis nur noch die Benutzerschnittstelle sichtbar bleibt. In derart technisierten Umgebungen ist die Verwendung von Tastatur und Maus für Benutzereingaben nicht zufriedenstellend. Andere Möglichkeiten zur Interaktion mit umgebenden Diensten stehen zur Verfügung, z.B. durch Verwendung eines Mobiltelefons oder durch Ausführung von Gesten und Bewegungen.

Die damit einhergehende Heterogenität zwischen der Benutzerschnittstelle und der Anwendung wirkt der Verwendung solcher Interaktionsformen entgegen. Sie erhöht die Komplexität des Entwicklungsprozesses wesentlich und erfordert eine detaillierte Beschreibung einer einheitlichen Gesamtlösung. Gängige Muster zur Erstellung von Software-Architekturen sind zu unspezifisch, insbesondere um die physikalische Verteilung abzubilden.

Diese Arbeit unterstützt die Herstellung von Interoperabilität und beschreibt detailliert das Design einer generischen Lösung zur Erstellung von Eingabegeräten für umgebende Anwendungen. Der Ansatz erweitert die Idee der Trennung von Benutzerschnittstelle und Anwendungslogik um die Definition virtueller Eingabegeräte, welche physikalisch von der zu steuernden Anwendung getrennt verwendet werden. Die Vereinheitlichung der Gestalt der Lösung und der Entwicklungsprozesse ermöglicht zusätzlich die Bereitstellung von Werkzeugen und automatische Erzeugung von Programmiercode.

Der zugrundeliegende Entwicklungszyklus, das Design der Architektur und die Verwendung der Werkzeuge wurden in zwei technischen Begutachtungen überprüft. Die Komplexität der Entwicklung und Aufwände zur Programmierung können mit Hilfe der bereitgestellten Artefakte deutlich verringert werden. Die Analyse des Programmiercode einer Beispielanwendung mit Hilfe von Software-Messgrößen bestätigte die erhöhte Effizienz.

To my beloved family.

Painting by my son Julian on the back of the latest draft of this thesis, October 2009.

Acknowledgements

This research would not have been possible without mental support, patience and willingness to make sacrifices from countless persons.

The loss of precious time with my family and friends was for me the most painful of all. The open-armed welcome and the laughter of my son Julian was a source of mental strength at hard times. I am much obliged to my wife Annabelle for her patience to keep my options open. I am very thankful to all members of my family for their strong mental support and call for perseverance.

I would like to express my gratitude to my adviser Prof. Matthias Jarke for his support, patience, and encouragement throughout my doctoral studies. His technical and editorial advice was essential to the completion of this dissertation. My thanks also go to my second adviser Prof. Jan Borchers for discussing previous drafts of this dissertation and providing many valuable comments that improved the presentation and contents of this dissertation. I would like to thank the members of my committee, Prof. Horst Lichter and Prof. Wolfgang Thomas.

I thank the whole group of "Mobile Knowledge" of the research group "Information in Context" at Fraunhofer FIT for creating such a creative, supportive, and friendly research environment. I am grateful to Dr. Andreas Zimmermann who was an important source of inspiration, knowledge and valuable feedback. I received a lot of input and ideas from discussions with him and Dr. Markus Eisenhauer in initial stages of my work. Many thanks to Prof. Reinhard Oppermann for his advice and reviews of the thesis. Your and Andreas' reviews lead to substantial improvements of this thesis. I also thank Ferry Pramudianto for the development of several input devices for the realisation of the Interaction-kiosk.

I am indebted to all participants in the reviews. You all did a great job in critical analysis of the artefacts under review. I appreciated to receive all your constructive comments and feedback. I also thank all attendees of the doctoral colloquium for their valuable feedback and intensive discussions.

The preparative user study for using handheld devices for mobile interaction with displays in home environments was conducted in close cooperation between Fraunhofer FIT and Lancaster University. Special thanks to Clara Fernandez de Castro and Dr. Enrico Rukzio for their excellent work. I thank all participants in the user studies for their attendance and valuable feedback.

This research was supported by the European Commission within the Network of Excellence "Interactive Media with Personal Networked Devices (InterMedia)", Project No. 038419.

Contents

List of Figures

List of Tables

List of Definitions

Chapter 1

Introduction

New trends start up from the combination of powerful mobile computer technology with high speed wireless networking. The trends in computer systems lead to location-independent personal computing in combination with devices embedded into the environment. When people are mobile, desktop computing using mouse and keyboard is accompanied by ubiquitous computing using remote input with wireless devices. In an ambient intelligence world, devices work together to support people in carrying out their daily activities in an easy, natural way using information and intelligence that are hidden in the network connecting these devices. The technology disappears into the surroundings until only the user interface remains perceivable by users. In Mark Weiser's [1991] vision, the computer disappears into the environment, performing tasks without explicit recognition by the user. On the road to ambient computing environments, this research addresses set-ups where the computer system is integrated into the environment but remains perceivable as computing or control device to the user.

For personal computing, no matter if non-portable or mobile, the WIMP-metaphor (Window, Icon, Menu, Pointer) has achieved the dominant position. Users interacting with personal desktop computers employ mouse and keyboard to manipulate the state of graphical interaction components while sitting in front of the machine. In this respect, mobile interaction does currently not differ significantly except that mouse and keyboard are not available in their original shape. Solutions in mobile computing simply replace mouse and keyboard with other input devices, like a stylus pen dragged on the display, a joystick, or an on-screen virtual keyboard. They address the creation of the same input using similar graphical interaction components like buttons, menus or text fields. The same holds true for other replacements like tracking head movements or aiming gestures in the air.

In contrast to the desktop paradigm, in which a single user consciously engages a single device for a special purpose, someone explicitly "using" ambient or ubiquitous services engages several computational devices and systems simultaneously and may not necessarily even be aware of doing so. Because ambient computing environments are characterised by ad-hoc settings of devices and services in the environment, the user interface depends on the context of the user, in particular it does not have a defined physical shape or fixed interaction metaphor. The selection of input devices will be performed in an ad-hoc manner, either of engaging personal devices of the user or other hardware

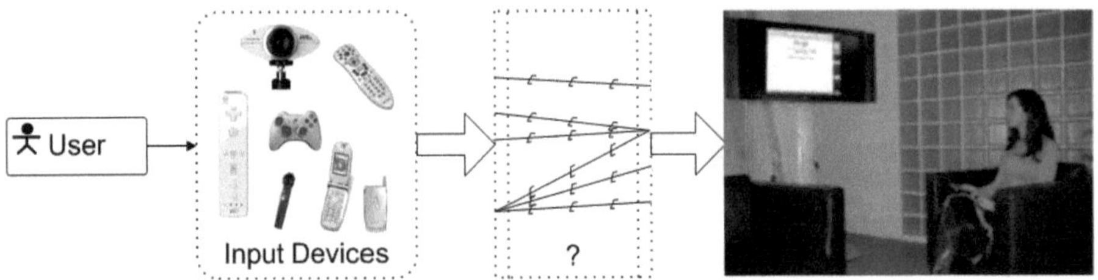

Figure 1.1: Remote interaction in ambient computing environments

devices found in the environment, or devices observing the voice or parts of the user's body (such as eyes, head, fingers, or hands) to conclude input expressions.

Figure 1.1 illustrates the set-up of a user interacting with services running on an environmental display. In particular, the user interface of the computing device remains perceivable by the user. On the left, the figure displays potentially used input devices, whereby the mapping of the devices to target services is put in question in the centre of the image. The achievements of this research will enable mobile and other devices capable of recognising user input expressions as input devices for controlling ambient or ubiquitous computer systems.

Chapter 2

Description of the Thesis

This work addresses user interaction with computing technology available in the current technical context of the user. Three terms coexist to denote such computing environments: ubiquitous, pervasive, and ambient. The research areas overlap and the terms are sometimes used interchangeable, like ubiquitous computing and pervasive computing by Satyanarayanan [2002]. In ambient intelligence, ubiquitous computing, or pervasive computing, intelligent systems continuously and imperceptibly modulate conditions of the environment. The technology disappears into the environment, and the user is not necessarily aware of interacting with a computer system. User input is implicitly expressed[1] or concluded from the context and behaviour of the user. On the lowest common ground on which to base this work, this thesis uses the term *service of ambient computing environments* to label any computing service that is available in the current technical context of the user.

Definition 2.1 (Ambient Computing Environment).
The computing technology is available in the environment of the user and perceivable as computer system. The user can interact with the computer system by expressing input and receiving output. User input is implicitly or explicitly expressed.

Examples: Ticketing machine on an airport / train / bus station, home media installation, projector in a meeting room, remotely user controlled heating system. ■

The focus is on explicit interaction with services requesting the engaged input device to have some specific properties, for example being able to (wirelessly) connect to the technology at different locations, offering powerful user interface realisations, and being popular to customers.

This chapter sets the boundaries of the thesis. It identifies the problems addressed in this work, formulates the thesis statement, and introduces the *modus operandi* of the conducted research. The research will follow the modus operandi to integrate the work on three issues: *Clarification of the research*, *elaboration of concepts and realisation*, and *transfer of solutions and evaluation* in real settings. It additionally confines the scope of the work and establishes a border to aspects that are out of scope. The end of the chapter provides the structure of this document.

[1] Also referred to as "non-command user interfaces" [Nielsen, 1993], "passive modes of interaction" [Oviatt, 2000], or "non-verbal implicit user interaction" [Eisenhauer et al., 2005]

2.1 Scenarios

This section introduces two scenarios to allow the reader to better understand the user's and developer's requirements [Rosson and Carroll, 2001]. It starts with a motivating scenario from the end-user's point of view introducing the use of available computational devices for comfortable control of services from a distance. The user study of a realisation of this scenario described in Section 2.2 was a main source of inspiration for this research work.

The second scenario illustrates the need for support to improve efficiency of the development process from the developer's point of view. It envisions the application of an abstract definition of user input to facilitate software engineering independent of input devices or modalities. In the course of this thesis, other chapters will repeatedly revisit this scenario to exemplify specific aspects.

2.1.1 Remote Internet Browsing

Anna has purchased a new personal computer that she connects with her computer-monitor and the television-screen. She uses the system as desktop device with the monitor for working on her master thesis as well as for relaxed watching videos on the television-screen. For working with the desktop she became a power user of the mouse, keyboard and short-cuts. For leisure activities indeed she got frustrated with the controls of the system. Because of the distance to the television, she is not able to browse the local file system searching for her favourite movies; there is also no comfortable use of the Internet browser from the couch to visit the movie sharing web-sites. All interaction needs to have precise mouse control of moving the pointer and clicking on links. Though wireless, her mouse is not designed to work from the couch because of missing a flat surface to operate the mouse on.

Anna downloads a software application from the Internet and installs the software on her personal computer. With the next synchronisation, she authorises the synchronisation tool to add a small piece of software to her pen-enabled smart phone. The installed software enables the device to simulate a mouse and keyboard control. The input is automatically translated into control commands and sent to the environmental device. By moving the stick on the touch-sensitive screen she can precisely move the pointer, by short touch on the screen she activates links. For entering small text, like the Uniform Resource Locator (URL) of a web-site, she can use the on-screen keyboard on the display of her smart phone for entering characters to the remote service.

2.1.2 Multi-modal Controls of an Ambient Media-Player

In a cooperative project, several partners work on an ambient media-player for home environments. The media-player is intended to run on a media-station connected with a large display and the HiFi system at home. The media-player reacts on five commands: Play, Stop, Pause, Fast-Forward, and Fast-Rewind. To combine expertise of partners, the consortium plans to have different user interfaces working with the media-player for controlling the service: A mobile phone, a small control panel integrated into a garment, a speech-control and a gesture recognition tool. It is challenging to have independent controls, in particular if physically distributed onto different hosts.

In the specification phase of the project it is important to develop a common understanding of the interface of the media-player service by all contributors. The company who contributes the media-player uses a shared interface description language defining the five commands the service understands. Furthermore, the media-company provides a network peer and the mechanism for listening to incoming events. The company publishes the specification to the partners who start to implement the remote software components. Because the media-company used a de facto standard for distributed systems, tools and coding examples are available for a wide range of client technology. Finally, all partners translate the specification into remotely invoking media-services.

2.2 Motivation

A preparative study for this thesis evaluated the user acceptance of a portable solution to control services on a remote display (see the scenario in Section 2.1.1). It generated mouse and keyboard input using a handheld device (i.e. a Personal Digital Assistant, PDA) instead of the traditional computer peripheral devices. The application has been specifically designed for home environments envisioning users performing multimedia tasks without being restricted by their location. The complete study, including a detailed description of the architecture and prototypical implementation, is presented in [Fernández De Castro, 2008; Lorenz et al., 2009a].

The goal of the study was to evaluate the user acceptance of three different interaction modes with a remote display using a:

- Wireless mouse and keyboard (Figure 2.1, left)
- PDA, joystick, and real keypad (Figure 2.1, centre)
- PDA, stylus pen, and virtual keyboard (Figure 2.1, right).

(a) Wireless mouse and keyboard

(b) Hardware buttons of a handheld device

(c) Touching the display of a handheld device

Figure 2.1: Modes for wireless interaction with a remote service

The participants were given two tasks related to Web-browsing activities requiring complex and rich combination of mouse and keyboard input. The usage of mouse/keyboard and the PDA with pen and virtual keyboard were on a similar level regarding user acceptance, satisfaction, and comfort. The recorded comments from the participants indicate that the handheld device was more fun and easy to use.

The combination of mouse/keyboard outscored the handheld device in terms of speed, particularly for entering text, pointing to the advantage of being familiar with the devices. The obtained results revealed that users made substantially more errors using the wireless mouse and keyboard than using the handheld device during the interaction with the remote display. The usage of mouse and keyboard was adopted quickly to the non-desktop use, but transferring it to the special set-up dramatically decreased its precise usage. In particular, the mouse needs a supportive surface for precise operation. Most participants adopted the lap-approach to cope with the lack of a hard flat surface. If they had difficulties using the mouse on their lap, people tried using their hands, the chair, or the underside of the chair as a surface, as the innovative applications of the device by the users in Figure 2.2 show.

More effort is needed in developing new interaction techniques in order to

> "be able to support a wide range of interaction styles, depending upon physical device availability and characteristics of the user as relative level of sophistication for the task, left or right handedness, etc. [, and] support the simultaneous availability of input devices [so that] the user can at his option use a mouse graphics tablet, keyboard or programmed function key to generate the same semantically and syntactically correct command." [Sibert et al., 1985]

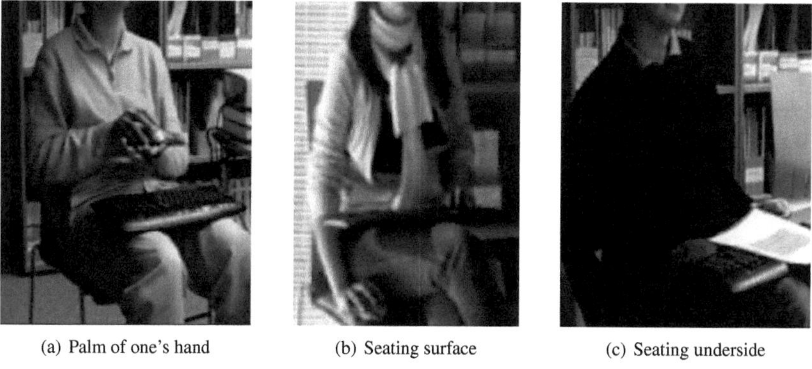

(a) Palm of one's hand (b) Seating surface (c) Seating underside

Figure 2.2: Innovative applications for using a wireless mouse in a preparative study

2.3 Problem Description

This thesis envisions users that are free to select devices that fit to their personal attributes and the current task. In parallel to appropriate appearance (*look*) of the user interface, a critical issue is the interaction (*feel*) with the system and careful consideration must be given to the control device intended for using the system [Carmichael, 1999]. Whether a control device is suitable for intended interaction depends on the experience and habit of the user. The design and implementation of interaction should *not be restricted to specific hardware* for input and output. If the physical shape of the equipment causes complaints or errors in operation, then the interaction could be improved either by revised design of the input hardware or by freedom to *switch to another input device* more aligned to personal attributes and capabilities of the user. Because of task-specific differences, interaction is improved by enabling the user to switch between input devices particularly *appropriate to the task and the environment.*

Current shifts in computer technology go hand in hand with re-thinking of user interface technology. The opportunity to switch between different devices, even crossing interaction styles, is considered to be key to enhanced interaction with services of ambient computing environments. Disconnecting the input from specific devices requires fundamental research in system's models and architectures, because

> "Lots of good research into input techniques will never be deployed until better system models are created to unify these techniques for application developers." [Olsen, 2007]

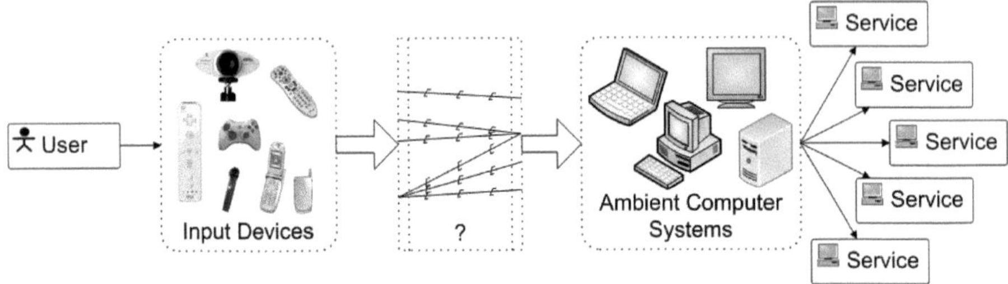

Figure 2.3: Transmission of user input from an input device to ambient computer systems

Current research lacks concepts to map input devices for interacting with services in the environment. The high distribution of modules, high level of specialisation of developers, and high heterogeneity in programming languages, platforms, and software development methods require complex integration for building the final system. Current system development lacks support for efficient development of distributed interactive systems.

2.4 Scope of the Thesis

For explicit user interaction, this thesis abstracts from mouse and keyboard input used in combination with graphical representation of the user interface. It generally addresses the problem of delivering input from any input device to a selection of interactive services. The location-independent remote access is illustrated in Figure 2.3. In its centre, the image illustrates the open question of adequately mapping remote input onto computer actions.

The focus is exclusively on the input side of human-computer interaction in ambient computing environments. The achievements of this work will empower distributing input events from any source to any service available in the environment without loosing its meaning to the service. The scope of this work therefore is on supporting developers in building interactive applications without prescription of specific input devices.

The input device engaged by the user is requested to provide a local user interface capturing the user input, the development of which is *not* in the scope of this thesis. It is the task of the user interface developer to ensure appropriate mapping from manipulating user interface components to user input expressions. The development of innovative services, potentially making use of innovative interaction styles, is also *not* in the scope of this thesis. To adapt the service behaviour and/or to create output for the user in response to the user input is implemented by the service developer independently of the outcome of this work.

2.5 Main Objectives

This work attempts to make a major step to improve human-computer interaction with ambient computer systems. The main objective of this thesis is to establish interoperability of user interface technology and services in ambient computing environments. It subdivides into establishing interoperability on an operative level of user interaction as well as on a technological level of device and software interoperability. One objective is to enable users to operate services of ambient computing environments using different modalities, interaction styles and interaction devices. The other objective is to elaborate technical solutions coping with different operating systems, programming languages, and system realisations.

The thesis copes with heterogeneity in system realisation by harmonising the development process, unifying the organisation of the software components, and mediating between distributed software modules. It implies three major tasks which are all in the scope of this thesis:

1. Define a generic solution to enable remote input to ambient computer systems independent of specific hardware and available metaphors. Enable reuse of the *design* of a solution.
2. Facilitate the instantiation of the general solution. Enable reuse of *technology*.
3. Provide back-end implementation hiding complexity of information encoding, data transmission on (wireless) networks, and information delivery. Enable reuse of *source code*.

In its main objective, this work enables system developers to address users who consciously engage an input device for performing a specific task. It encourages developers to create interfaces that depend on the meaning of the input rather than on the specific input device. Potentially in parallel to current standard input devices, delivered software routines take care of transmission of input not bound to a specific location.

2.6 Thesis Statement

To decouple the input device from the service logic, remote input devices need to declare *what* needs to be done by the service, without prescribing *how* to do it in terms of sequences of actions to be

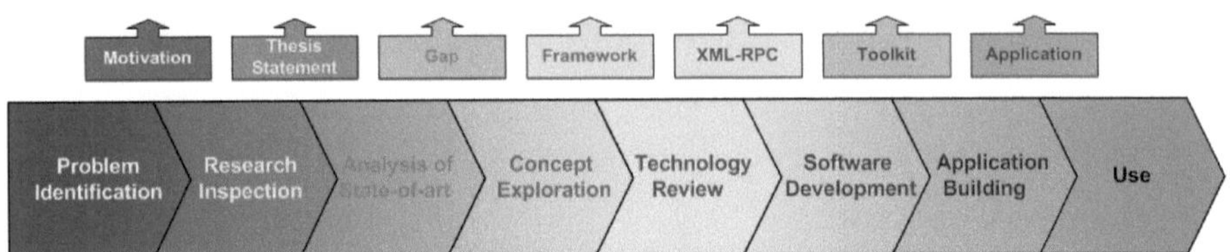

Figure 2.4: The research process

taken by the service, and without prescribing specific user interface *systems and technology*. The user of the service may require to express what needs to be done by the service *synonymously* employing different hardware, software and input modalities.

> **Thesis statement** Declarative non-homonymous communication between the user, the user interface technology and the processing service is key to synonymous use of user interface technology in human-computer interaction with services of ambient computing environments.

In linguistics, a *homonym* is one of a group of words that share the same pronunciation but have different meanings, and are usually spelled the same. *Synonyms* are different words with identical or at least similar meanings. The thesis statement excludes the homonymous use of input expressions, i.e. having the same or similar input expressions with different meanings to services, and the homonymous use of interface technology, i.e.having the same or similar user interface for different input expressions. It consciously opens synonymous use of user interface technology, i.e. allowing different user interface technology to generate the same input expression.

2.7 Modus Operandi

Figure 2.4 illustrates the research process for the development of this thesis. The image shows the sequence of eight activities in the horizontal line accompanied by the output of each activity on top of the transition to the next activity.

The sequence of activities starts with the identification of aspects for improving human-computer interaction with ambient computer systems. The recognition of open issues in this interaction guided the work described in this thesis. The research work started with the inspection of the research field and the formulation of the thesis statement. The analysis of the current state of the art of research, existing approaches, concepts, technologies and solutions was the next activity. This analysis provided the basis to discover the gap between the state of the art and the research goals.

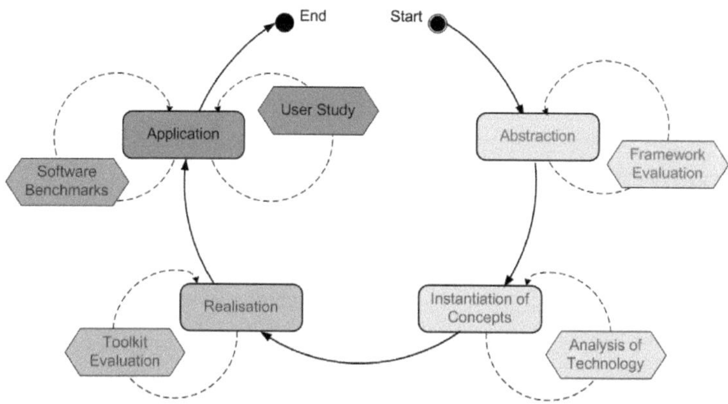

Figure 2.5: The research path

The next step was to explore the conceptual basis for improvements, and determine approaches for transforming concepts into software applications. As its main contribution, the thesis defines a framework for open human-computer interaction with ambient computer systems. Building software applications according to the framework deserves technological support. The development activities performed in this work provide tools for realising interactive distributed systems being coherent with the specified architecture.

The sequence of activities ends with the application of the achievements of this work to build applications. The final activity was therefore characterised by the generation of shared source code for and the analysis of the benefits for software developers, and a real life application evaluated with users.

2.8 Research Methodology

The research path, illustrated in Figure 2.5, magnifies four activities of Figure 2.4 from conceptual work towards creation and evaluation of solutions. The research work inside the activities is organised in an clockwise circle. The research work is represented by boxes, whereas the evaluation of each research step is connected in trapezes. Before moving to the next activity, a cycle of evaluation triggers an iterative process of reflection and potential refinement. The four activities are:

Abstraction The main concept used is *abstraction.* Abstraction is a mechanism and practise to reduce and factor out details so that the focus is on the main principles. This thesis uses abstraction to extract the essentials of the problem and to retain only information which is relevant for a particular purpose. On the highest level of abstraction, it results in a framework defining a generic architecture of an abstract solution, wherein formerly concrete details are left undefined.

On the highest level of abstraction, the framework is evaluated in a technical review.

Instantiation of Concepts Decreasing the level of abstraction for implementing solutions requires the instantiation of the concepts. Distributed system's technology serves for default implementation of common aspects of the framework. The code-base derived from this technology supports the integration of different implementations on a defined platform.

Three different approaches of message sending, remote procedure calls, and applying to the simple object access protocol are assessed in the course of this work based on a list of assessment criteria.

Realisation Based on the instantiation of concepts, delivered software tools support building specific solutions. On the lowest level of abstraction, a toolkit enables developers to create solutions in a defined programming language.

The software tools to derive programming code and work on software solutions are evaluated in a software walk-through.

Sample For proof of concepts and measuring the efficiency of development, an application example has been realised and analysed: The Interaction-kiosk using a set of six independent controls for a gaming application. To assess the benefits of the code-base for generating specific solutions, the code-base is assessed with objective and subjective benchmarks of software quality. The use of the controls was analysed with 42 users in a user study.

2.9 Outline of this Thesis

The thesis is composed of five main parts:

1. The Introduction

   The first part introduces to the topic, the motivation of the work, and the thesis itself (Chapter 1 and Chapter 2).

2. The Concepts

   The second part elaborates the need for support of development of interactive systems and formulates the underlying concepts of the thesis. Chapter 3 identifies the stakeholders in the life cycle of interactive systems, and explains the need for support for a selection of stakeholders. The conceptual part of this thesis moves on to review the current state of the art in Chapter 4. Based on the elaboration of the theoretical background and definitions, the design of a framework defining a generic solution to integrate capabilities for receiving input from remote input devices is illustrated in Chapter 5.

3. The Instantiation of Concepts

   The third part describes tools and technology supporting software developers in realising systems based on the concepts. This part performs a review of technology from development of distributed systems in Chapter 6, and describes a collection of tools supporting the development of distributed interactive client/server applications (Chapter 7). It also describes the extension of auto-generated solutions.

4. The Results

   The last technical part illustrates the results of the research. Chapter 8 illustrates objective and subjective measurements of an application developed based on the outcome of this thesis, and the results from a user study of the prototype. Chapter 9 introduces different approaches for evaluation of software products, and describes two kinds of evaluation: The technical review of the framework, and the software evaluation of the toolkit.

5. The Conclusions

   The last chapter draws the conclusions of thesis and derives future work (Chapter 10).

Chapter 3

Supporting Development of Interactive Systems

This chapter elaborates the background knowledge and concepts used in this thesis. Other parts of the thesis will repeatedly revisit these concepts and definitions, and adopt them for their specific purposes.

The chapter starts with the description of the *life cycle for interactive systems*. It identifies a set of actors in this life cycle, labelled as stakeholder, some of which are directly supported by this work. The chapter explains three levels of complexity to be exploited by stakeholders with different development skills: *Programming abstractions, tools*, and *full access to programming code*. Relating to the complexity levels, the last section defines four software partitioning schemes that reduce complexity and support reuse of design and programming code for building specific solutions: *Library, architecture, framework*, and *toolkit*.

3.1 Adapted Life Cycle of Interactive Systems

The general system life cycle describes all activities from identifying a user's need to removing the solution from the operational environment. It is defined by a standard from IEEE:

Definition 3.1 (System Life Cycle).

The period of time that begins when a system is conceived and ends when a system is no longer available for use. [IEEE 610, 1990] ■

The activities for designing the interaction and user interfaces are not explicitly addressed in the standard definition. The *adapted life cycle of interactive systems* used in this work is an adapted instance of the general system life cycle to reflect interactivity of the system, of which the input part is of central concern in this thesis.

3.1.1 System and Interaction Design

In the standard view, the term "design" covers the structure of a software system labelled as *architectural design* in this thesis. In addition, the working relationships among the components need to be defined by *functional design* [IEEE 610, 1990]. Overall, the term *system design* addresses the combination of architectural design and functional design. For an interactive system, system design alone cannot deliver all documentation needed for the implementation [Winograd, 1996].

Definition 3.2 (Interactive).
Pertaining to a system or mode of operation in which each user entry causes a response from or action by the system. [IEEE 610, 1990] ■

Developers of interactive systems tend to focus on the functions and the technology that makes them possible rather than on the interfaces that allow people to use them [Moggridge, 2006]. The effects of the design of software that interacts with users include the experience the users have in working with the software [Winograd, 1997]. Kapor [1996] proposed an architectural model of software design distinguishing design from engineering. Developers need to think about designing interfaces that are right to the users and the task, rather than thinking first about the way to build the system.

Designing an interactive system therefore includes the specification of user-interface components, their relationships with functional components, and information exchange between the system and the user (input/output). This activity is addressed by the term *interaction design* in this thesis. It extends *interface design* with the definition of the behaviour:

> "When we design a computer-based system or device, we are designing not just what it looks like but how it *behaves*. We are designing the *quality* of how we and it interact. This is the skill of the interaction designer." [Smith, 2006]

Interaction design activities require expertise different from pure system design and user interface design, in particular to fulfil specific requirements such as: Clear mental model, reassuring feedback, navigability, consistency, intuitive interaction [Smith, 2006]. In order to integrate the identified components, interaction design activities have influence on system design activities.

3.1.2 Activities

The adapted life cycle of interactive systems used in this thesis consists of the following seven activities.

Concept Exploration The initial activity of identifying, describing and evaluating the needs of the user.

The concept exploration delivers a set of problems the user want to have solutions for.

Requirements Analysis The activity of studying the user needs to arrive at a definition of capabilities required by the user to achieve an objective.

The requirements analysis delivers a set of functional requirements and non-functional requirements.

Design The activity of defining the architecture, components, interfaces and data for the system, and the user interaction with the system.

The design delivers a set of documents, diagrams, schemes, specifications, and constraints.

Implementation The activity of creating and debugging a software or software component from documented design.

The implementation delivers a set of software modules.

Integration and Test The activity of integrating software modules into a final software product, and evaluating the software product under realistic conditions.

Integration and test delivers a system realising a tested solution to the user needs.

Installation and Operation The activity of installing the integrated software product in its operational environment, and employing it in this environment for satisfying the user needs.

Support and Maintenance The activity of supporting the user in operation of the system, monitoring user satisfaction and correcting problems.

3.2 Stakeholders in the Adapted Life Cycle of Interactive Systems

The activities identified in the previous section involve different persons, teams or companies to perform specific tasks. The persons involved in each activity are often experts in specific tasks of a particular activity. This thesis refers to eight of such persons or teams, which are labelled as "stakeholder".

Definition 3.3 (Stakeholder).
A stakeholder in the adapted life cycle of interactive software is a person, group, or organisation that can cause an impact on the realisation of an interactive software system. ∎

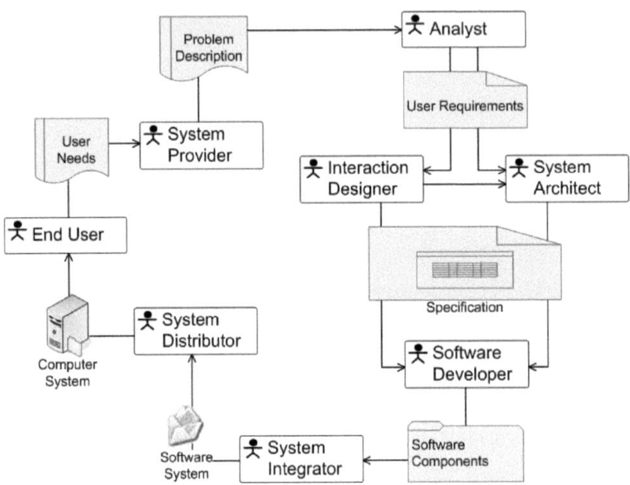

Figure 3.1: Stakeholders in the adapted life cycle of interactive systems

Eight stakeholders are associated with activities from the adapted life cycle of interactive software systems. Figure 3.1 illustrates the eight stakeholders in white single boxes. The yellow items illustrate artefacts, such as documentation, source code, executable systems, or personal assistance, being exchanged between stakeholders. Section 3.3.2 selects five stakeholders supported by this work.

Olsen [2007] proposed the identification of *Situation, Task and User* () for the evaluation of user interface development. The next paragraphs describe each stakeholder according to a similar scheme of Stakeholder, Situation and Task (SST):

1. The stakeholder.
2. The situations in which the stakeholder is required to perform the task.
3. The task the stakeholder performs.

System Provider The system provider performs the initial activity of identifying, describing and evaluating the needs of the user. The system provider usually creates a business case for profitable fulfilling these needs. The system provider also performs the activity of supporting the user in operation of the system, monitoring user satisfaction and correcting problems. The system provider will often perform all or parts of the other activities as well depending on size of the company, business model, and available expertise. If not performed by the system provider himself, the system provider initiates performing the other activities by third parties.

SST (System Provider):

Stakeholder

Any stakeholder that creates a computer system for users.

Situation

A need of the intended user group has been identified. The system provider is requested to create a computer system building a solution.

Task

Create a beneficial computer system fulfilling the requirements of the intended user group, including all or parts of

- Requirements analysis
- System realisation and documentation
- Deployment to users, guidance and user support
- Evaluation

Analyst The analyst performs the activity of studying the user needs to arrive at a definition of system capabilities required by the user to achieve an objective.

SST (Analyst)

Stakeholder

Any stakeholder that specifies user requirements to an intended computer systems.

Situation

An idea of a potential computer system is available. The analyst is requested to define a set of functional and non-functional requirements for the system.

Task

Identify a list of requirements to the computer system including

- Structured analysis of user needs and user intentions
- Evaluating scenarios, use-cases and requirements with users
- Prioritising requirements, identifying level of satisfaction or dissatisfaction

Interaction Designer The interaction designer performs the activity of defining user-interface components, the relationships among user-interface components, their cooperation with functional components, and information exchange between the system and the user (input/output).

SST (Interaction Designer)

Stakeholder

Any stakeholder that designs the interaction of a user with a computer system.

Situation

The functionality and behaviour of an intended computer system are specified. The interaction designer is requested to define the way of interacting with this computer system.

Task

Define the interaction of a user with a computing system, including

- Specification of input semantic and input style
- Specification of output of the computer system and output modality
- Selection of used hardware for input and output

System Architect The system architect performs the activity of defining the system architecture, components, interfaces, data, and the working relationships among the components.

SST (System Architect)

Stakeholder

Any stakeholder that defines the architecture of a computer system.

Situation

The functional requirements of an intended service are defined. The system architect is requested to define the architecture of the computer system that is able to fulfil the user requirements.

Task

Define the architecture of a computer system, including

- Identification of required hardware and software components
- Definition of the structure of the computer system
- Definition of cooperation of components and the information flow inside the computer system
- Definition access points for communication with the outside world

Software Developer The software developer performs the activity of creating and debugging a software or software component(s) from documented design.

SST (Software Developer)

Stakeholder

Any stakeholder that develops software components of a computer system.

Situation

The structure of an intended computer system is specified. The software developer is requested to build specific software components of the system's architecture.

Task

Develop the software components of an intended computer system, including

- Software specification and documentation
- Implementation
- Debugging

System Integrator The system integrator performs the activity of integrating software modules into a final software product, and evaluating the software product under realistic conditions.

SST (System Integrator)

Stakeholder

Any stakeholder that integrates software components into a final computer system.

Situation

All components of a computer system are realised and ready for use. The system integrator is requested to build the final computer system

Task

Integrate the software components into the final computer system, including

- Integration of software modules
- Integration of third party modules, libraries, databases, and services
- Verification and Validation

System Distributor The system distributor performs the activity of installing the integrated software product in its operational environment.

SST (System Distributor)

Stakeholder

Any stakeholder that delivers an instance of a computer system to users.

Situation

The computer system has been build, tested and is ready for delivery. The distributor is requested to deliver the computer system to users, and enable users to run the system.

Task

Deliver the computer system to members of the intended user group, including

- Creation of the installation guidelines and user instructions
- Packing of the final solution, and create installation scripts and short-cuts
- Delivery of the solution to customers

End-User The end-user performs the activity of employing the software product in its operational environment to achieve an objective.

SST (End-User)

Stakeholder

Any person who interacts with a computer system.

Situation

The user has access to the software of the computer system. The user delivers input to the software in order to control the behaviour of the service.

Task

Work with the computer system to achieve an objective.

3.3 Supporting the Stakeholders

This work aims at empowering stakeholders to compose technology according to the diverse needs of its users. Similar objectives are addressed in the field of *End-User Development* [Fischer, 2002; Lieberman et al., 2006], which aims at empowering end-users to tailor and configure information technology to their specific and changing needs. A main objective of this work is to reduce the complexity of tailoring technology by the stakeholders participating in the development process. This section identifies three levels of complexity of performing activities by the stakeholders.

3.3.1 Levels of Complexity

Addressing users at different stages of expertise and development skills, three levels of complexity that avoid big leaps in complexity were introduced in the literature [like Henderson and Kyng, 1992; Mørch, 1997]. Zimmermann [2007] summarised to *"select between predefined behaviours, compose a desired application out of existing modules, and fully access the code base of an application"*

This property of avoiding big leaps in complexity to attain a reasonable trade-off is called the *gentle slope of complexity* [Beringer, 2004; Wulf and Golombek, 2001]. Zimmermann [2007] explains: "*Users have to be able to make small changes in a simple way, while complex changes should only involve a proportional increase in complexity*". Regarding stakeholders like a developer, a designer, or an architect as the end-user of the achievements of this work, Zimmermann's four complexity levels of "Code Base", "Programming Abstraction", "Configuration", and "Tools" are condensed to three software artefacts on different levels of abstraction. The artefacts can be exploited complementary:

Programming Abstractions Well-defined concepts allow for structured programming through reducing the details of the underlying implementation by experts. Consistent specification of basic artefacts allow for automatic generation of programming code in different languages, and use of common software fragments for recurring processes.

The main concept used in this thesis for programming abstraction is the design of a framework described in Chapter 5.

Tool Support A set of tools equip stakeholders with instruments and user-interfaces for specifying the system behaviour, tailoring the software modules, generating the source code, and deploying and testing the prototypes.

This thesis delivers a set of tools to design the information exchange between the user interface software and the processing service, translate the design into code fragments, and test and deploy the source code. The toolkit is explained in Chapter 7.

	Abstractions			*Tool Support*					*Code-Base*
Activity	**Generic Architecture**	**Specification Language**	**Shared Technology**	**Modelling**	**Programming**	**Compiling**	**Testing**	**Deploying**	
Concept Exploration									
Requirements Analysis									
Interaction Design	x	x		x			x		
System Design	x		x						
Implementation			x		x	x			x
Integration and Test							x	x	x
Installation and Operation								x	x
Support and Maintenance									

Table 3.1: Support for the activities of the adapted life cycle of interactive systems

Code-Base The code base offers a large collection of reusable software components to experienced developers. Guidelines for extension and reuse of software fragments enables tailoring the software to special purposes.

Two parts of reusable software components are generated by this work: Unified libraries coping with physical distribution (XML-RPC, used in Section 6.4.1), encapsulated with auto-generated source code available for further extensions which mediates between the user interface software and the processing service (see Section 7.7).

The gentle slope of complexity is achieved through the flexible use of the underlying technology. The appropriate position along the continuum between abstractions, automatic code generation and full code control will be dedicated by the stakeholder's needs, expertise and current situation. Table 3.1 illustrates the support for each activity from the adapted life cycle of interactive systems. It lists the activities of Section 3.1.2[1] and assigns potential support for the stakeholders performing these activities, grouped into the corresponding complexity levels, marked with an "x".

3.3.2 Required Support

From inspection of user needs and analysis of user feedback, user requirements are identified that the system is requested to fulfil. Though the identified user needs guide all development, and the end-user

[1]The design activity is decomposed into system design and interaction design.

benefits from systems that are developed using the concepts and tools described in this thesis, it does not explicitly address end-users of interactive services of ambient computing environments.

Stakeholders performing the activity of concept exploration (i.e. system providers) or the activity of studying the user needs to arrive at a definition of capabilities required by the user to achieve an objective (i.e. the analyst) are also not part of the target user groups. User requirements analysis is a sub-cycle of creating scenarios and use-cases, deriving lists of requirements, and retrieving user feedback for quality assurance. Special tools, concepts and templates are available for tasks of structured analysis and definition of user requirements.

In terms of the adapted life cycle of interactive systems, the thesis focuses on activities of *software development*. As the starting point, a list of user requirements is available. The target group of this work is then a sub-list of five items from the list of stakeholders: The interaction designer, the system architect, the software developer, the system integrator, and the system distributor. Each member of this group performs specific activities of developing interactive systems requiring specific support on different complexity levels.

Interaction Designer

Programming abstractions

- Semantic modelling of user input
- Selection of input and output devices

Tool support

- Support for rapid prototyping

System Architect

Programming abstractions

- Process design
- Template for the software architecture of similar applications
- Data model

Software Developer

Tool support

- Programming support
- Derivation of stubs and skeletons for distributed software components
- Syntax verification

Code-base

- Libraries for frequently used back-end implementation
- Default solutions

System Integrator

Programming abstractions

- Handling distributed components of the application

Tool support

- Building scripts
- Test of the system and communication between the components

System Distributor

Tool support

- Packing of software libraries
- Installation scripts
- Configuration support

3.4 Technical Foundations

The preceding section identified ways to reduce the complexity of developing interactive systems. This section defines the relevant terms from the field of software design and engineering. Each subsection starts with a general definition from the online dictionary *Encarta MSN* [@Encarta, 2008b]. The review of related work allows to render the terms more precisely for the use in this thesis.

3.4.1 Library

The creation of reusable software components, implementing functions independently from a specific application, is a major step forward to improve efficiency of software development. In general, collections of re-usable software artefacts are covered by the term *library*, which refers to:

> "a collection of things for use on a computer, e.g. programs or diskettes, or a collection of routines or instructions used by a computer program". [@Encarta, 2008d, clause 3]

A library is a generalised set of related algorithms. Examples include code for manipulating strings and for performing complex mathematical calculations. Libraries focus exclusively on code reuse [Hong and Landay, 2001]. In object-oriented software design, the term *class-library* is used to address a collection of re-usable components providing useful functionality to others. To include other approaches of software design, a more abstract term of *software-library* is used in this thesis, covering class-libraries as a specific sub-collection:

Definition 3.4 (Software-Library).
A controlled collection of software and related documentation designed to aid in software development, use, or maintenance. ■

Software libraries are the main building units of the code-base.

3.4.2 Architecture

In computer science, the term *architecture* generally refers to the structure of all or part(s) of a computer system. It describes

> "the design, structure, and behaviour of a computer system, microprocessor, or system program, including the characteristics of individual components and how they interact". [@Encarta, 2008a, clause 3]

The specification of the architecture is a major step of the system design phase. This thesis therefore applies the standard definition of IEEE, which includes guidelines to understand, use and improve an architecture:

Definition 3.5 (Architecture).
The fundamental organisation of a system embodied in its components, their relationships to each other, and to the environment, and the principles guiding its design and evolution. [IEEE 1471, 2007, definition 3.5] ■

In software engineering, an architecture is tied up with a specific purpose, it is precisely built for a defined function [Ludewig and Lichter, 2007]. The next section elaborates a definition of the term framework referring to a generic architecture.

3.4.3 Framework

The development and use of *frameworks* is a well-known technique to achieve reusability on a high level of software development. For recurring development of similar software applications it makes sense to not only reuse code fragments but to elaborate the fundamentals of a potential solution first. In principle, a framework describes

> "a set of ideas, principles, agreements, or rules that provides the basis or outline for something intended to be more fully developed at a later stage". [@Encarta, 2008c]

A framework is a set of classes that embodies an abstract design for solutions to a family of related problems [Johnson and Foote, 1988]. It integrates reusable components and extensible interfaces, i.e. design solutions supporting certain variations in the specialisations [Pree and Sikora, 1997]. According to Gamma et al. [1994] it is

> "A set of cooperating classes that makes up a reusable design for a specific class of software. A framework provides architectural guidance by partitioning the design into abstract classes and defining their responsibilities and collaborations. A developer customises the framework to a particular application by sub-classing and composing instances of framework classes." [Gamma et al., 1994]

Frameworks concentrate on *design reuse* by providing a basic structure for a certain class of applications. This work has a special interest in the design of solution(s) independent of hardware and software. Therefore this document uses the following definition:

Definition 3.6 (Framework).
A framework is the generic design and body of a solution for a set of similar problems. It is a formal object that is defined by a generic architecture, tailorable code-base, and connection points in a way that is logically independent of any particular realisation. ■

In contrast to software libraries, frameworks prescribe the control flow of the application. On the highest level of abstraction, the design of the generic architecture is described in Chapter 5. It is filled with a code-base successive decreasing the level of abstraction in Chapter 6.

3.4.3.1 Hot and Frozen Spots

Because they represent an abstract design of solutions, frameworks are not executable per se. Using a framework means to integrate application specific code and control with the modules of an instance of the framework and its control flow:

> "Frameworks shoulder the central responsibilities in an application but provide ways to customise the framework for specific needs." [Hong and Landay, 2001]

The user-defined components usually extend or call predefined framework components called *hot spots* and *frozen spots* [Pree, 1997]. The hot spots are abstract interfaces or methods in the architecture where the programmers using the framework add their own code to specify the functionality of their own project. When developing a specific software system using a framework, the hot spots are specialised according to the specific needs and requirements of the system.

Some features of the framework cannot be altered. These points of immutability constitute the frozen spots of a framework. Frozen spots remain unchanged (frozen) in any instantiation of the framework. Unlike hot spots, frozen spots comprise pieces of code already implemented within the framework calling one or more hot spots.

3.4.3.2 Using Frameworks

The process of framework-based creation of an application, referred to as the *framework specialisation* [Santos et al., 2007], is centred around the identification of the relevant hot spots and their customisation. Because the hot spots are dictated by the framework's architecture, it is difficult for an application developer to identify the relevant hot spots and understand how they should be specialised. Depending on the usage of the hot spots, two approaches for using a framework are available, and one combination of the two: The black-box approach, the white-box approach, and the grey-box approach.

Black-Box Approach Hiding all details, the internal realisation of the framework's components are not visible and no internal knowledge is required for the use of the framework. This approach is also referred to as *closed framework* [Ludewig and Lichter, 2007]. The stakeholder using the framework creates and customises instances of components of the framework, and activates internal processes of the black box. Because the developer accesses static interfaces of the framework, *framework related tools* can support the developer in the composition of relevant components.

The main advantage of this approach is that complexity of recurrent processes are hidden from the stakeholder using the framework. The main criticism is that black boxes provide too little information insufficient to implement more interactive components [Büchi and Weck, 1997].

The black-box approach is applied to the framework in Section 5.6.1.

White-Box Approach Revealing all details, the internal realisation, mechanisms, and control of the framework's components are visible. This approach is also referred to as *open framework* [Ludewig and Lichter, 2007]. White-box frameworks consist of partially-implemented components, where hot spots occur at abstract methods. The developer derives components from general components of the framework, and overwrites abstract methods with specific method bodies. To have profound knowledge of the internal processes is therefore required for using white-box frameworks. Because the developer extends the code of the hot spots, *software development tools* can support the developer in creating object hierarchies and programming.

The main advantage of this approach is its openness for extension and overwriting. The main criticism is that white boxes reveal too much information [Büchi and Weck, 1997]. It may demand too much of a stakeholder using the framework to understand all components, especially if it has a complex behaviour and interacts with many other components [de Bruin, 2000].

The white-box approach is applied in Section 6.4.1 for defining the architecture of solutions using the code-base and/or solutions generated with the toolkit.

Grey-Box Approach In between of pure black and white boxes, grey boxes [Lichter and Schneider, 1993; Büchi and Weck, 1999] only expose those details of a component that are required to assess different usages of a component. A grey box reveals parts of its internal body as detailed as necessary where needed. Other parts remain rather abstract. This hybrid approach enables both code extension by overwriting hot spots as well as module integration by invoking hot spots.

The grey-box approach is applied to the framework in Section 5.6.2.

3.4.4 Toolkit

A toolkit refers to a set of tools, libraries, information and guidance for its application for a particular purpose. In general, a toolkit is

> "a collection of information, resources, and advice for a specific subject area or activity".
> [@Encarta, 2008e, clause 2]

More focusing on software development, the resources are denoted by

> "a set of programs, scripts, macros, documentation, and other aids to help a developer build applications faster". [@ODLIS, 2008]

Toolkits unite frameworks with code-bases through providing a reference implementation that offers a set of basic building units. The framework delivers the design, whereby libraries submit collections of implemented software routines. The toolkit manages the creation and operation of reusable components, but leaves some of the responsibility to the developer of the targeted application as well [Zimmermann, 2007]. This thesis uses a combination of the definitions to focus on aspects of supporting the development of specific solutions from abstract design and shared technology.

Definition 3.7 (Toolkit).
A toolkit is a compilation of reusable software, specification of interfaces, and advice for developing software systems for a specific problem. ■

The toolkit developed in this thesis comprises five tools including advice for developing software systems. It is described in Chapter 7.

3.5 Summary

This chapter examined the theoretical background for the thesis. The chapter explained the adapted life cycle of interactive systems and elaborated an image of supporting actors with different development skills. The description of different levels of complexity established an understanding of the support for the stakeholders. Three software artefacts were identified to be developed in the course of the thesis in order to reduce complexity on three levels: Programming abstractions (framework and shared technology), tool support (toolkit), and full access to programming code (reference implementation generated with the toolkit, code-base, software libraries).

In the course of this thesis, a *framework* for interaction with services of ambient computing environments is designed. It specifies the *generic architecture* and defines the interplay between the components for the family of interactive systems using remote input devices. Recurrent functions are implemented in *libraries* of common technology. To support the realisation of software systems based on the framework, a *toolkit* delivers artefacts for specification, (automatic) code generation, and other aids for system development. Table 3.2 summarises the addressed activities from the adapted life cycle of interactive systems, and the supporting artefacts.

Level of Abstraction	**Scope**	**Activity**	**Artefact**	**Level of Generalisation**
Concept	Define a generic solution	• Design of the Development Process • Design of the the Software Architecture	• Sequential use of the tools: Model - Code - Build - Test - Deploy • The framework	Generic architecture
Model	Support for creating instances of the generic solution	• Interaction Design • Data Modelling • Rapid Prototyping	• Infrastructure (XML-RPC) • Toolkit (Modelling) • Toolkit (Testing)	Specification and Infrastructure
Solution	Back-end implementation for realisation of specific solutions	• Coding • Compilation • Testing • Deployment • Integration	• Toolkit (Coding) • Toolkit (Building) • Toolkit (Testing) • Toolkit (Deploying) • XML-RPC Adapter • Libraries	Java-Application

Specialized Implementation ⟼

Conceptual Abstraction ⟼

Table 3.2: Summary of supportive artefacts

Chapter 4

State of the Art

The research fields touched by this thesis are manifold. The application of wireless input devices for controlling remote services started with hardware based remote controls, like the TV remote control at home, the car locking system with remote control unit, or nowadays the smart bathtub or oven operated via Short Message Services (SMS).

In home environments, the selection of items can be sufficient if the state of the device is just alternated, for example to switch a device on or off; for non-binary states it is not sufficient. The zoo of remote controls on home's coffee table indicates high relevance of remotely expressing specific input to environmental devices. Excluding mouse and keyboard input of a PC, the type of remote input can be categorised with rapidly decreasing percentage of use:

1. Action events like On/Off, Up/Down, Play/Stop. Such control commands are present at almost all remote controls.

2. Numbers and short texts, for example to operate the phone, switch TV-channels, name movie recordings on a DVD-Recorder, or Short Message Service.

3. Almost no usage of longer text and pointer controls.

This work assumes that smarter devices are usable to perform smarter tasks in computing environments where the application of wired mouse and keyboard is not possible because of the usual distance to the object. Smart wireless devices can do more if software based solutions are available to implement more sophisticated user interfaces to remote services. A mandatory feature then is the logical separation of the service logic from the user interface, which has a long history in graphical user interfaces already, including patterns for software architectures of interactive systems. To bridge the distance between distributed components in ubiquitous and ambient computing environments, infrastructures, middlewares and toolkits are available for prototyping and hosting interactive systems.

4.1 Controlling Remote Services

In Mark Weiser's vision of ubiquitous computing, the technology is integrated in the environment [Weiser, 1991]. In his famous example of the "dangling string", the system delivers information to network administrators in a non-obtrusive manner [Weiser, 1994]. In this example, the information flow is directed from the system towards the user. In contrast to the scope of this research, the user has no opportunity to provide input or control the system.

Iftode et al. [2004] identified the need for a simple, universal solution to control different applications in the environment of the user, which end-users are likely to accept easily. The remote device should be programmable and support dynamic software extension for interaction with additional embedded services. For controlling the service, many approaches allow users to design their own remote control by creating new graphical interfaces that are downloaded to the remote device after compilation. Beside haptic input capabilities it is also possible to use speech recorded by a mobile device to control a remote system. Using for instance the Personal Universal Controller [Nichols et al., 2002] a user can speak the name of a command through which this is executed by the system. Myers [2002] illustrated how users are able to select from different interaction styles and devices, such as GUI on a handheld device, an interactive Braille, or a headset that supports speech recognition. The controller communicates with the appliance to control, downloads a specification of its functions, and generates a remote-control interface. The focus here is on automatic creation of the user interface from a service description language: The handheld device is becoming self-programming.

Rukzio [2006] identified four main remote interaction styles to interact with objects in the real world: Touching, Pointing, Scanning, and User-mediated object selection. By touching, the user moves a mobile device in very short range of the object to select; by pointing, the user points towards the desired object. For scanning the user selects the object by hand from a list of available items. In user-mediated object selection, the user directly enters the unique identifier of the desired object, which increases the reliability of the selection. Other systems [like Zimmermann and Lorenz, 2008] added more sophisticating capabilities by analysing the movements of the user to infer the desired object.

In Rukzio's studies, user-mediated object selection was seen as the most reliable; nevertheless, it was often not chosen because of the low fun in entering identifiers by hand. If the user has a choice of several actions to be performed on the item, all approaches require an additional step to select the desired action. For more complex services, touching and pointing loose simplicity in interaction and are difficult to use for controlling the system's behaviour. For scanning and user-mediated object selection, the interaction drifts from item-selection towards being a Universal Remote Control. Another interesting result of Rukzio's work is that the preferred style correlates with the position of the user in relation to the object:

1. If the object is in close range without moving, the users preferred touching.

2. If the object is not in range but in the room, they preferred pointing to the object. The users did not like to move to the object in order to apply touching.

3. If the object is in another room the users preferred scanning for services and selecting the appropriated one. The users did not like to move to the other room in order to apply touching or pointing.

Research in projects like IBM's "Universal Information Appliance" (UIA [Eustice et al., 1999]) or XWeb [Olsen et al., 2000] result in the definition of a set of incompatible description languages like MoDAL (an XML-based language used by UIA) and the "User Interface Markup Language" (UIML [Abrams et al., 1999]). These sometimes went under the term "model-based", where the programmer provides a specification (model) of the application, the display and the user. The specific user interface is thus decoupled from the application logic, but only valid for this specific application.

For development of GUI-based desktop applications there exist common techniques and events that have a clear meaning to an application. For example, independent events like mouse-clicks can be delivered to any service; the (physical) mouse or mouse-button do not know about the meaning to the application. The mouse could be therefore replaced with any other physical device that posts correct mouse-events. Most prominent candidates to replace mouse and keyboard in transition to explicit remote interaction are currently the use of mobile and handheld devices, or the recognition of gestures performed with parts of the user's body.

4.1.1 Mobile and Handheld Interaction Devices

Already in 1999, Eustice and Lehman [1999] detailed the requirements that a wearable device must meet in order to become a portal into the user context such as input and output mechanisms, local data storage and network communication. As a conclusion, any wearable device with the minimum functionality could act as remote control for all appliances. They already envisioned that users should have the freedom to select from a wide range of devices depending on the situation or preference.

Many studies in smart environments affirmed that users can easily interact with their context using handheld devices. Nichols [2001] and Nichols and Myers [2003] presented positive results after performing an exhaustive study of the efficiency of users using handheld devices to remotely control a stereo and a telephone/digital answering machine. Some authors introduce the mobile phone as the user's favourite device for remote controlling [like Myers, 2002; Koskela and Väänänen-Vainio-Mattila, 2004]. Others have already presented software solutions for Personal Digital Assistants

(PDAs) that simulate a remote control, certifying that from the user's point of view the handheld interfaces are easier and clearer to use than remote controls or complex button panels [Roduner et al., 2007]. The "Physical Mobile Interaction Framework" (PMIF [Rukzio et al., 2005, 2008]) provides several solutions to implement the four interaction styles[1], for example to use NFC/RFID for touching, laser pointer and visual codes for pointing, or bluetooth and WiFi for scanning the environment. It enables to find smart physical items to be the subject of manipulations by the user. A survey of different interaction techniques that use mobile phones as input devices to ubiquitous computing environments is available in [Ballagas et al., 2006].

Lumsden and Brewster [2003] criticised that "*the interfaces and associated interaction techniques of most mobile and wearable computers are based on those of desktop GUIs*". They request a paradigm shift in interaction techniques beyond mouse and keyboard as mechanisms of interaction. Using the taxonomy of desktop input devices defined in [Foley et al., 1984][2], Ballagas et al. [2008] structured an analysis of mobile input techniques with five dimensions: graphical subtask (position, orient and select), dimensionality, relative vs. absolute movement, interaction style (direct vs. indirect) and feedback (continuous vs. discrete). The review of the relationships between input techniques gives insight to the key design factors of each technique. The design space helps designers of ubiquitous computing applications to select the most appropriate input mechanism to use in a given application.

4.1.2 Gesture-Based Interaction

In psycholinguistic research, Kendon [1986] classified gestures into three categories: *Arbitrary*, *Mimetic*, and *Deictic*. Mimetic gestures are motions that form an object's shape or representative features [Wundt, 1973]. Meanwhile deictic gestures are used to point at objects, and arbitrary on the other hand is a metaphoric gesture whose meaning has to be learnt before. These gestures normally convey abstract ideas and events. Stokoe [1960] mentioned that gestures are represented by hand shape, position, orientation, and movement In the context of Human Computer Interaction, Wu and Huang [1999] concluded that hand gestures mainly can be classified into: conversational gestures (for example sign languages), controlling gestures (e.g. pointing and navigating), manipulative gestures and communicative gestures. Manipulative gestures like teleoperation are useful and natural for dealing with virtual objects. Communicative gestures are vague in human interaction and involve psychological study. Communicative gestures consist of preparation, stroke, and retraction. Because stroke contains the most information it is required to be distinguishable from the other gesture phases.

Head-tracker solutions [like Kjeldsen, 2006] are designed to work with gestures for replacing traditio-

[1] i.e. touching, pointing, scanning, and user-mediated object selection, see page 34

[2] i.e. Position, Orient, Select, Path, Quantify and Text Entry

nal pointing devices. Using a Web-cam, it allows users to point and click by simply aiming their face. A combination of pointer position and keystroke input device is described by Ahmad and Musilek [2006], using miniature video cameras that track finger position where the user can type or point in the air.

Sweep [Ballagas et al., 2005] lets users move a camera-phone along the desired direction of the cursor motion. By comparing consecutive frames of the camera, it offers indirect control of the cursor position. Direct Pointer [Jiang et al., 2006] allows direct manipulation of the cursor with continuous visual feedback, closely resembling the laser pointer. It enables to use cameras equipped on handheld devices, such as mobile phones and PDAs. It captures a view of the screen with the handheld camera. If the cursor is identified at a different location in the frame, its position should be updated so that it will move back to the centre of the camera frame. The primary advantage of this technique is that it only requires equipment that is readily available: an electronic display, a handheld digital camera, and a connection between the two. Comparable systems use a pre-calibrated, fixed camera to visually track the bright dot on the display [Olsen and Nielsen, 2001; Oh and Stuerzlinger, 2002]. All these systems have the advantages of natural interaction and immediate feedback. Depending on the depth of objects in the camera images, short-distance motions may generate different distances for the cursor to move, making control difficult. Additional effort is required for the implementation of key strokes and text input.

4.2 The Separation of the User Interface

The normal use of the word "interface" is to name the well defined relationship between two entities. To enable interaction, an interface defines the communication boundary between the entities in terms of an abstract representation of each entity. Computer scientists are aware of several interfaces, such as hardware interface, network interface, data interface, software interface, and user interface. This work focuses on the latter one: The interface between a computer user and a computer system.

> "The user interface is that part of a system that the user comes in contact with physically, perceptually, or conceptually." [Moran, 1980]

Until about 1975, interacting with computer systems was built on electronic switches, magnetic tapes, or punch cards. In transition to the area of personal computers, users were provided with a text console to type commands as plain text. For decades, the interaction has been managed without graphical user interfaces. It is challenging for non-expert users to know a wide range of commands including parameters. Other input devices than the keyboard were not available to make the computer doing the job that the user asked to do. The term "user interface" comes into play:

> "The *functionality* defines what the program can do, and the *user interface* defines how users tell the program what to do, and how the program tells users what it did." [Szekely, 1987]

To enable the computer to play its role in this interaction, the user interface refers to hardware components (input/output devices) but also software components receiving input, performing data processing, and delivering information back to the user. The central concern of separable user interfaces is the assumption that

> "it is possible to identify components that perform functions that should not be seen as part of the interface." [Edmonds, 1992a]

With the advent of microprocessors and semiconductor memory the nature of computer graphics changed entirely. Because almost every personal computer has graphics capabilities, the potential of computer graphics to provide an interactive medium was recognised. The notion of User Interface Management Systems (UIMS) was developed for building high-quality user interfaces for a variety of graphical applications. The end-user will not see the UIMS but only the user interface. In the back, the UIMS will manage all aspects of the user interface. It implies that the user interface must have sufficient access to application internals in order to keep the user aware of the application semantics (the application objects, operations and effect of the interaction).

As an important conceptual step in this field, Newman [1968b] developed a logical device ("The Light Handle") for increasing/decreasing numerical numbers by simulating the effect of winding a handle or rotating a knob. Employing any coordinate input device (at that time for example the RAND tablet [Davis and Ellis, 1964] or SRI mouse [English et al., 1967]), the user provides input of a specific type to the computer system. In other terms, Newman constructed a graphical interaction object abstracting from physical input devices, which was a major milestone in the development of desktop user interfaces.

In transition to remote interaction with services, this work follows the path of separation. The developer of interactive systems must create a logical separation between the application and the user interface.

> "Separation lets specialists develop the user interface and the application independently, promotes interface consistency across applications, and allows application functions to be added or combined in new ways" [Hurley and Sibert, 1989]

In the evolution of UIMS four major requirements to UIMS were elaborated [Thomas and Hamlin, 1983]:

- The user interface implementation should be separated from the application code.
- The user interface and its supporting software should control the flow of the application rather than the application code itself.
- Tools should be developed to assist user interface developers.
- User interfaces should be specified using a separate dialogue description tailored specifically for user interface design.

As research has progressed, the emphasis has expanded beyond the narrow question of productive user interface implementation to encompass the entire user interface design process. The next section will introduce some of the early architectures to achieve separation of the user interface.

4.2.1 Architectures

Moran [1980] proposed an important model for the specification of user interfaces. From his definition[3], the user interface can be decomposed into three components: *Physical interface*, *communication*, and *conceptual component*. In this view, only the conceptual component needs direct contact to the functional aspects of the system. On a semantic level, the concepts represent the system's functional capabilities and provide operations to the user for manipulating the system's state. This work has been influential to the development of architectures for separable user interfaces as requested by UIMS.

The first proposal of a user interface software architecture was probably developed by Edmonds [1982]. The proposed architecture built directly upon Moran's concepts. The I/O processors transform physical input actions from the user into corresponding internal representations, and vice versa transform internal representation of processing results into physical output action(s) displayed to the user. The dynamic processor determines the action(s) that the computer system should take. The background tasks are the set of possible functions that may be performed by the background application.

4.2.1.1 The Seeheim Model

Another architecture further elaborates the separation of the user interface from functional code. The *Seeheim model*, illustrated in Figure 4.1, consists of three components: Presentation, Dialogue

[3] see page 37

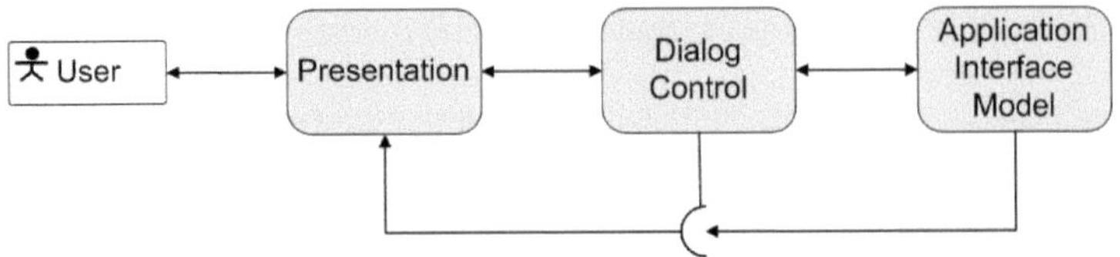

Figure 4.1: The Seeheim-Model for User Interface Management Systems [Green, 1985]

Control and Application Interface Model. The *Presentation* covers all issues for controlling the visual appearance and physical device for the actual interface. The *Application Interface Model*, also referred to as *semantic interface*, defines the interface between the UIMS and the functions of the application. It is a representation of the application from the viewpoint of the user interface. In between, the *Dialogue Control* defines the structure of the dialogue between the user and the application. It receives an input stream from the presentation component and the output stream from functional calls of the application, defines the interaction and routes the information to the appropriate destinations. It serves as a mediator between the presentation component and the application itself. In general, all information flow must pass through the dialogue control, except output from the application back to the user might be forwarded directly to the presentation component. If the data is not to be processed by the dialogue control, only having control on the information flow is considered more efficient.

The Seeheim model got widely accepted as base reference. Most of the UIMS architectures build upon this model, enhancing it with additional features. For an overview on early architectures and systems see [Edmonds, 1992b]. Commonly, the early architectures, including the Seeheim model, suffered serious problems in facing the demands of direct manipulation, of which user's action should directly affect the objects on the screen [Shneiderman, 1983; Hutchins et al., 1985]. With the rising interest in direct manipulation, researchers decomposed the structure of an interactive application into lexical, syntactic, and semantic levels. Derived from research in language processing and compiler construction, this approach more represents the issues of user interface construction than a valid system architecture.

4.2.1.2 Lexical Issues

The lexical level of user input is generally viewed as a set of logical input devices. The characteristic of the lexical level is that

> "it attempts to isolate the logical or software view of a device from its actual physical implementation." [Olsen, 1992]

The lexical level specifies the interplay of three types of devices:

- The logical device: The identification of the device and type of value it delivers, and the software interface for accessing the value.

  Example: "Scroll_X" *

- A physical device: An actual piece of hardware capable of creating the value.

  Example: A sliding controller. *

- A virtual device: A software simulation of a logical device.

  Example: A horizontal scroll-bar. *

Each logical device has a *measure* that simply represents its current value. In addition, logical devices can have a *trigger* that indicates that the device's measure is now important to the software [Rosenthal et al., 1982].

> *Example: The measure of the logical device "Scroll_X" is the current horizontal position, represented as integer value. The trigger is an event indicating that the value of the scroll bar was changed by the user, triggering the application to move the content inside the active window.* *

Of key importance on the lexical level is the mapping of the physical device to the logical device in the presentation description. Some researchers asserted that any physical device could be simulated by a virtual device [Foley and Wallace, 1974; Wallace, 1976]

Sampled and Event Devices Devices, where the application determines when it is important to ask for the current value of the measure, are referred to as *sampled devices*. The other way around, most of current applications treat input devices as *event devices*, for which the user interface specifies the time that the changed measure becomes significant to the software to control [Anson, 1979, 1982]. Current windows systems are usually build on event devices in combination with physical devices of mouse and keyboard. The CREASE-model (*conceptual relation*, *entity*, *action*, *state* and *event* [Hurley and Sibert, 1989]) supports the description of an application in a logical view, which is independent of the user interface and the application. The event is defined here as follows:

> "An event is a discrete unit of communication between two entities. An event is generated by an action performed by the entity sending the event, may trigger an action performed by the entity receiving the event, and may provide data." [Hurley and Sibert, 1989]

4.2.1.3 Semantic Issues

The interaction with logical, physical or virtual devices is meaningless to the computer system unless it is mapped to specific application code. A generalised mapping to application code allows the use of the user interface in a wide range of settings. Two major models exist for the semantic interface, interconnecting the dialogue control and the application functions. Both models are not exclusively used but share components in many settings.

The Command Model In its simplest form, the command model is a set of named commands to be called, often directly mapped to procedures of the specific application code.

> "The command model views the application as a server which provides a set of command procedures that can be called by the user interface in order to get actions performed." [Olsen, 1992]

If the application program accepts parameters, commands can be enhanced with the same set of parameters. This introduces a hidden dependency, because changes in the application code introduce the need to update the command invocation accordingly. A solution to this problem is to pass the event record as parameter to the application. In this case, the application code is required to be able to interpret the events coming in from the user interface components. In a more complex form, the dialogue control creates messages encoding semantic actions that are interpreted by the application. The use of an interpreted language allows to directly deriving the semantic interface from the dialogue description.

The Data Model The data model is usually built of structured data objects or records.

> "The data model views the application as a data structure to be manipulated by the user interface." [Olsen, 1992]

The data objects are assigned with named fields that contain dynamic values of specific types. The types range from basic values (like integer or character) to structured data (like enumerations and arrays), and complex objects. The dialogue control accesses the fields of the data records in reading or writing mode. In object-oriented design, where information hiding is a major feature, data manipulation would only be feasible if the data object provides accessing methods. In this case, data model and command model overlap.

4.2.2 Discussion

User Interface Management Systems emerged at the transition from textual to graphical human-computer interaction. UIMS proposed to separate the user interface components from the functional code. The separation makes user interface development more efficient because the design, building, and evaluation of the user interface are separated from the code of the application. It also enables to implement different interaction methods, potentially using different graphical representations, for similar user input. By using abstractions of input devices, creating graphical widgets, and introducing event-mechanisms, the research in this area build the ground for today's object-based creation of graphical interfaces on windows-based displays.

Because the research originates from computer graphics, it was from the very beginning bound to graphical interfaces on a personal computer. For decades, the setting of the user operating mouse and keyboard in front of the PC was standard. With the advent of mobile technology, this setting was enhanced, mainly by three aspects: users became location-independent, mobile interaction was missing mouse and keyboard hardware, and users interact with remote services embedded in the environment. Architectures, mechanism and features of UIMS that have confirmed validity build a solid ground but need to be adapted to changes in technology and human behaviour.

We stand at the border of the transition from local interaction with a computer system to location-independent remote interaction with systems available in the environment of the user. The separation of the user interface is the key concept used for the design of the framework in Section 5.5. The perception that any physical input device can be simulated by software-based virtual devices is a basic rationale for this work. The design of the framework will revisit the lexical issues, define virtual event-based input devices and use the command model for defining the semantic interface.

4.3 Architectural Patterns for Designing Interactive Systems

The primary goal of UIMS was to reduce the effort required to create a new user interface. As an important early work, Newman Newman [1968a] distinguishes between *reaction handlers* and *procedure components*, and introduced a *network definition language* for defining the user interface together with its links to the functional part of the system. This section reviews more recent architectural patterns to link the user interface components to the functions of the application.

4.3.1 The Model-View-Controller

The Model-View-Controller (MVC) is the oldest and perhaps the most common pattern. First ideas were developed by Reenskaug in 1979 for separating the visual appearance and the user input components from other objects in Smalltalk-80. The main idea was to

> "tear the original object apart, so that one object represents the information, one is responsible for the presentation and one for capturing input from the user. The first was called the *model* object, the second was called the *view* object and the third was called the *controller* object. This gave the freedom to have many different presentations and input facilities for the same object, and even to have several views of a given model on the screen simultaneously." [Reenskaug, 1995]

The pattern was widely accepted not only inside the Smalltalk-80 community and object-oriented design approaches. More oriented to the realisation of large or complex system, it uses a modular approach of three components: The *Model* represents the data, functions and behaviour of the system, the *View* (visually) presents the model to the user, and the *Controller* updates the model on behalf of the user. Each model can be combined with several view/controller pairs, whereas each view-controller pair is bound to only one model. Figure 4.2 illustrates the diagram adopted from Krasner and Pope [1988]. According to the image of Dix et al. [2004], the user, the input device, and the display device are integrated into the view. Furthermore, the image illustrates the use of several controller-view pairs as shown by Lewis et al. [1995].

The approach uses the *Observer*-pattern[4] [Gamma et al., 1994] to notify and update all dependants when one object changes state. The object maintains a list of dependants (the observers) and notifies them automatically calling one of the observer's methods.

Drawing from the MVC approach, Ulmer and Ishii [2000] have developed an interaction model for tangible user interfaces (TUI) called "Model-Controller-Representation (physical and digital)" (MCRpd). This model divides the view element into two sub-components: physical representations and digital representations. Where the MVC pattern highlights the GUI's separation between graphical representation and control, MCRpd highlights the TUI's integration of physical representation and control.

[4]also known as "publish-subscribe", or "subscribe-inform"

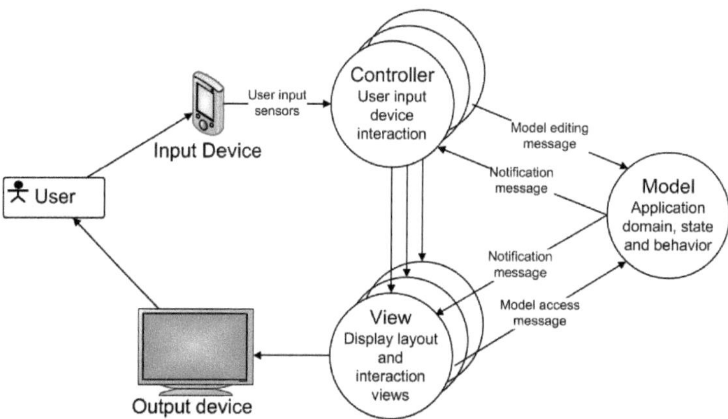

Figure 4.2: Model-View-Controller state and message sending with multiple view-controller pairs

4.3.2 Presentation-Abstraction-Control

Similar to the Model-View-Controller pattern, the Presentation-Abstraction-Control pattern (PAC [Coutaz, 1997]) distinguishes three parts of an interactive system: The graphical user interface (*Presentation*, similar to view of MVC), the data model (*Abstraction*), and the communication and control (*Control*). It enhances the MVC pattern with a hierarchical structure of modules called "agents", each consisting of a triad of presentation, abstraction, and control. The agents only communicate with each other through the control part. The hierarchy uses three layers: A single top-level agent performs all global tasks of the system, the bottom-level agents provide the indivisible functions of the interactive system, and the intermediate-level agents combine several bottom-level agents to a sub-system. In this model, it is possible to support different interaction modalities by integrating several presentation and interaction components [Tandler, 2004].

A comprehensive explanation to PAC and its derivatives PAC-Amodeus and PAC* is provided in [Calvary et al., 1997].

4.3.3 Abstraction-Link-View

To define systems that are used by multiple users from multiple computing devices, the approach of the Abstraction-Link-View pattern (ALV [Hill, 1992]) builds dynamic relationships between the application semantic and the user interface. The application semantic is labelled as *Abstraction*, the user interface is denoted by the term *View*. The developer declares a set of constraints - often relationships between objects - and the constraint system is responsible for finding an assignment of values that satisfies the constraints. Constraint systems allow very high level descriptions of behaviour that turn out to be well suited to tasks of particular importance to user interface implementation making connections between data objects and interactive views of those objects. The *Links* are in charge of expressing constraints between the views and the shared abstraction and of maintaining their mutual dependencies by a bidirectional propagation of events. As a result, these systems can provide a general mechanism for relating or connecting data values and data structures that can be employed in a number of ways to support a number of different application areas.

Using the ALV pattern, the Rendezvous architecture [Hill, 1993; Hill et al., 1994] supports construction of applications intended to simultaneous work of cooperating persons in a distributed setting. An example of an application build with the Rendezvous system is a graphical editor that can be operated by multiple users at a distance [Brinck and Hill, 1993]. To concurrently operate applications in a multi-threaded setting, Bharat and Hudson [1995] use distributed dependency graphs for the constraint algorithms.

4.3.4 Discussion

The Model-View-Controller pattern highlights the GUI's strong separation between the digital representation provided by the graphical display, and the control capacity mediated by the GUI's mouse and keyboard. The classical pattern implements all components separately, which often is not the case in practise. Because of implementation details, view and controller are often realised together in single software bundles, like the components in JavaSwing. Because of the strong coupling between components, it does not scale well, and involves multiple threads and objects. In contrast to PAC, inputs and outputs are processed by two distinct parts of controller and view. There is no expression of dependencies between the functions.

The strength of the PAC pattern is the separation of the interactive system into distinguished parts (the agents). This approach well supports extendibility of a system by adding more agents, and the maintenance of the system. The disadvantages are the higher complexity and communication effort between the agents. In particular the control components of the agents become complex.

The key to the power of ALV is the constraints. The constraints convey information automatically among the views and abstractions when needed. The programmer does not have to indicate when the information must be conveyed. This is inferred by the constraint system. It guarantees that all redundant copies of information are kept consistent. As the main disadvantage, a very powerful constraint system and a multi-process object system are needed to implement ALV. Because the constraints in the links are used for inter-process communication, the realisation of the links requires the definition of a programming language for implementation of the constraint objects.

Limits Architectural patterns do not deliver a detailed specification. Each pattern is more a way to describe accumulated experience from well-tried solutions to a common problem [Sommerville, 2007]. They illustrate good designs in a way that it is possible for others to reuse the experience. The design support is limited because of missing details for most of the components.

In a detailed design description using the MVC-pattern, the clarification of model, view and control remains an abstract definition of the organisation of the components and their roles. Though almost every object-oriented graphical user interface framework employs a mechanism designed similar to the MVC pattern [Booch, 1991], the design of the solution does often not distinguish between model, views and controls. It rather integrates readily available graphical components like buttons, menus, or text fields, delivered from a graphical user interface framework. The ALV pattern is not showing more details than a common Client/Server architecture, where the application abstraction denotes the server and the views act as the clients. The use of the constraints conflicts with methods of event- and sampled devices, which most designers and developers of interactive systems currently are familiar with.

Aim of this Work Beyond the definition of a template to create an architecture, this work aims at the full design of a generic architecture for enhanced interoperability of separated user interfaces with services. It stretches a model across physically distributed devices to enable remote controllers to send model editing messages (see Figure 5.3 on page 62). To increase the detail level, it uncovers components taking care of the communication between the model and its controllers and views. The approach will implement the widely accepted event-device method.

4.4 Infrastructures for Ubiquitous Computing

Ubiquitous applications need interfaces between many different devices and end-user applications. The challenges to be covered by a software infrastructure are manifold, for example Niemelä and Latvakoski [2004] proposed "interoperability, heterogeneity, mobility, survivability and security, adaptability, self-organisation, and augmented reality with scalable contents"; da Costa et al. [2008] condensed ubiquitous computing issues and challenges to ten issues[5]. It is questionable if software infrastructures will ever be able to adequately address this amount of issues.

[5] which are: Heterogeneity, Scalability, Dependability and Security, Privacy and Trust, Spontaneous Interoperation, Mobility, Context-Awareness, Context-Management, Transparent User Interaction, Invisibility

Kindberg and Fox [2002] identify two key characteristics of ubiquitous computing systems: Physical integration and spontaneous interoperation. They examine how these properties affect the design of software for ubiquitous computing environments and discuss future directions:

> "Ubicomp system designers should divide the ubicomp world into environments with *boundaries* that demarcate their content. A *clear system boundary criterion* - often, but not necessarily, related to a boundary in the physical world - should exist. A boundary should specify an environment's scope but does not necessarily constrain interoperation." [Kindberg and Fox, 2002]

4.4.1 iROS

Following the boundary principle, the Interactive Room Operating System (iROS [Johanson et al., 2002]) is a meta-operating system tying together devices that have their own operating systems. It is a middleware supporting communication through the event heap, which is a central server distributing incoming events to appropriate recipients.

Data-Heap The data heap is used to store persistent information. It allows applications to place data into a store associated with the local environment. It also facilitates management of different data formats and conversion of data into the best format supported by the retrieving application.

Event-Heap The event heap [Johanson and Fox, 2002] is responsible for coordination of applications and services. Derived from a tuplespace model [Carriero and Gelernter, 1989], it manages a central repository to which applications post events, and stores and forwards the events as messages. The events are collections of name-type-value tuples. Events have an expiration time to allow for automatically remove unconsumed events. Applications can access the event heap using standard TCP/IP technology.

iCrafter The iCrafter handles the generation and selection of user interfaces for services, along with a system for service advertisement and service invocation. The user interface manager allows users to select the service to control and automatically returns the best interface for the user's device. The iCrafter is explained in more detail in [Ponnekanti et al., 2001].

A running iROS system is associated with a specific physical interactive workspace.

4.4.2 iStuff

Supporting rapid prototyping, iStuff [Ballagas et al., 2003] is a software platform and toolkit designed to simplify the exploration of novel interaction techniques for the post-desktop era. It provides a general toolkit of physical user interface components that can be used to construct more complex physical user interfaces [similar to Greenberg and Fitchett, 2001; Marquardt and Greenberg, 2007]. The system is compatible with many platforms and programming languages, and highly extensible by integration of the components based on the iROS middleware. Nevertheless, the iStuff hardware is usually too large to be integrated into devices of daily use.

The derived architecture "iStuffMobile" [Ballagas et al., 2007] is a platform combining (physical) sensor enhanced mobile phones and interactive spaces. The mobile phone is then capable of sensing (local) user activity (e.g. key pressed) that is posted as events on the heap.

4.4.3 EIToolkit

The EIToolkit [Holleis, 2009] is a platform to combine devices and implementations with a variety of different underlying technologies. Similar to the event heap of the iROS platform, it defines a common communication area to exchange information between input devices and service to control in a distributed setting. Connectors between interaction devices and services are implemented by stubs, similar to the notion of a proxy or a driver for a specific device. The design unifies the protocol for information exchange with the communication board for both the interaction device and the service. Though the stubs encapsulate all the information needed to communicate with the service they represent, the semantics of this information is not well represented.

4.4.4 BEACH

The BEACH application model and framework [Tandler, 2001, 2004] provides the functionality for synchronous cooperation and interaction with room elements with integrated information technology. "BEACH", the Basic Environment for Active Collaboration with Hypermedia, provides the software infrastructure for environments supporting synchronous collaboration with many different devices. It offers a user interface that also fits to the needs of devices that have no mouse or keyboard, and which require new forms of human–computer interaction. BEACH builds on shared documents accessible via multiple interaction devices concurrently.

4.4.5 GAIA

The Gaia project [Roman and Campbell, 2000] developed a software infrastructure for ubiquitous computing environments called "active spaces". As part of the system, a component-based meta-operating system has been developed, which is an operating system for the whole environment built on top of currently existing operating systems (GaiaOS [Roman et al., 2001]). To form an application model, the Model-View-Controller pattern has been extended to "Model-Presentation-Adapter-Controller-Coordinator" (MPACC [Roman, 2003]).

4.4.6 metaUI

The meta-User Interface (metaUI) is an attempt to form an unified ambient interactive space, which is "a dynamic assembly of physical entities coupled with computational and communicational entities to support human activities" [Coutaz, 2006]. It is an overarching interactive system based on the concept of dynamic coupling of interaction resources necessary and sufficient to control the state of an interactive ambient space. The objects involved are either of *digital* (applications, files, services), *mixed-by-design* (i.e. physical entities and digital services are coupled by the system designer), or *mixed-by-construction* (i.e. physical entities and digital services are coupled by the end-user) [Barralon et al., 2007]. It revealed that almost all UIs manipulate pure digital objects mixed-by-design with external user interfaces, i.e the user interface components of the metaUI are not mixed with user interface components of the domain-specific service.

4.4.7 Discussion

Current infrastructures are interconnected with special environments, often with single room installations where users meet at a dedicated place (the interactive spaces). The system boundary is strongly connected with a spatial boundary. The creation of the interactive environment is a crucial task dedicated to experts. The installation, maintenance and securing the service part is a burden to customers in real settings different from self-contained lab environments. The full potential of mobile interaction devices is not explored if the solution is only feasible in a particular lab-setting. The transfer of sophisticating solutions from the lab to real-life settings is not addressed by most infrastructures. The installation of the software at the input device by laypersons would require the delivery of complete software bundles and guidelines.

Limits Spatial constraints and requirements to the infrastructure, and complex installation processes reduce practical use. Infrastructures based on proprietary formats and protocols narrow the interoperability to controlled lab settings, and impede the exchange of technology and know-how between independent development teams. The systems do not provide features for deploying the service nor for creating a software bundle for the input device. The platforms are very much purpose oriented and do not support the understanding and modelling of the fundamentals. They focus on quick development of systems using the platform rather than on support of designing activities.

Aim of this Work The specialisation of the elaborated architecture with specific technology pays particular attention to the required infrastructure. The use of standard formats for data encoding replaces proprietary formats, enables for higher integration of components from different developers, and enables the use of existing tools and parsers.

The approach of maintaining full application servers is replaced by light-weight server instances informing observers on the server host; the delivery of client software bundles to work on small and mobile devices will be a special feature. The generation of test instances on either side supports rapid prototyping.

In addition, this work aims to provide tools supporting development on different level and expertise. The definition of input expressions is supported by graphical user interfaces, code fragments using shared components are auto-generated by tools. Furthermore, the creation of a code-base of components for inter-process communication enables to share and reuse technology on code level. The source code of accepted prototypes will form a repository for demonstrations, reuse, and further extensions.

4.5 Summary

Current approaches often depend on particular input devices and/or interaction styles. The mobile phone / handheld devices are in the focus of attention, leaving other devices untouched, even if considering multi-modal input like speech and gestures.

Extending the approach of separation of the user interface and the application logic, the used approach puts special emphasis on the logical and the physical separation of user input components from the service logic. It aims at designing for a mixed-by-construction approach where the end-user couples physical devices and digital services. Physical input devices potentially run instances of several virtual input devices (for example one to operate a movie player, one to request information from an airport guide, one to communicate with a ticketing machine, one to control the air condition). Each service vendor is able to install, run and charge for the service independent from others.

The technology used should require low resources, and should be well supported for many programming language. The generated solutions will not rely on any proprietary infrastructure on the service host, everything needed will be bundled into a single software application that can be used on any host able to implement the server-role in a client/server application (in particular to open listening ports for incoming connections requests). Proxy approaches mediating events with web-service or event heaps are considered to not scale well if requiring a fully fledged server.

Chapter 5

Design of a Framework for Interaction in Ambient Computing Environments

This chapter explores the fundamentals of the interoperability of input devices and services of ambient computing environments. Revealing the nature of remote input delivery facilitates understanding the process and the components participating in this process. It facilitates interaction designers to elaborate the input semantics, to select the input metaphor and hardware, and to design the user interfaces. The identification of components generally required to build a solution, and the relations between those components, enable the system architect to specify a solution around available parts. A basic structure of the a desired solution enables system integrators to look for libraries, databases and other third party modules needed on either side of the client/server architecture.

Beyond the use of input devices associated with graphical user interfaces, this work investigates how the user can at his choice use *any physical device* to generate the same *semantically and syntactically correct input*. One fundamental idea is to have a direct mapping from semantic events to actions after the receiving object of the event has been identified. The other fundamental idea is that the user interface should be defined not in terms of syntax or states of the service but in terms of the meaning of the interaction to the service. The realisation of both aspects is described in this chapter. It already implements the evolution of the architectural design and documentation in consequence of the review of an intermediate version in Section 9.2.4.

5.1 Design Requirements

This section illustrates the process of defining the fundamental structure of the framework, identifies the components and interfaces and describes the characteristics of a system. The main requirements to the design of the framework are determined by Definition 3.6: *Abstraction*, *Architectural Design*, and *Being independent of Hardware and Software*.

Abstraction The framework is required to detailed describe the generic design of solutions. All components and specification need to be independent of any specific application or intended use-case.

The generic design is required to be tailorable to similar problems. The framework is required to allow for quick understanding of the underlying principles and ideas, rather than for quick implementation of solutions.

The framework is furthermore required to support the definition of the set of potential user input expressions. To enable interchanging of the user input technology, the framework is required to logically separate the user input definition from any service logic of ambient computing environments.

Architectural Design The framework is required to define a valid architecture for transmission of user input from an input device to services of ambient computing environments. By Definition 3.5, the architecture is required to identify the components of a valid solution and define their relationships to each other.

Three parts of components are required for a valid solution: A user input part, a data exchange part, and a service notification part. The architecture is required to support physical distribution of the user input part and the service notification part. By definition of the data exchange, the architecture is required to bridge the boundaries of physical distributed components. To ease the development of specific solutions, the architecture should simulate local event flows on both the user input part and the service notification part.

Being Independent of Hardware and Software The architecture must not dictate the use of any device, programming language, operating system, network technology or other technical detail of realisation.

5.2 Aspects of Human-Computer Interaction in Ambient Computing Environments

Five main aspects set the future directions for user interface technology in ambient computing environments. The elaboration of theses aspect in this section direct influences the design of the framework. Each aspect is exemplified regarding the basic application from the scenario for the "Ambient Media-Player" (Section 2.1.2):

Example: A Media-Player is running on a PC with TV-output. To start the playback of a media-file, the player understands clicking on a "Play"-button with the mouse, entering "Ctrl-P" with a keyboard or saying "Play" into the microphone. *

(1) The service to control is independent of the physical device the user employed. The source can be any physical device that is able to deliver the input to the service.

Example: To the Media-Player it makes no difference whether the user employed the mouse, the keyboard or the microphone to trigger execution of the "play"-method. ∗

(2) The service to control is independent of the input modality the user has chosen. The service reacts to the meaning of the input, not to the way of its creation. The user can therefore select any style that can be transformed one-to-one into the right format.

Example: To the Media-Player it makes no difference whether the user has pressed "Ctrl-P", clicked on the "Play"-button or spoke the command to trigger execution of the "play"-method. ∗

(3) The input device is independent of the service to control and the particular behaviour of the service. The input devices therefore can apply a "fire-and-forget" mechanism to deliver input events regardless of the receiving services.

Example: Whenever the user pressed "Ctrl-P", clicked on the button, or spoke "Play" neither the keyboard, the mouse nor the microphone cares if the movie starts playing or not; they know nothing about movies. ∗

(4) The user consciously manipulates the user interface elements to tell the service to control what to do, with specific interest in reaction and behaviour of the service.

Example: To get the movie playing, a user might press "Ctrl-P", click on the button, or say "Play". The intention of the user was not using the input device but starting the movie. If the movie does not start, the user will get upset. ∗

(5) The user consciously selects an input device, style and modality with particular consideration of the physical shape, functionality, usability, and look-and-feel depending on

- Situation: In different situations, a user might employ different input devices and/or modalities to control the computer system. If the situation changes, the user might want to change the input device and/or modality as well, preferably without interruption of the current task.

  Example: In front of the PC, the user might use the mouse; sitting on the couch, the user might employ a spoken command. ∗

- Task: Input devices and/or modalities have specific strengths and weaknesses. A user who is in doubt about the usefulness of the input device and/or modality for a specific task might try another device. Vice versa, a user switching to another task might want to switch the input device and/or modality as well.

  Example: For starting the playback, the user might employ the speech recognition - for browsing the file system searching a movie, the user might switch to the mouse. ∗

- Preferences: Users might select input devices and/or modalities just because of personal feelings, habits, interests, joy, experiences, or concerns.

  Example: The user might find it strange to chat with a computer system and prefer to use mouse or keyboard if possible. ∗

- Capabilities: Users might reject specific input devices and/or modalities because of personal ability to operate it.

  Example: A physical impaired user might not be able to operate a mouse but capable of speech. ∗

The five aspects have influence on the design of the framework. Aspects (1) and (2) enable the physical separation of user interface and service without prescribing specific user interface technology. Aspect (3) enables the use of pure input devices without prescribing how to do it in terms of sequences of actions to be taken by the service. Aspect (4) requests to declare the meaning of executable actions and the effect of the user interaction. Aspect (5) requests to express what needs to be done by the service synonymously employing different hardware, software and input modalities.

5.3 Design Decisions

Figure 5.1 illustrates five design decisions for using remote input devices together with services of ambient computing environments. These decisions separate the input channel of the user interface from the output channel of the service. They set the channels for feedback to the user interaction for the local user interface and for the ambient service. The last two decisions address the format of the data transmission and the way of information exchange.

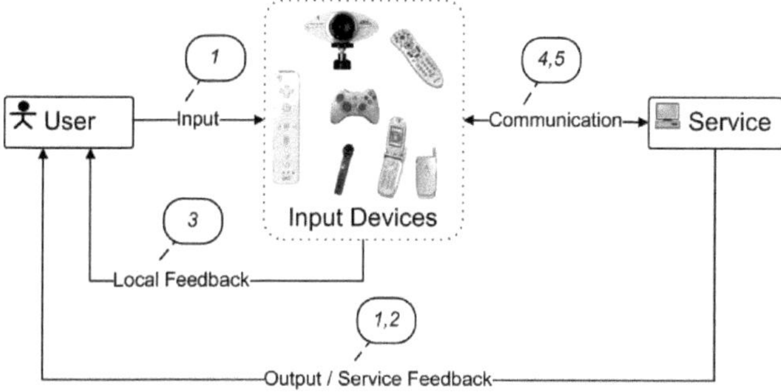

Figure 5.1: Visualisation of the five design decisions

(1) Pure Input Devices Input devices are the physical counterpart engaged by the user to express the demands to the service. They define pure input devices, which are not required to handle or render output on behalf of the service to control. Some input devices, like gesture or speech recognition tools, might not have the capabilities to render specific output appropriate.

Example: The user expresses the demand to start the playback of a video. The ambient media application to control starts to render the audio and the video output, regardless of the input device. ∗

If this rule is violated, it cannot be assured that the output is delivered to the user. If the employed input device is not able to render the output, the behaviour of the service to control is potentially becoming inconsistent.

(2) Direct Feedback from the Service to the User Common rules for good interaction design recommend response to the user on the internal state of an application and progress. The feedback from the service is sent to the user, not to the input device. Again, some input devices might not supply the capabilities to render a specific type of feedback.

Example: The user expresses the demand to start the playback of a video. The ambient media application to control cannot start playback because no video file is loaded. A visual error message appears on the screen of the service, not at the input device. ∗

If this rule is violated, the service becomes dependent on the user interface of the input device. The user interface is not interchangeable with another implementation or modality without updating the service.

(3) Local Feedback from the User Interface In realisation of the interaction design, input devices are free to provide own feedback to the user. This feedback must be independent of the service of the ambient computing environment and its internal logic.

Example: The user activates a button on the mobile phone to express the demand to start the playback of a video. The local user interface highlights the corresponding icon on the display to acknowledge the user activity. *

If this rule is violated, an input device becomes dependent on the service to deliver the feedback that might be necessary to operate or understand the local user interface.

(4) Post Discrete Events Some user interaction approaches analyse continuous streams of data, such as audio or video data, in order to recognise the user input. A recognition engine searches the data stream for specific patterns with special meanings of input. The continuous stream is therefore transformed into discrete input events. The service to control does not respond to the continuous stream; it is triggered by discrete input events from the recognition engine.

Example: The user performs a thumb-up gesture to increase the volume of the playback of a video. A camera observes the movements. When a gesture is identified, the gesture recognition tool delivers the associated event to the ambient media application to control, not the video stream captured by the camera. *

If this rule is violated, i.e. if the service of the ambient computing environment performs recognition of events, then the input device becomes dependent on the internal logic of the service to control for performing the recognition process.

(5) Bi-directional Client/Server Communication The realisation of the client/server approach must provide a bi-directional communication channel. The direction from the client device to the device to control is needed to deliver the user input. The direction back to the client device is requested to retrieve the status of the data transmission and event consumption. Because of the first three design decisions, the channel back is an internal channel of the client/server approach. It is not open to the service logic for sending feedback or service output.

Example: The user expresses the demand to start the playback of a video. The input device posts the event to the ambient media application to control. If the service does not deliver an answer, the input device re-posts the event assuming that the service did not receive the first copy. After the input device received the acknowledgement from the service, it displays the success message at the display. *

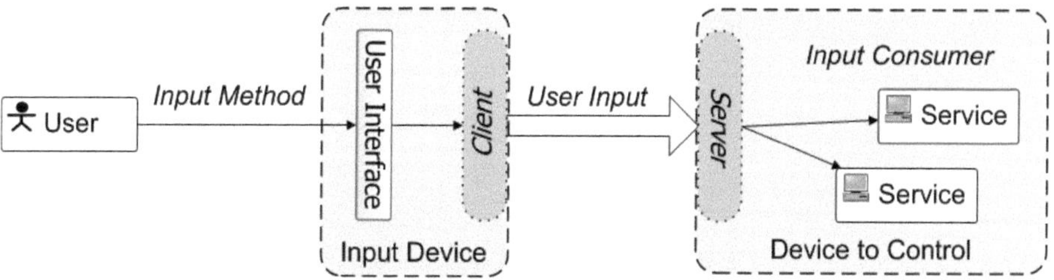

Figure 5.2: The technical components

If this rule is violated, the user interface is not able to identify success or failure of the event delivery. Furthermore, the user interface cannot inform the user about the current status of input processing.

5.4 Identification of Technical Components

This section identifies the technical components required for the architectural design. Figure 5.2 illustrates their places in the process.

5.4.1 Hardware Components

From the hardware perspective, the system boundary encapsulates two devices interconnected by a network channel. One device hosts the user interface for expressing user demands, and the other device hosts the service to control. The device engaged by the user is labelled as *input device* in this thesis; the host of the services of the ambient computing environment is labelled as *device to control.* Because of physical separation, both hardware components are connected with each other by a network channel. In case of a single device hosting both the user interface and the service, they must also use the network channel encapsulated by the system hardware boundary.

Definition 5.1 (Input Device).

The computing device that the user engages to control a service. A user interface realisation is running on the input device as the counterpart of the user interaction.

Examples: Mobile phone, laptop, microphone, traditional computer systems. ■

Definition 5.2 (Device to Control).

The computing device that is available in the current technical environment of the user. A controllable application is running on the device to control as the final recipient of the user interaction.

Examples: Small items providing information (sensors), output devices (displays, speakers), traditional computer systems. ■

Coupling of Devices The approach assumes that the communication peers are known. In future environments with a high number of interactive items in the environment of the user, the decision to couple an input device with the computing environment should be in control of the user. The hosts of available services of ambient computing environments can be made perceivable by the user for example by scanning [Rukzio, 2006], by spotting on interactive objects [Jentsch, 2009], or by augmentation of a camera image [Reiners, 2009]. Metaphors for the exploration of interactive items in the environment are described in [Reiners et al., 2009].

5.4.2 Software Components

From the software perspective, the system boundary encapsulates five software components. One component resides on the input device to realise the user interface. The user engages this realisation of the input method to express the demands to the service of the ambient computing environment. The recognised input expression is delivered by internal communication between a client component residing at the input device and a server component residing at the device to control.

Definition 5.3 (Input Method).
An abstract definition of a way to express input from the user to the service, including the modality used with the input device. The potential meaning, interpretation and reaction depend on the service implementation.

Examples: Common GUI-based methods (for example clicking a certain button), voice commands (like spoken word "up"), gestures (like "Thumb up") or any other method. The examples could be interpreted to increase the volume by an audio player, but other services could implement their own interpretation (for example to move the cursor upwards). ■

Definition 5.4 (User Interface).
A realisation of an input method. It covers the hardware and software available to the user to operate the system. The user interface is supposed to adhere to common usability guidelines.

Examples: A button of a GUI, a voice recognition tool, a gesture recognition engine. The system's interpretation of activating a specific feature must be predictable by the user, e.g. to increase the volume by an audio player. ■

Definition 5.5 (Client).
The role of the information provider in the client/server approach. The client is the application running on the input device, receiving input from the user interface and delivering the input in a feasible manner to the event-consumer.

Examples: Networked adapter, TCP/IP-Socket, Web-Client. ■

Definition 5.6 (Server).
The role of an information receiver in the client/server approach. The server is the application running on the device to control informing dependants on user input.

Examples: Networked adapter, TCP/IP-Socket listener, Web-Server. ■

Definition 5.7 (Ambient Service).
An interactive application (short *service*) running on any device to control. The user consciously interacts with the service in order to get information, adjust settings or control the behaviour.

Examples: A GUI-based application, multi-media station, automatic home application, ticketing machine, airport information system. ■

Data Transmission Components Additional software components are required for data transmission from the client to the server. The user input determines the information exchanged between the distributed components. Usually, the ambient service is the input processor; however the consumption of the user input might trigger transforming and posting it at cascading internal mechanisms, for example implemented by proxies. The process terminates when all input processors finish performing the user input.

Definition 5.8 (User Input).
The object delivered by the client to the server. The object has a source, a specific type and additionally contains object-specific data.

Examples: Button clicks, keyboard strokes, or mouse movements. The object include additional information like the character assigned with a pressed key or the position where a mouse click occurred. ■

Definition 5.9 (Input Processor).
The component processing the user input. ■

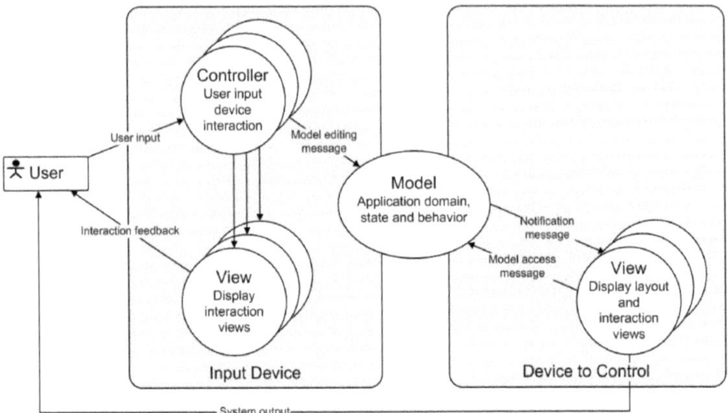

Figure 5.3: Adopted Model-View-Controller

5.5 Specification of the Framework

From the user perspective, the system boundary encapsulates a user interface realisation and an ambient service, perceived like a single interactive application. In accordance with the five design decisions, the specification of the framework identifies the required components of a system realisation, defines the relationships between the components, and illustrates the control flow within the system.

The key concept used in this thesis for the design of the generic framework is *separation*. The user interface components are logically and physically separated from the internal logic of the service of ambient computing environments. Vice versa, the service logic is decoupled from the realised interaction metaphor and used interaction style. The architectural design in this work extends the Model-View-Controller pattern (MVC, see Section 4.3.1) for separating the user interface from the application logic.

In the first step, the extended concept separates the input elements, i.e. the controller of the MVC-approach, from the physical device and location of the host of the service of the ambient computing environment. This allows to move the controller to any computing device able to connect to the model and the view. Like for the MVC-approach, several controllers can connect to one service, potentially using different interaction metaphors for receiving input from the user.

The model is *stretched* over the physical devices, virtually bridging the hardware boundaries in Figure 5.3. It receives model editing messages from the controller residing at an input device, and triggers notification messages to the application. The visual appearance and physical device of the presenta-

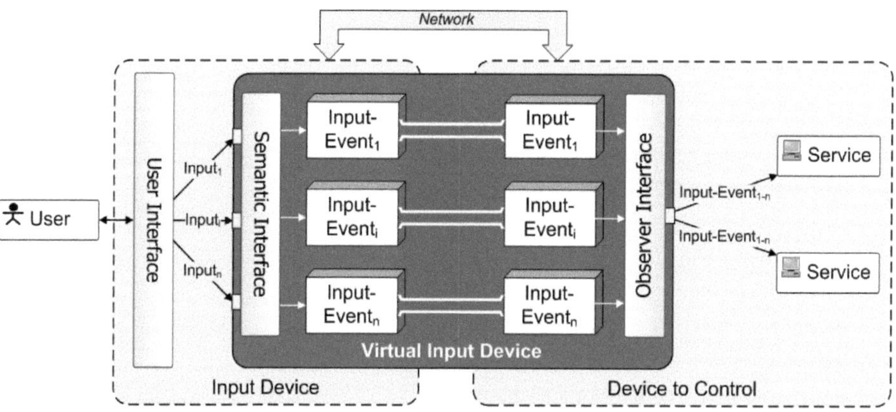

Figure 5.4: The framework

tion of the application, i.e. the views of the application, are designedly left untouched. Additional views appear on the input device in order to implement local feedback to the user. The hardware of the host of the controller, and its software realisation play a minor role. The source of the input remains abstract and is therefore labelled as "*virtual*" in this document.

Figure 5.4 illustrates the derived architecture of the framework. In the centre of this image, the *virtual input device* spreads across both hardware components, covers the input events and introduces virtual event delivery mechanisms. The system boundary of the virtual input device is denoted by the grey box in the background of the image. The hot spots of the framework, where programmers add their own code to add the functionality specific to their own project, are illustrated as small rectangles at the left and right border of the box representing the virtual input device.

Definition 5.10 (Virtual Input Device).
A virtual input device is a source of meaningful user input without constraints for physical shape of the device, type of user interface or interaction style. ■

In terms of the lexical issues of Section 4.2.1.2, the realisation of a virtual input device is a software simulating logical devices implemented by the user interface software. The next section identifies the components of virtual input devices.

5.5.1 Components

A virtual input device covers three main components: The definition of the input event, a semantic interface and an observer interface. The user interface is not part of the specification of the virtual input device because it addresses a specific realisation of an input method. Moreover, any user interface realisation accesses a software realisation of a virtual input device.

5.5.1.1 The Input Event

The delivery of an *input event* covered by a virtual input device is equal to the propagation of a model editing message in the stretched MVC-approach.

Definition 5.11 (Input Event).
An input event is a named command to be called by the user interface in order to get actions performed. Each input event has a name, an identifier of the source device, and a list of parameters to update the model of the application. ■

The name of the event defines a logical input device. The source of the input event usually is the software realisation of the virtual input device, or an identifier of the user interface or user interface component. The host of the component stated as the event source represents the physical input device creating the value. Noticeably, it is not necessarily the device engaged by the user if a proxy approach is applied.

5.5.1.2 The Semantic Interface

The input events determine the hot spots of the framework. They depend on the model of the virtual input device and must be implemented to specialise the framework. The implementation can either be done manually, by integrating a shared code-base, or automatically derived by tools. To facilitate a single point of implementation, the *semantic interface* comprises a set of methods for all input events defined by the model of the virtual input device. The activity of defining the semantic interface is labelled as *semantic modelling* in this thesis.

The semantic interface might be directly derived from the application programming interface of a specific service. However, to not depend on a specific service implementation, the semantic interface should rather define the user expressions valid for several instances of the same type of service. Furthermore, the semantic interface might be completely independent of any application interface model, for example defining pointer movements and pointer selections consumed by any graphical user interface.

Definition 5.12 (Semantic Interface).
The semantic interface defines the interface between the user interface software and the functions of a virtual input device. ■

The software realisation of the semantic interface is the unique point for user interface software to access the software realisation of a virtual input device. This work distinguishes five different types of client implementations accessing the semantic interface, depending on their location and behaviour.

Local Client The client implementation accessing the semantic interface resides at the same host as the server part.

Example: A traditional mouse driver. $*$

Remote Client The client implementation accessing the semantic interface resides at another host than the server part.

Example: An application mapping finger movements on an interactive table to movements of a remote mouse pointer. $*$

Location-independent Client A special case of the remote client. The location of the remote client implementation is not relevant, and might not be known by the server part. The location of the client remains unchanged while accessing the semantic interface.

Example: An application mapping finger movements on the touch-pad of a laptop to movements of a remote mouse pointer. The laptop can connect to systems at different locations but is not moved while the mouse pointer is controlled. $*$

Mobile Client A special case of the location-independent client. The location of the client implementation might change unpredictably while accessing the semantic interface, and without explicit notification. Special handling is needed when the technical context changes due to the movement.

Example: An application mapping pen movements on a touch-sensitive screen of a mobile phone to movements of a remote mouse pointer. The mobile phone can be moved to another place while the mouse pointer is controlled. The control migrates to the closest available system. $*$

Proxy Client A special case of one the three types above, where the client implementation is not linked directly with the input method. The proxy client receives events from the user interface software and forwards the events to remote services on behalf of the user interface.

Example: An application receiving the outcome from a gesture recognition tool, which is connected with a camera. The application distributes the commands on behalf of the recognition tool. ∗

5.5.1.3 The Observer Interface

This work adheres to the observer pattern of Gamma et al. [1994] for notification of dependants on input events. The *observer interface* provides the mechanism to register services of ambient computing environments as dependants, and notify them if state changed. It is the hot spot of the framework at the server side.

Definition 5.13 (Observer Interface).
The observer interface defines the interface between the virtual input device and the dependants on the user input. ■

This work distinguishes six different types of server instances implementing the observer interface, depending on their behaviour and instantiation process, four of which are illustrated in Figure 5.5. The last three approaches are derived from the proxy approach.

Single Server Single active objects use dedicated server instances. Usually, it is one single service receiving specific input from single or multiply clients. There is a single processing line on the server. Dedicated services allocate unique communication ports. The server exits when the processor exits.

Example: A single movie player application waiting for specific control commands. ∗

Shared Server Multiple active objects share the same server instance. Multiple services receive input from multiple clients. Different input devices access fixed communication ports. The server instance branches into different processing threads inside a single process. The server exits when the last processor exits. The shared server can be simulated using a single server instance and registering several dependants at the observer-interface.

Example: A multi-media application switching between media players. ∗

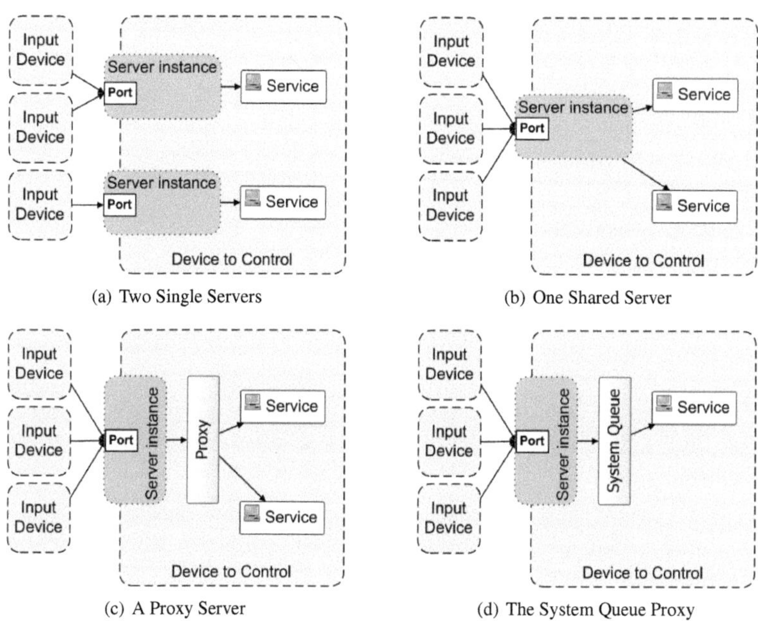

(a) Two Single Servers

(b) One Shared Server

(c) A Proxy Server

(d) The System Queue Proxy

Figure 5.5: Server types

Proxy Server A special case of a single or a shared server, where the dependants do not directly receive the events from the server instance. Only the server instance itself is registered at the observer interface, forwarding the messages to the dependants, and perhaps transforming it into another format. This approach mainly aims at the integration with legacy code, i.e. applications of which the developer has no access to the source code. Three methods use the concept of the proxy server:

System Queue Proxy Incoming events are integrated into the local event queue of the operating system. This approach enables high integration with standard graphical user interface technology. It enables event delivery to any service already available on the operating system without changes of the service. The service to control must run in the front in order to receive the events. The creation of events is restricted to meaningful default events available in existing user interface specifications, i.e. key pressed events, character typed event, mouse moved events and mouse clicked events.

Example: A server instance that integrates external mouse-events into the event queue of the local operating system. ∗

Short-cuts Proxy Incoming events are transformed into local keyboard short-cuts. This approach enables high integration with complex applications that provide short-cuts to access its functions. Because it uses the same approach as the system queue proxy to generate the keystrokes, the service to control must run in the front in order to receive the short-cuts. When the short-cuts of the application change, the mappings of incoming events to short-cuts need to be modified. If the current active application uses a different mapping, then posting an event can lead to misbehaviour of this application.

Example: A server instance that integrates keystrokes for "Ctrl-p" into the local event queue of the operating system if triggered by receiving a "play"-event. $*$

Application Interface Proxy Incoming events are transformed into method invocations of the application's programming interface (API). This approach enables purposely informing dedicated applications, even if they run in the back. Strongly coupled with a specific application, the proxy needs to have access to the application to control, in Java for example by using the Java Native Interface (JNI). If the programming interface changes, e.g. if a new version of the application is installed, the mapping and the invocation need to be modified.

Example: A server instance that uses JNI to get access to a dedicated movie player application, and invokes its "play"-method if triggered by receiving a "play"-event. $*$

5.5.2 Control Flow

The user interface software instantiates the software realisation of the virtual input device, which is the destination for the user input from the point of view of the user interface. The user interface software accesses the implementation of the semantic interface of the virtual input device to propagate an event, and returns to be ready for the next input from the user.

The consumption of the input event by the instance of the virtual input device internally triggers the propagation of input events to the event notification part at the server side. The software instance of the virtual input device handles the connection management with the remote service and sends the events over the network.

The server part of the virtual input device receives the data from the network. The software realisation of the observer interface manages a list of dependants, and notifies any service enrolled in this list by invocation of the event performing method.

5.5.3 Specification of Virtual Input Devices

The specification of virtual input devices are encoded in XML. The meta-syntax Extended Backus-Naur Form (EBNF [ISO 14977, 1996]) is used for definition of the XML-syntax.

A virtual input device is defined by its name and a list of events it delivers. The event list must not be empty.

virtual_device ::= "<virtual_device>"
device_name event_list
"</virtual_device>".

The name of a virtual input device or an event is a string starting with an upper case letter. The name of a parameter of an event is a string starting with a lower case letter. If the name is not a single letter, it concatenates any digit, letter, or the special characters "-" and "_".

device_name ::= "<device_name>"
upper_case_char {name_char}
"</device_name>".

event_name ::= "<event_name>"
upper_case_char {name_char}
"</event_name>".

parameter_name ::= "<parameter_name>"
lower_case_char {name_char}
"</parameter_name>".

Any virtual input device provides at minimum one event. An event list is a non-empty list of events. Each event must provide at minimum one parameter delivering an identifier of the source of the event as string.

A parameter list is a non-empty list of parameters. The provision of a parameter describing the source of an event is mandatory.

event_list ::= "<events>"
event {event}
"</events>".

parameter_list ::= "<parameters>"
source_parameter {parameter}
"</parameters>".

An event is defined by an event name, and a parameter list.

event ::= "<event>"
event_name parameter_list
"</event>".

A parameter is defined by the parameter type, and the parameter name.

source_parameter ::= "<parameter>"
"<parameter_type> string </parameter_type>"
"<parameter_name> source </parameter_name>"
"</parameter>"

parameter ::= "<parameter>"
parameter_type parameter_name
"</parameter>".

The parameter type is one of "string", "integer", "boolean", or "double".

parameter_type ::= "<parameter_type>"
"string" | "integer" | "boolean" | "double"
"</parameter_type>"

The characters, digits and other containers are defined as follows:

name_char ::= char | "_" | "-".

char ::= digit | upper_case_char | lower_case_char.

digit ::= "0" | "1" | . . . | "8" | "9".

upper_case_char ::= "A" | "B" | . . . | "Y" | "Z".

lower_case_char ::= "a" | "b" | . . . | "y" | "z".

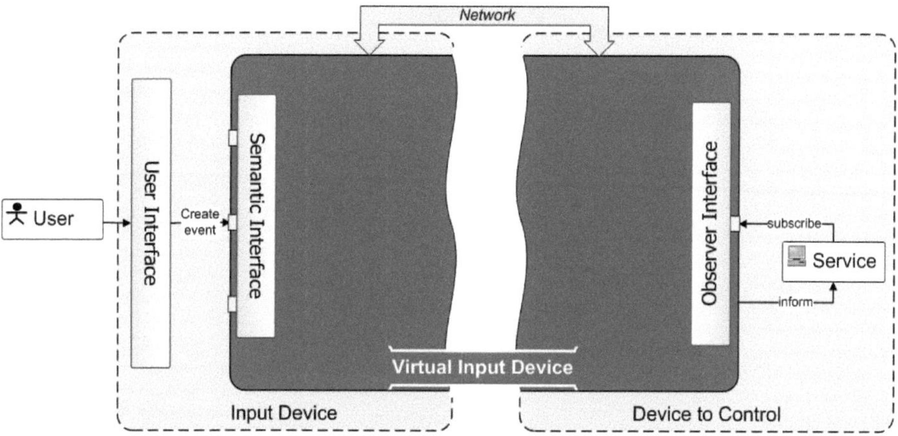

Figure 5.6: The framework as black box

5.6 Application of the Framework

Determined by the model of the virtual input device, the stakeholder using the framework connects the user interface with the semantic interface of the virtual input device, and/or registers services at the observer interface for notification. This section illustrates the use of these hot spots of the framework independent of technology. It adopts the black-box and grey-box approach from Section 3.4.3.

5.6.1 Black-Box Framework

Figure 5.6 illustrates the framework as a black box. The application of this approach provides an abstract view on the process of distributing input events

The virtual input device implements a bridge between the input device and the device to control. The user interface software invokes a method of the semantic interface, and the dependants on the input are informed by the software realisation of the virtual input device. All components implemented to build this bridge, their relationships and the internal control flow are of no interest in this view and remain imperceptible. It is not possible for the stakeholder using the framework to adjust the behaviour.

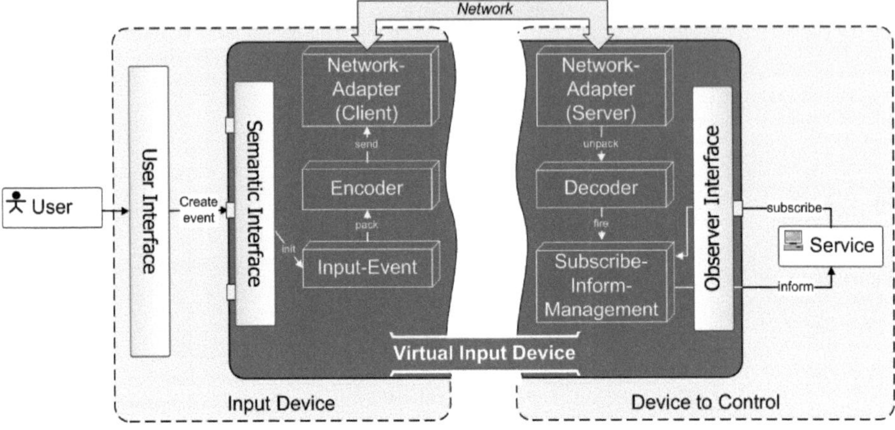

Figure 5.7: The framework as black box with open top cover (grey box)

5.6.2 Grey-Box Framework

To overcome limitations of a pure black-box approach, the grey-box approach exposes those details that are required for different usages of the virtual input device. Figure 5.7 therefore opens the top cover of the black box.

This view reveals the components required on both sides of the distributed instance of the virtual input device. Revealing those details enables precise refinement of the architecture. Though it is still abstract, independent of hard- or software, a stakeholder the framework is able to identify the components that are required for implementation. In terms of a software architecture, this view provides a prototypical architecture, tailorable to specific purposes.

5.6.2.1 Components

The virtual input device from Definition 5.10 is refined to contain six software components. To implement the process of controlling a service using a remote input device means to create instances of those components, independent of the technology, operating systems or programming languages.

Input Event The implementation of a method of the semantic interface for a single measure of the virtual input device. This component generates the envelope containing the measure and its value sent to dependants. The software realisation of the virtual input device implements its delivery.

Encoder The component converting the event into a corresponding representation for network transmission. The process is labelled as *marshalling* in the field of distributed systems (see Section 6.2.3).

Network Adapter (Client) The component sending the encoded data to the network. In particular, this component abstracts from network technology, protocols and connection management (connection establishment, message sending).

Network Adapter (Server) The component that receives the data from the network. In particular, this component abstracts from network technology, protocols, and connection management (waiting for connection requests, accepting connections, and managing channels).

Decoder The component converting the data from its network representation to the original input event. The process performed by the decoder is labelled as *de-marshalling* in the field of distributed systems.

Subscribe-Inform Management The implementation of the observer interface. This component manages a list of dependants on the input from virtual input device, handles registration and de-registration of dependants, and delivers the instance of the input event to each subscribed observer.

5.6.2.2 Control Flow

The user instantiates the process of event delivery by interacting with the user interface software on the input device. The user interface software recognises the interaction and invokes a corresponding method of the virtual input device to initialise the propagation of the user input. Internally, the instance of the virtual input device creates an input event, which is transformed into the corresponding representation for network transmission. The network adapters of client and server exchange the data over the network, potentially using handshake implementation for improving quality of service.

On the device to control, the services register at the subscribe-inform management component as dependants on the input from the virtual input device. When receiving data from the network adapter, the original input event is unpacked from the network representation. The inform mechanism iterates through the list of dependants and invokes the processing method of each observer.

The process ends, when all input processors subscribed as observers have received a copy of the input event.

5.7 Summary

The design of the framework aimed at fundamental understanding of the mechanism for delivering input events in ambient computing environments. On the highest level of abstraction, the framework introduces the use of virtual input devices. The approach enhances the idea of separating the user interface from the application logic with the feature of separating the user interface also from the application hardware and physical constraints.

Because the framework is abstract by definition, developers need to know how to specialise the framework to special purposes. The application of the framework starts with a metamorphosis into black- and grey-box images revealing the components and hot spots of the framework. In both views, the components and control flow are still defined in a general manner, independent of hardware and software used for realisation.

Chapter 6

Elaboration of a Code-Base Managing Physical Distribution

The application of the framework as grey box revealed six components required to realise an instance of a virtual input device. In addition to providing a better understanding of the architecture, the grey box specification allows using standard software components covering most of the complexity:

> "We can use frameworks to develop middleware and to build software that runs on that middleware." [da Costa et al., 2008]

This chapter analyses approaches and technologies from distributed system development for their suitability to facilitate the specialisation of the hot spots of the framework, i.e. the semantic interface and the observer interface. The aim of the technology is to support interoperable interaction between different software applications, running on different platforms, programming languages or hosts [Orfali et al., 1999]. Directly mapped to code-bases for different programming languages and operating systems it supports the stakeholders "Software Developers" and "System Integrators". Software developers are relieved from implementing aspects of distributed software by hand, such as connection handling, data transmission, or message parsing. System integrators are enabled to use reference implementations for specific software modules required to be part of a solution.

To illustrate differences between the approaches, the example of invoking a `playMedia(String)`-method of an ambient media-player service is continuously used. The scenario of the "Ambient Media-Player" is introduced in section 2.1.2.

> *Example: A multi-media server runs a media-player service. A small application running on a mobile phone provides the controls (e.g. Play, Pause, Stop) for the media-player. On user request, the client on the mobile phone delivers commands to the service on the media-player service using wireless networking.* $*$

This example allows to concentrate on the underlying principles to be transferable to different programming languages and sophisticated services. Because of its wide distribution and consistence on different operating systems, all reference implementations are provided in the programming language

Java. This thesis uses the terms *JavaSE* (Java Standard Edition) and *JavaMobile* (Java Platform Micro Edition) to distinguish code for server and desktop applications from code designed to run on mobile devices. The JavaSE source code of a `MediaPlayer` class providing the `playMedia`-method is exemplified in Listing B.1 on page 185.

This chapter starts with an overview on the history of the concepts of distributed systems. It then describes a collection of assessment criteria, and analyses candidates accordingly.

6.1 Overview

The underlying inter-process communication technology of distributed systems allows a computer program to execute a subroutine or procedure of another address space (commonly on another computer on a shared network) without the programmer explicitly coding the details for this remote interaction. The fundamental concepts are derived from, and largely identical to, the basic capabilities of more mature middleware technologies from the area of distributed computing. White [1976] proposes a

> "high-level, application-independent protocol and software framework that would extend the local programming environment to embrace modules in other computers within a resource sharing computer network, and thereby facilitate the construction of distributed systems and encourage the sharing of resources." [White, 1976]

The procedure call model views a process as a collection of remotely callable subroutines or procedures. Each procedure is invoked by name, can be supplied a list of arguments, and returns to its caller both a boolean outcome, indicating whether it succeeded or failed, and a list of results. New model extensions were added to the protocol implemented as procedures, rather than as additional messages. The evolution lead to the remote invocation of system processes:

> "Before a program in one machine can use resources in another, it must either create a new process in the remote machine, or gain access to an existing one. In either case, the local process must establish an IPC[1] channel to a resident dispatching process within the remote system, specify the program to be started or contacted, and identify itself so that its access to the program can be established and billing carried out." [White, 1977]

[1]Inter Process Communication

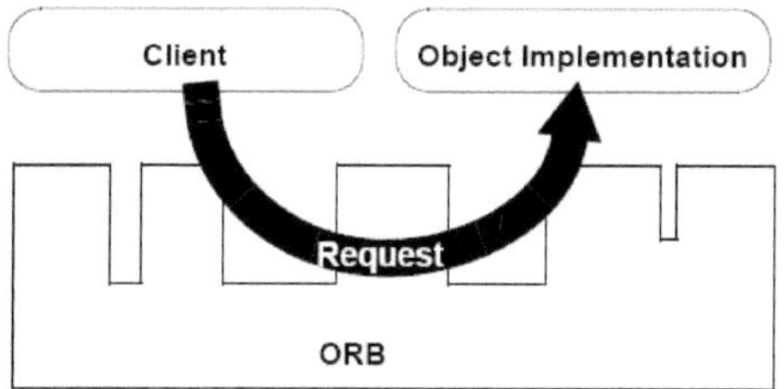

Figure 6.1: A request being sent through the Object Request Broker [@OMG, 2002]

6.2 Terms

The distributed application is written as a client/server application of a set of communicating objects. When the client application invokes a method of a remote service, a registration component locates the instance of the service class, invokes the requested method, and returns the results to the calling client. Figure 6.1 illustrates the basic approach using an instance of an Object Request Broker (ORB [@OMG, 2009]).

6.2.1 Client Stub

The client stubs provide access to the operations of a remote object in a way that is easy for programmers to predict. Programmers use client stubs to invoke functions of a remote service in a local process.

Definition 6.1 (Client Stub).
The client [...] stub provide the static interfaces to object services. These pre-compiled stubs define how clients invoke corresponding services on the servers. From a client's perspective, the stub acts as a local call - it is a local *proxy* for a remote server object. [Orfali et al., 1999] ■

This thesis uses the term *stub* to label client stubs.

6.2.2 Implementation Skeleton

The server stubs provide static interfaces to each service exported by the server [Orfali et al., 1999]. While implementing the service logic, the classes of the services implement the interfaces exported for the server. The Object Management Group (OMG) calls the server stub *skeletons*: Programmers derive services from the implementation of server skeletons adding code to implement the service logic.

Definition 6.2 (Server Skeleton).
For a particular language mapping, and possibly depending on the object adapter, there will be an interface to the methods that implement each type of object. The interface will generally be an up-call interface, in that the object implementation writes routines that conform to the interface and the ORB calls them through the skeleton. [@OMG, 2002, Chapter 2] ■

The existence of a skeleton does not imply the existence of a corresponding client stub.

This thesis uses the term *skeleton* to label server stubs and/or server skeletons.

6.2.3 Marshalling

The client stub includes code to invoke the method on the server from a higher level programming language without taking care of the underlying protocols, data encoding, and network representation. The remote method is simply invoked from the client program to obtain a remote service.

Definition 6.3 (Marshalling).
[Marshalling] means that the [client stub] encodes (and decodes) the operation and its parameters into flattened message formats that it can send to the server. [Orfali et al., 1996] ■

6.3 Assessment of Technology

This section compares three approaches to find the most promising technology for the purpose of using input devices for controlling remote services of ambient computing environments. It describes the three approaches of *Message Sending*, *Remote Procedure Calls*, and *Web-Services based on the Simple Object Access Protocol*. Other candidates were excluded for several reasons. JavaRMI [@JavaRMI, 2009] is not supportive because of its dependency on the Java programming language. The Distributed Component Object Model (DCOM [@COM, 2009]) is only feasible for addressing Microsoft's COM components and therefore not suitable to talk to non-Microsoft systems. The Common Object Request Broker Architecture (CORBA [Vinoski, 1997]) is very complex and requires significant effort to implement. It is well-suited to sophisticated desktop and enterprise applications rather than for interoperation with small clients. Though available in sufficient number, the ORBs differ widely from vendor to vendor. It is extremely difficult to write interoperable CORBA code if important features are inconsistent across ORBs.

6.3.1 Assessment Criteria

Five assessment criteria are used to elaborate the suitability of different approaches.

Development Overhead Any implementation not necessary for realisation of the object's functionality is treated as overhead. The realisation of an input method on a client input device should be relieved of implementing network access, information encoding and data transmission. The effort to connect a realisation of an input method with the semantic interface should be small. The realisation of forwarding the call to a processing object on the server should not require connection handling, unpacking, and parsing. To support the development, there should be a large range of background implementation, templates of stubs and skeletons, parsers and other tools available for as many programming languages and operating systems as possible. Documentation should be available and helpful.

Deployment Overhead Beside installation of the client and service application on the devices and hosts, there should only be a small overhead introduced by the realisation as interactive distributed application. Any effort for installing and configuring additional software including required tools, packages, libraries or application-servers is considered a deployment overhead, if introduced by the use of a distributed approach. For some services (like smart items) the deployment overhead is the main criterion, for other services (like central home media servers) it is of lower interest. The deployment overhead includes any maintenance-effort needed after installation for updates or frequent calibration.

Interface Definition The server skeleton should pair with the stub on the client. The semantic interface between client and server components should be well defined and documented. Developers should be able to perceive all accessible methods provided by the service. For any remote invocation it should be possible to check the message format before sending. For any incoming data it should be possible to check whether it is consistent with the interface definition. Wherever available, it is preferred to be consistent with standards, even if this required a justifiable extra-effort.

Name Service A name service provides a method to identify and locate available communication peers. This function is required in unknown environments and to access changing services in an ad-hoc manner. In more or less static environments or environments deployed by one specific vendor the use of a name service can be potential replaced with fixed port mappers.

Extensibility The implementation should be extensible and reusable. The reuse of user interface software and service implementations on other devices of according capabilities should be possible without introducing additional effort. It should be possible to add new input events to the semantic interface, and to add user interface implementations and additional physical input devices. It should also be possible to associate additional service implementations with a set of user interface realisations.

6.3.2 Message-Sending Approach

The message sending approach is the simplest way to deliver information from a client (on the input device) to a server. The server offers a communication port accepting incoming connection requests. After the connection is established, the client sends data via the connection in a format that the server-side (hopefully) is able to parse. The server reads the data stream from the network connection and a parsing component extracts the information for further processing.

Example: Listing B.2 and B.3 show the code fragments for a control message to start playing a media file. *

Development Overhead The development overhead is high. The developer has to implement everything from scratch: Network connection handling at both sides, message creation at the client side, message sending / reading, message parsing. There are no pre-implemented stubs or skeletons at hand.

Example: The fragment of the server implementation in Listing B.2 contains 18 non-empty lines of code, of which 4 lines are dedicated to port-handling, 5 lines implement reading a message from a port, 8 lines are needed for parsing the message, and only one non-empty line of code (i.e. line 30) is used to jump into the processing branch.

The fragment of the client implementation (Listing B.3) consists of 6 non-empty lines of code. Two lines are dedicated to port handling, one line is needed to create the message, and 3 non-empty lines of code implement sending the message to the server. *

Deployment Overhead The deployment overhead is minimal. Because the developer has to implement everything from scratch, there are not even libraries on either side needed that are not part of the language-core. The only required activity is to define and publish the port where the server is waiting for connections.

Interface Definition There is no explicit definition of the client/server-interface. The semantic interface is hidden in the message parser on the server-side: The code and tokens defined in the parser determine the interface accepted by the server. The correct format and syntax of the message, the control command, and parameters are also encoded inside the code of the parser.

Example: The code of the lines 27-35 in Listing B.2 accepts commands "`play_media`" as well as "`Play_Media`". If the developer would have used `equals` instead of `equalsIgnoreCase`, it would not except anything else than the exact former one. Another developer would have used the exact name of the method to be invoked (i.e. the term "`playMedia`"). ∗

The only way to understand the correct command, parameters and syntax is to look at the code. It is not possible to check messages for consistency with the specification before sending. There is also no possibility to check incoming messages whether they are conform to the specification, nor to scan if a message and its parameters are in the correct format with correct types.

Name Service A name service is not available. The address of the target service is defined by the address and the port number of the communication peer.

Extensibility The user interface implementation as well as the service implementation can be transferred to another device of according properties. If the new device does not support the programming-language or operating-system, a complete re-implementation is necessary.

Adding a new user interface only requires establishing a network connection from the input device to the server port. Any new service can be made available on a new address or port. Adding a new input event to the semantic interface requires to add the corresponding message type to the server-side parser. In consequence, there potentially exist different incompatible versions of the language inside the code of old and new versions of client and server implementations.

Advantages and Drawbacks The main advantage of this approach is its simplicity: The developer(s) of client and server define their own network protocol and implement the required components. They are free to add anything they want to the message specification. Changes can be done quickly by just adding a new keyword or parameter to a message. The messages do basically not have any overhead that needs to be transmitted and distinguished from information while parsing.

Another advantage is its independence of operating systems and programming languages: The messages could be created and sent from any system having access to the networking layer. The same holds true for programming languages. For transmission of data packets the developer must carefully consider different representation in different operating systems / programming languages, such as big-endian integer vs. little-endian, signed or unsigned numbers, or different representations of character strings.

The main drawback of the approach is the hidden interface definition: Nobody except the developers of the message parser knows about available services, message formats and parameters. There is no way to check for provided functions and correct syntax without access to the source code of the server-side parser. Changes in the format are not visible to others, and new keywords added to the client/server interface do only appear in the source code. There is hardly any prospect for third parties to implement a new user interface and integrate into an existing system.

Usage Fields The message sending approach is a good candidate for running services on small devices with very limited memory, because the approach does not require extra installations or packages. It is the first candidate if network transfer is of major concern: If it refrains from structuring the data in the message, the message size is minimal. The message sending approach is feasible in static environments where the development of services is from one source: The developer will easily be able to integrate several input devices and target services into one overall system. Third parties will have barriers in adding their own components if the documentation of the parser is not outstanding and up-to-date.

6.3.3 Remote Procedure Calls

On top of the message sending approach, *Remote Procedure Calls* (RPC [Srinivasan, 1995]) use structured text messages for remotely invoking procedures on the server. The goal is to relieve the developer from low level networking, message creation and message parsing. Ideally, the developer on the client side invokes remote procedures as if they are provided locally; in turn, the developer on the server side only provides implementation of the functionality that is invoked on request. Though the interaction components are distributed on several devices in ambient computing environments, the processing looks like having a local user interface for the service.

Because it can be sent as plain text messages, a popular format for coding parametrised method calls is the *Extensible Markup Language* (XML [@W3C, 2008]). As standard of the *World Wide Web Consortium* (W3C), XML comes with a well defined structure that allows type proving, and many parsers in different programming languages and operating systems are available. The input event is translated into an XML-document (like the example in Listing B.4 on page 187), and posted to the server. On the server, an XML-parser extracts the data, a handler mechanism looks for the desired object, and invokes the desired method with the parameters.

The use of XML for realisation of remote procedure calls (XML-RPC [@XML-RPC, 2008]) is a de-facto standard supported by the Apache foundation. It provides stub and skeleton for a wide range of programming languages. With the aid of this libraries, the effort on the client side is reduced to create an instance of the provided adapter and invoke its `execution`-method. On the server-side, the processing class for incoming user-interaction will be registered to the adapter as method-handler.

Example: Listing B.5 shows a code fragment for adding the handler mapping to a web-server. The code in line 15 defines to map all calls dedicated to `MediaPlayer` to the implementation `MediaPlayer.class`. Listing B.6 on page 188 shows the corresponding code fragment of a caller implemented in JavaMobile. The code of line 14 remotely triggers the server to search for the mapping for "MediaPlayer", and dynamically invoke the method "playMedia" of the mapped class. *

Development Overhead Without recommended use of libraries, the development overhead is higher than for the message sending approach. RPC requires translation of method calls, parameters and return values into a pre-defined representation. The overhead is substantially reduced, if the solution is based on an available library, providing functions for network handling, encoding/decoding and data transmission. Some extra effort arises because there are only few parameter types supported and some parameter types need to be translated into another representation before sending. In the example, the code saving is about 30-50% compared to the message sending approach.

Example: The fragment of the server implementation in Listing B.5 contains 9 non-empty lines of code, of which 6 lines are dedicated to administration of a web-server, and 3 are needed to add the appropriate handler mapping.

The fragment of the client implementation (Listing B.6) consists of 4 non-empty lines of code. One line is dedicated to set the properties of the server connection, 2 lines are needed to create the message, and one line sends the message to the server. *

Deployment Overhead The deployment overhead is very low. Like the message sending approach, RPC uses a static port that needs to be defined and published. In addition to the source code, some packages for stub and skeleton need to be included. There is no need to do any installation on either side.

Example: It is necessary to integrate small packages for JavaMobile (about 26kB) on the client and packages for JavaSE (about 200kB) on the server-side to execute the code of Listing B.5 and Listing B.6.

Interface Definition Despite the use of XML, the semantic interface of the service is not explicitly defined. The actual interface is encoded in the handler mapping on the server (line 13-16 in Listing B.5). Because each incoming call is directly mapped to a method of one of the handlers, the specification of the *Application Programming Interface* (API) of the handler-classes are good candidates to make the interface available to others. If the API, e.g. created with JavaDoc, is up-to-date, it describes the classes, methods and parameters of available services. From this point of view, there is no difference to basic Java-programming of non-distributed applications.

Name Service A name service is not available. By definition, RPC uses fixed port mappings for available services. The server will be available at the address and the port number of the communication peer.

Extensibility The user interface implementation as well as the service implementation can be transferred to another device of according properties. If the new device or host does not support the programming-language or operating-system specific implementation, then a partially re-implementation using an appropriate XML-RPC library is necessary.

Adding a new user interface only requires establishing a network connection from the input device to the server port. Any new service implementation can be made available on a new address or port, or can be registered as an additional handler to an existing server instance. Adding a new input event to the semantic interface can be done either by extending an existing handler class, or by adding a new handler for the special purpose.

Advantages and Drawbacks The main advantage of this approach is its powerful way to express method calls including parameters with low implementation overhead. There are many reference implementations available for a wide range of platforms and programming languages. There is no extra effort to implement (un-)packing and network communication. Although it is not able to process standard interface definition languages, the client/server interface is available for third parties to integrate own devices and services if the handler classes are well defined and documented.

The structured format allows human readers to trace, debug and understand the communication. It also enables to generate procedure calls by sending messages by hand, for example on small devices for which XML-RPC is not available or not feasible.

The main drawback is the missing interface definition and name service. The former avoids validation of messages before sending and type checking of transmitted parameters at the client. The use of the standard representation enables validation of the message format; it does not enable to check whether such a method exists on the server or not. The missing name service introduces the requirement to know the server address beforehand. This avoids moving of services from one server to another without updating the clients.

Usage Fields Remote Procedure Calls are used in a wide area, ranging from clients and services designed for small devices to integrated environments with high-end computing capabilities. It supports the integration of different input devices and services, because the interface can be made available by professional software documentation of the server-side code. In enhancement of the message sending approach, building systems by different vendors becomes an option. Specifically adding new input devices or input methods is well supported, for example to enable any personal mobile device to act as input device for a fixed set of services. Because it does not support a name service, the available services should not change frequently.

6.3.4 Web-Services based on the Simple Object Access Protocol

The *Simple Object Access Protocol* (SOAP [Snell et al., 2001]) is a distributed middleware technology that uses a lightweight and simple XML-based protocol to allow applications to exchange structured and typed information across the Web. It comes with a robust XML grammar with a rich palette of XML Schema data-types and a host of enterprise capabilities through a flexible header architecture [Alonso, 2004]. SOAP is similar to CORBA's Internet Inter-ORB Protocol (IIOP [Ruh et al., 2000]) in the sense that it is a protocol for conveying messages between applications. It is designed to support automated web services based on a shared, decentralised, and open web infrastructure. There are three main parts in the SOAP architecture [@W3C, 2000]:

1. An envelope that describes the contents of a message and how to process it.
2. A set of encoding rules for expressing instances of application-defined data-types.
3. A convention for representing remote procedure calls and responses.

SOAP applications can be written in a variety of programming languages (such as Java, C++, C, Perl, and C#), used in combination with a wide range of Internet protocols and formats (such as HTTP, SMTP, and MIME).

Development Overhead The development overhead is low if implementations for stub and skeleton are available. Tools exist for several programming languages to generate source code from the specification of the client/server interface. Without the use of tools, the back-end implementation required for using SOAP is extremely high.

Example: Tools like from Apache's `WSDL2Java` *[@Apache, 2008b] translate a WSDL-file (like Listing B.10 on page 190) into Java code for stub and skeleton. Among other files, it produces two files for the skeleton of the server:* `MediaPlayer.java` *(Listing B.7) and* `MediaPlayer-SoapBindingImpl.java` *(Listing B.8). The only thing the developer has to do (beside specifying the interface) is to replace line 12 of Listing B.8 with own code. For mobile clients, Sun's Wireless Toolkit (WTK [@Sun, 2008]) provides a code generator translating WSDL-descriptions into a JavaMobile-stub that can be used like in Listing B.9.* ∗

Deployment Overhead The deployment effort on the client side is low. The tool support includes the libraries for building executables and running the generated code.

Example: Based on the reference implementation of JSR-172[2]*, the client does not even need to deploy additional packages to be installed.* ∗

The deployment overhead on the server-side is extremely high. The use of SOAP-based web-services requires the installation, configuration and maintenance of a full web- or application server. It will be impossible for a layperson to install everything on his device(s) without expert-help.

Examples: Apache Tomcat, Glassfish Application Server or IBM WebSphere. ∗

Interface Definition The interface is defined in the *Web Service Description Language* (WSDL), which is a W3C-standard [@W3C, 2001, 2007]. The WSDL-specification is very complicated, numberless parts are separated into different sections. It is hard to understand the defined interface with parameters and return types at a glance.

Example: Listing B.10 illustrates the WSDL-file to specify the interface of the `MediaPlayer` *application.* ∗

[2] Java Specification Request 172: J2ME Web Services APIs [@JSR172, 2009]

A developer can hardly define a complex client/server interface in WSDL by hand. In contrast, developers usually go the other way around, define the interface in a high-level programming language first, and use tools to create the WSDL-file from the specified interface. This approach leads to interfaces that are very much oriented to the capabilities and the look-and-feel of the specific language, which might not be replicable in other programming languages.

Example: Tools like `Java2WSDL` *[@Apache, 2008a] translate Java interfaces into WSDL.* $*$

Name Service A name service is available as *Universal Description, Discovery and Integration* (UDDI [@UDDI, 2008]).

Advantages and drawbacks The main advantage of SOAP-based web-services is their power for highly sophisticated solutions of remote method invocation. The provided name service allows to discover and invoke services that do not have fixed network addresses, whose address is unknown, or needs to be mapped dynamically. If a web-server is already running, this approach enables to integrate web-services with other web-applications (local or remote), web-sites, or other Internet-services. If the web-server uses the standard-port, the services are easy to find on a well-defined port.

The main disadvantage is the requirement of a full web-server installation. It is neither realistic to install a web-server for serving just a small service, nor for the use of low-power server hosts. In addition, the effort to implement the functionality is only well-balanced with the effort to install everything for complex services. If a web-server exists but is available to the public (e.g. a company's web-server), extra maintenance will be required to separate local web-services from public available ones.

Usage Fields SOAP-based web-services are designated for environments where a web-server hosting services is already available, or there the installation of the web-server is reasonable for the installation of the service. SOAP-based web-services should also be considered for applications that need to have a name service. SOAP-based web-services are not feasible in environments where many small services exist on different hosts.

6.3.5 Conclusion

Between a basic message sending approach and a fully fledged web-server, XML-RPC appears to be the best compromise, in particular if a name service is not mandatory. It offers everything needed to remotely operate a service, has low extra-efforts, and uses a well documented standard format for description of method calls. Libraries for client and server parts are ready for integration for a wide range of programming languages. In contrast to enhanced SOAP-based web-services, no software-installation is required on either side. This would be unrealistic for many intended service hosts that are not designed to run web-servers. Table 6.1 summarises the advantages and drawbacks of the three approaches.

6.4 The Code-Base using XML-RPC

This work uses an object-oriented approach to realise the architecture illustrated in Section 5.6.2. Based on the object-oriented design, the code-base implements adapters to control the communication between client and server components. It uses XML-RPC because of its simplicity, power, and light-weight realization. The software encloses the common XML-RPC adapter from Apache [@Apache, 2009].

6.4.1 White-Box Framework

The object-oriented architecture to realise the grey-box framework is illustrated in Figure 6.2. It forms the reference architecture for realisation of instances of the framework. According to the white-box approach (Section 3.4.3), it reveals all details of internal realisation, mechanisms, and control. The design of the client/server architecture facilitates auto-generating components by using the toolkit defined in Chapter 7.

The main disadvantage of XML-RPC, i.e. the missing interface specification between client and service, is approached by the use of virtual input devices. The semantic interface discloses the functions of the virtual input device and provides access to the internals by the dependants on that device.

6.4.1.1 Components

The key components are determined by the model of the virtual input device. This specification is represented by the interface `VirtualInputDevice` on the bottom of Figure 6.2. The interface is implemented directly by a client software part and by a server software part. This approach enables software components on either side to consistently work with private instances of the same object. This specification also determines the shape of the dependants on the virtual input device, which are commonly labelled as "listener" in Java. The observer object specification is translated into the `VirtualInputDeviceListener` illustrated at the bottom right of the image.

	Message-Sending	**Remote Procedure Calls**	**SOAP-based Web-Services**
Development overhead	$\ominus$ High	$\oplus$ Low	$\odot$ Medium
Deployment overhead	$\oplus$ Very low	$\oplus$ Low	$\ominus$ High
Interface-Definition	$\ominus$ No explicit definition $\ominus$ Interface hidden in the code of the message parser.	$\ominus$ No explicit definition $\odot$ Interface definition is equal to API-specification of server methods.	$\oplus$ Interface specification in WSDL $\ominus$ Working with complex WSDL-files feasible for experts only.
Name service	$\ominus$ Not available. Server must explicitly made available on fixed communication port.		$\oplus$ Available (UIID)
Extensibility	$\ominus$ Difficult for third parties. Requires access to server source code.	$\odot$ Good if the API is well documented.	$\oplus$ Very high because of the use of standards.
Usage	• Useful if network traffic is of concern (no communication overhead for message structuring). • Useful for vendor-specific solutions where client and server are developed by one team.	• Useful for almost all services that do not require a name service.	• Useful for complex services. • Useful if solutions are integrated into existing web-server. • Useful for services made available to the public.

Table 6.1: Comparison of distributed system's technology

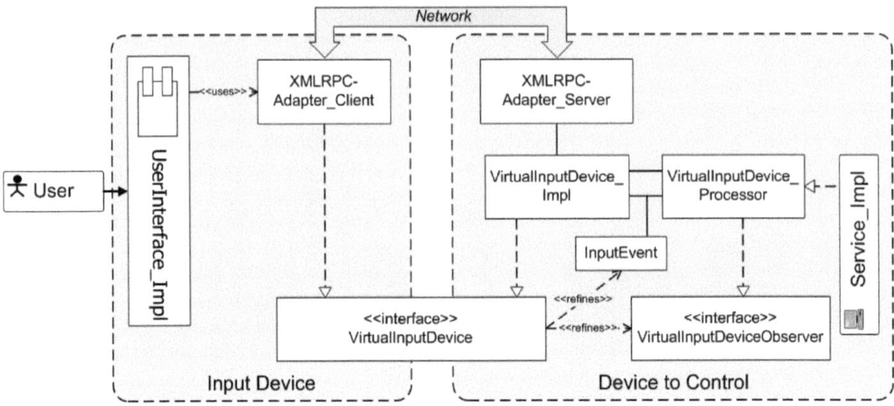

Figure 6.2: Object-oriented architecture instantiating the framework using XML-RPC (white box)

VirtualInputDevice The software interface of the virtual input device.

VirtualInputDeviceListener The specification of a component that depends on input events from this virtual input device.

The architecture maps the components identified for the grey-box view on the framework (Section 5.6.2) to common implementation of XML-RPC. It uses XML to encode input events for network transmission. Both network adapters of Section 5.6.2.1 are implemented by XML-RPC adapters, which contain encoding and decoding of the input events.

UserInterface_Impl The realisation of the user interface. The implementation uses an instance of the XML-RPC adapter of the client to post events.

XMLRPC-Adapter_Client On the client side, the architecture integrates an XML-RPC adapter for delivery of input events on demand. The adapter realises two components of the grey-box architecture: "Encoder" of the input event, and "Network-Adapter (Client)". It implements the model of the virtual input device to allow for using the hot spot of the framework's client side like a single method invocation of the client's adapter. The architecture therefore specifies the <<*implements*>>-relationship from the XML-RPC adapter to the software interface of the virtual input device (on the bottom of the image).

XMLRPC-Adapter_Server For receiving and decoding the transmitted data, the architecture also integrates an XML-RPC adapter on the server side. The adapter implements two components of the grey-box architecture: "Decoder" of the input event, and "Network-Adapter (Server)". This adapter waits at a specific network port for incoming events, and informs the software implementation of the virtual input device about the event.

VirtualInputDevice_Impl The object implementing the virtual input device on the server side. The implementation manages a reference to the XML-RPC adapter of the server to get informed about incoming events. The main task of the object is to implement the component "Subscribe-Inform Management" of the grey-box view. Because it implements the model of the virtual input device, services of ambient computing environments are able to subscribe directly to the software realisation of a virtual input device.

InputEvent The implementation of the input event. The input event is determined by the model of the virtual input device, and instantiated on demand by the software realisation of the virtual input device. The method of informing observers is equal to post an instance of the input event.

VirtualInputDevice_Processor The component processing the instance of the input event. The processor is a component that

(a) implements the `VirtualInputDeviceListener` interface, and
(b) is registered as dependant at the implementation of the observer interface.

Service_Impl The realisation of the service of ambient computing environments. It implements the event performing methods according to the specification of the events. It therefore can be derived from the `VirtualInputDevice_Processor`, overwriting the default methods to perform the events. Otherwise, the service implementation is required to implement the interface `VirtualInputDeviceListener` and register at the observer interface itself.

6.4.1.2 Control Flow

The user interface software manages an instance of the client's XML-RPC adapter of the virtual input device. When the user manipulates the state of the user interface items, the user interface software delivers events directly to the client's XML-RPC adapter implementing the semantic interface of the virtual input device. The adapter internally establishes a connection to its server side counterpart, and remotely calls the corresponding procedure according to the XML-RPC format and protocol.

On the device to control, the XML-RPC adapter lists on a defined port for incoming event. An entry is added to the property handler of the adapter mapping the name of the virtual input device to its software realisation. This component is informed by the XML-RPC adapter about incoming events through invoking the corresponding method. The software realisation of the virtual input device creates a new instance of the received input event, and informs any processor registered as dependant on the virtual input device.

6.4.2 Connection of Applications with the Code-Base

The aim of the architecture is to support delivery of input from the user to a service of ambient computing environments. The architecture can be approached from two directions: Connect a user interface software with the semantic interface, and register a service implementation at the observer interface. The former is implemented by the client stub component, the latter by the server skeleton.

6.4.2.1 Connect a User Interface with the Client Stub

For a new or modified model of a virtual input device, the client adapter of the code-base needs to be modified to implement the semantic interface. The user interface software is connected with the client stub by instantiation of the `XMLRPC-Adapter_Client`-component and invocation of its methods. Because the adapter implements the model of the virtual input device, complexity is reduced to a single method call.

Example: Examples of the code for JavaSE and JavaMobile are provided in Listing A.3 on page 179 and Listing A.4 on page 180. *

If using the toolkit described in the subsequent chapter, the auto-generated client adapter implements the semantic interface already.

6.4.2.2 Connect a Service with the Server Skeleton

The adapter for the single server instance as well as for the realisation of the system queue proxy are readily implemented. The process to register a dependant at the observer interface comprises three steps:

1. Implement the event performing methods. One option is to derive the component from the class `VirtualInputDevice_Processor` and overwrite the event performing methods with own functions. The other option is to implement the `VirtualInputDeviceListener`-interface by hand.

   Example: An example of a device-listener in JavaSE is provided in Listing A.6 on page 181. It is implemented by Listing A.7 on page 181. *

2. Register at the server adapter. This is usually done by invoking a special registration method of the class `VirtualInputDevice_Impl`, the implementation of which updates the list of registered dependants on the virtual input device.

   Example: An example of the registration in JavaSE is provided in the constructor of a processing class in Listing A.8 on page 183. ∗

3. Add a mapping to the XML-RPC adapter of the server instance. This step maps the name of the virtual input device to the implementing class. The mechanism realised for adding handler mappings vary across implementations of XML-RPC.

   Example: An example in JavaSE based on an XML-RPC realisation from Apache is available in the `addInputListener`-method in Listing A.7 on page 181. ∗

The code auto-generated with the tools explained in the next chapter cover the last step already. It automatically adds an entry to the server instance to map the name of the virtual input device to the class `VirtualInputDevice_Impl`.

6.4.3 Code-Base of Shared Technology

Realisations for a number of virtual input devices were developed in the course of the thesis in JavaSE and JavaMobile, for example the virtual movie controller used in Chapter cha:The-Toolkit and the virtual game controller used in Chapter cha:User-Study. For the latter, a rudimentary code-base for C# was added in the course of the application development.

To work with legacy code, the code-base additionally contains the implementation of a system queue proxy that can be used without further updates. The the full implementation of a virtual keyboard device and virtual pointer device are included (see Section 7.6.4.2).

Additional programming languages are still needed to support the mainstream systems and devices, like stubs for mobile and handheld devices (e.g. for C#/.NET, C/C++, SymbianOS C++, Java for Android, or Objective-C) and skeletons for server (e.g. C#/.NET, C/C++, or PHP).

6.4.4 Repository of Reference Implementations

User interface implementations of the examples are available mainly for Java-enabled mobile devices and gesture recognition tools. Reference implementations were collected in a repository for the use of the following user interface implementations:

- Reference implementation to work with gesture tools
- Default implementation for Mouse/Keyboard simulation using the realisation of the system queue proxy

6.5 Summary

The design of the software architecture aimed at managing the physical distribution of components. The approach of remote procedure calls using XML as format for network messages is particularly promising. This approach allows to use a standard message format, does not require installation of supportive infrastructures, and is well supported with libraries for many programming languages.

The white-box architecture further decreases the level of abstraction. The architecture selects XML-RPC for covering the complexity of network communication and message encoding. This represents the metamorphosis of the framework specification into a middleware for distribution of user interfaces and services. The code-base comprises implementations of frozen spots of the framework for using JavaSE, JavaMobile and C#. It forms the basis to facilitate development on code level. The decrease in effort for creating the application example is elaborated in Section 8.4 on page 133.

Chapter 7

Tool-Support for Generating Solutions for Special Purposes

This chapter describes a set of tools for constructing systems based on the framework defined in Section 5.5. The aim of the toolkit is to partially automate the translation of an abstract specification into a concrete solution for a specific purpose.

> "Toolkits build on frameworks by also offering a large number of reusable components for common functionality." [Hong and Landay, 2001]

With the aid of the toolkit, the code-base is extended with program code transforming the hot spots of the framework into frozen spots. Any stakeholder using the framework can connect own functions without paying attention to the internals of software realisation of the semantic interface and the observer interface.

The chapter starts with placing the toolkit in the right place of the adapted life cycle of interactive systems. The components required to instantiate the framework's architecture for specific solutions are identified, and the tools and guidance to build solutions are described. All items described in this chapter are identical to the items examined in the walk-through the toolkit described in Section 9.3.2.

7.1 Software Development Cycle for Interactive Systems

The toolkit is intended to support activities of a cycle of software development for fulfilling user input requirements, illustrated in Figure 7.1. From the adapted system life cycle elaborated in Section 3.1, the software development cycle receives input from activity "Requirements Analysis", and performs the activities "Design", "Implementation", "Integration and Test", and "Installation and Operation". The result of the cycle is an interactive system using remote user input for controlling services of ambient computing environments.

The Outer Cycle The outer circle of the figure fulfils the functional requirements of remote user input delivery. In this work, a user requirement defines the need of a user to express input to a service running in the user's environment.

In the specification phase, the developer transforms the functional user input requirements into a description of input functions the user(s) requested. The information exchanged between the user interface software and the interactive service is defined in form of events. The events are generated according to the semantic model. The model of the information exchange leads to programming code realising associated components for event invocation, data transmission, and notification of dependants. For checking syntactic correctness, preparing execution of tests, and finally building the application, the source code is compiled into executable code running on a specific machine. Before deploying, testing functions for checking communication and event delivery are executed and the behaviour of the application is verified. If the implementation passed through the tests, the binaries, libraries and scripts of the application are packed for delivery to users, who might re-submit user input requirements to the development process.

The outer cycle defines a clockwise process of subsequent activities; developers performing activities on the outer cycle would usually not step back on the outer circle for changing code directly, or re-building the solution without changes of the model.

The Inner Short-cuts In the intended process, the model is of major concern. All other components depend on the model, and software tool might automatically generate components derived from the model. Therefore, the inner short-cuts in Figure 7.1 link any other activities back to semantic modelling in order to refine the model. Changing the semantic model always requires to re-start the whole process from semantic modelling on clockwise.

The short-cuts enable developers to quickly try different solutions, and fine-tune the model. In practise, developers will do this several time until they are satisfied with the solution. Then they will go on to deploy stub and skeleton for building their final application.

7.2 Required Features

The aim of the toolkit is to support the complete software development cycle and to deliver five main features according to the activities introduced above. The required features of the toolkit are derived from identification of supported development activities. Tool support has been identified as required by several stakeholders, i.e interaction designer, software developer, system integrator, and system distributor. This section identifies the features to be delivered by the toolkit.

Modelling Input Semantics The toolkit is required to support interaction designers in creation of the model of of virtual input devices without special knowledge. The design of the virtual input device

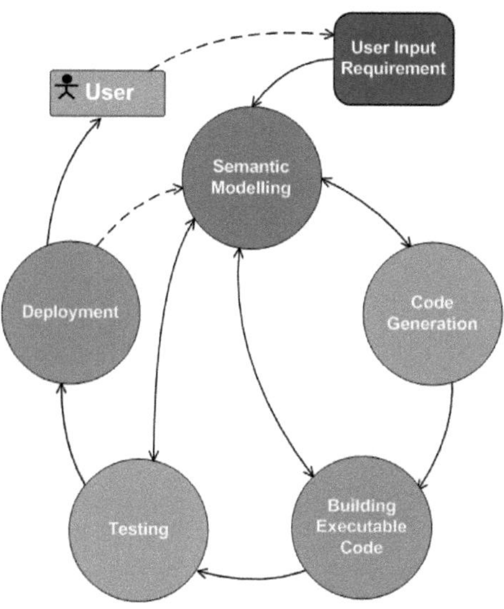

Figure 7.1: The software development cycle supported by the toolkit

must be convertible into in a machine-readable representation for persistent storage of the model. The model must be recoverable from its persistent storage, and the user of the toolkit must be able to re-work on the specification.

Generating Executable Code The toolkit is required to convert the model of virtual input devices into a common programming language. The automatic code generation covers input creation, data encoding / decoding, data transmission and event delivery. It uses the object-oriented software architecture and the XML-RPC code-base identified in Chapter 6. The toolkit is required to compile generated code into executable code, supporting compilation and verification of the generated solution.

Extending Automatically Generated Code The toolkit is required to support extension of auto-generated code by software developers. The process of delivery of events from the input device to the service needs to be interlinked with the components of the user interface on the target input device. The server-side counterpart needs to be open for registration of event processing services.

<table>
<tr><th></th><th></th><th>Required Feature</th><th>Supported Activity</th></tr>
<tr><td rowspan="14">Mandatory</td><td>(1)</td><td>Creation of valid virtual input device</td><td rowspan="3">Semantic Modelling</td></tr>
<tr><td>(2)</td><td>Persistent storage of virtual input device</td></tr>
<tr><td>(3)</td><td>Recovery from persistent storage</td></tr>
<tr><td>(4)</td><td>Translation of the model into source code</td><td rowspan="3">Code Generation</td></tr>
<tr><td>(5)</td><td>Mechanism for extending the client software</td></tr>
<tr><td>(6)</td><td>Mechanism for extending the server software</td></tr>
<tr><td>(7)</td><td>Translation of the programming code into executable binaries</td><td>Building executable code</td></tr>
<tr><td>(8)</td><td>Generation of client default instances</td><td rowspan="4">Testing</td></tr>
<tr><td>(9)</td><td>Generation of server default instances</td></tr>
<tr><td>(10)</td><td>Local test of event flow</td></tr>
<tr><td>(11)</td><td>Test of event flow between distributed client and server parts</td></tr>
<tr><td>(12)</td><td>Generation of client libraries</td><td rowspan="3">Deployment</td></tr>
<tr><td>(13)</td><td>Generation of server libraries</td></tr>
<tr><td>(14)</td><td>Creation of start-up scripts for client and server</td></tr>
<tr><td rowspan="3">Optional</td><td>(15)</td><td>Representation of virtual input devices in a syntax that is understandable for human editors</td><td rowspan="3">Semantic Modelling</td></tr>
<tr><td>(16)</td><td>Representation of virtual input devices that is compatible with the use in external editors</td></tr>
<tr><td>(17)</td><td>Graphical editing virtual input devices</td></tr>
</table>

Table 7.1: Required features to support the development

Testing Communication and Information Flow The toolkit is required to generate default client and server instances available for testing of communication and event delivery between distributed components. This feature supports system integrators and system distributors in testing the set-up of hardware and software components.

Deploying Code-Bases of Solutions The toolkit is required to pack binaries, scripts and libraries for deployment of all back-end implementation for mobile and non-mobile platforms. The deployed packages should be ready for integration with specific solutions.

Table 7.1 summarises the list of required features for the toolkit. It separates the mandatory features identified above from optional features for semantic modelling. The optional features (15)-(17) point to the usability of the main feature of modelling virtual input devices.

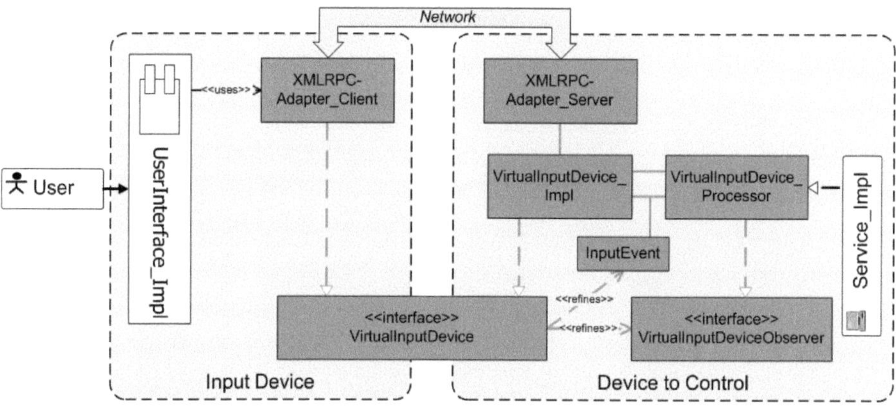

Figure 7.2: Class diagram of objects auto-generated by the toolkit from the model of the virtual input device

7.3 Auto-Generating Components

Using the common architecture and same components for different solutions enables automatic derivation of programming code from the model of the virtual input device. All components and dependencies highlighted in orange in Figure 7.2 are automatically generated by the toolkit from the model. The components remain unchanged from the design of the software architecture in Section 6.4.1 on page 88. In result of the code-generation, the hot spots of the framework defined in Section 5.5 are transformed into frozen spots. The frozen spots are then ready to be called by the functions provided by the implementer.

The advantages of this approach are manifold. In does not only harmonise the process of development, it also unifies the shape of the software, documentation and application programming interfaces. It uses consistent naming after the name of the virtual input device and its specified events, and unifies the naming extensions of the components. It also generalises the behaviour of the software components and sequences of system actions. The unique way to use stub and skeleton supports learning of their usage and extension, and facilitates knowledge transfer for working with other virtual input devices.

7.4 Design Decisions

The toolkit translates the model of virtual input devices into program code in Java[1]. Because the architecture elaborated in Section 6.4.1 is independent of any particular language, it is at any time possible to implement the concepts in any other language, or even to translate the generated programming code from one programming language into another one.

The toolkit does not support sophisticated source code editing[2]. Software developers are often power users of purposively selected Integrated Development Environments (IDE). The toolkit however focuses on semantic modelling of solutions, test of prototypes, and deployment of the code-base enabling programming by extension. Users of the toolkit are recommended to work on a sophisticated model rather than to enter programming code. The purpose of the toolkit is to translate the model into unified code fragments, which are intended to be integrated into any IDE of the developers choice.

The toolkit supports clients running on desktop-PCs (*"Desktop Client"*) and clients running on mobile devices (*"Mobile Client"*). Desktop clients are implemented in JavaSE in particular aiming at provision of *Local Client* and *Proxy Clients* of the list of potential client instances described in Section 5.5.1.2. Mobile clients use JavaMobile in particular to implement *Remote Clients* and *Mobile Client* from that list.

From the list of potential server instances described in Section 5.5.1.3, the toolkit only supports the single server instances and a realisation of the system queue proxy. The realisation of the system queue proxy is labelled as "*System Queue Server*" by the tools in order to express the included server functionality to the user of the toolkit. The user can directly launch it from the testing tool, as explained in Section 7.6.4.2.

Shared server instances are created by using a single server instance and adding additional observers. Realisations of short-cuts or application interface proxies were not considered because both depend on a dedicated application. The creation of correct keyboard short-cuts, or correct access of the API, cannot be effectively auto-generated in a general fashion.

7.5 Description of the Toolkit

The aim of the toolkit is to help developers building interactive ambient applications more efficient by using a set of programs, scripts, macros, documentation, and other aids. The solutions generated by the toolkit directly instantiate the prototypical architecture of Section 6.4.1.

[1] i.e. JavaSE and JavaMobile as introduced in Chapter 6

[2] This design decision was criticised by the reviewers in the walk-through of the toolkit, see Section 9.3.2.3.

7.5.1 Supported Technology

The toolkit fully supports Java implementation, i.e. Java Standard Edition (version 1.5 or higher) on non-portable devices (server and desktop client instances), and Java MicroEdition MIDP 2.0 on mobile devices (remote and mobile client instances).

7.5.2 Implementation of the Toolkit

The toolkit itself is implemented in Java, version 1.5. It consists of two main packages: The package "common" implements technology commonly used *by auto-generated* source code, and the package "toolkit" implements the graphical user interface and the tools *to auto-generate* source code.

The toolkit uses a template-based approach to generate source code. To generate executable code, 16 templates contain default code for classes, methods, or code fragments. The templates have place holders that are replaced with source code at run time of the toolkit. The templates allow for comfortable update of implementation details, format, or documentation of the auto-generated source code without changing the source code of the toolkit. A package "toolkit.shared" contains the classes to file in a template and file out a generated source file.

Overall, the toolkit contains about 5500 Non Commenting Source Statements (NCSS). The tool JavaNCSS [@JavaNCSS, 2009] was used to count the of statements and declarations in the Java source code[3]. Figure 7.3 shows that most code is dedicated to implement tools for auto-generating source code (43% of the toolkit package), and the implementation of the graphical user interface (40%) to operate the tools. The relatively large size of source code for the GUI results from the need for a graphical modelling tool which is the starting point of the whole process.

Almost 1000 statements are used to implement common technology (17%), of which the most effort was spent for the implementation of the system queue proxy instance.

The package "common"

This package contains classes that are used at run time by the auto-generated code. In particular, this package defines default XML-RPC adapters for both clients (the desktop client and the mobile client) and the two server types (the single server and the realisation of the system queue proxy). The implementation of the system queue proxy additionally contains the realisation of five default devices, including the required adapters to post events to the system queue. The corresponding models of virtual input devices are described in Section 7.6.4.2.

[3]It is approximately equivalent to counting ";" and "{" characters in source files.

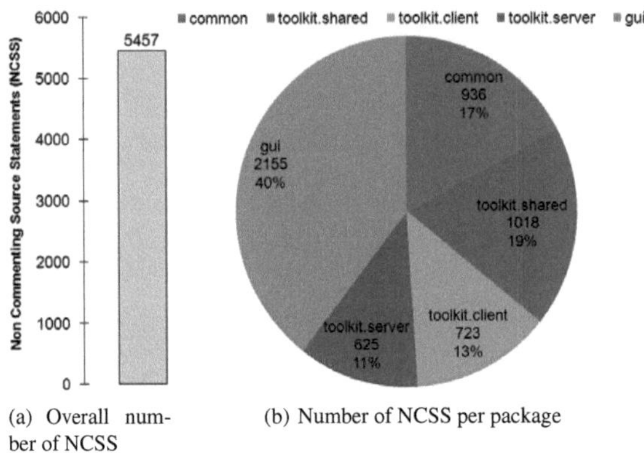

(a) Overall number of NCSS

(b) Number of NCSS per package

Figure 7.3: Non commenting source statements of the toolkit

The package "toolkit"

This package contains three sub-packages for generating source code for client and server implementation and shared components.

The package "toolkit.shared"

This package contains 13 classes required for both the client and server implementation, and tools required for code-generation. The most important classes are:

VIDReader Reads and parses the XML-representation of a virtual input device.

VIDWriter Converts the model of a virtual input device into its XML-representation.

JavaTemplateReader Reads a template and returns the content as String. It supports encryption of text files for restricted use of the toolkit.

JavaInterfaceWriter Generates a Java interface from the model of a virtual input device. Extracts the name and all events from the model and defines a single Java method for each single event.

LicenseManager Manages the access to features and code for four different licenses:

- Trial license: Full modelling is supported (create, write, change). Temporarily build is supported. Running the server and clients inside the toolkit is enabled. The preview and export of source code is disabled. The export of the byte code, and any deployment is disabled. Server and client instances shut down after 30 minutes automatically.

- Evaluation license: Extends the trial license with code preview in the toolkit and deployment of the server and client instances, which shut down after 30 minutes.
- Full license: Extends the evaluation license with full code export and removes the 30 minutes limit from server and client instances. The preview and export of the source code for the XML-RPC adapters is disabled.
- Partner license: Extends the full license with the full code preview and export.

The package "toolkit.client"

The package contains seven classes to generate source code for the client implementation.

Three classes generate source code for the desktop client:

JavaSE_XMLRPC_Writer Generates the XML-RPC adapter for the client in JavaSE. The adapter implements the Java interface representing the virtual input device. Each method of the adapter has a body to post the event to the server.

JavaSE_ClientGUIWriter Generates a basic user interface implementation using Java-Swing. Each control implementing an event from the model of the virtual input device is represented by a single tab in a tabbed pane.

JavaSE_ControlWriter Generates a graphical panel with a basic user interface implementation. Each event from the model of the virtual input device is implemented by a single control. On activation of the button by the user, the control triggers the XML-RPC adapter of the client to post the event.

Three classes generate the source code for the mobile client:

JavaME_XMLRPC_Writer Generates the XML-RPC adapter for the client in JavaMobile. The adapter implements the Java interface representing the virtual input device. Each method of the adapter has a body to post the event to the server.

JavaME_MIDletWriter Generates a MIDlet in JavaMobile of a basic user interface implementation. The MIDlet provides a menu containing all controls defined for the virtual input device.

JavaME_ControlWriter Generates a graphical form in JavaMobile to be accessed by the MIDlet. Each event from the model of the virtual input device is implemented by a single menu item. On activation of the item by the user, the control triggers the XML-RPC adapter of the client to post the event.

One additional class has been added from the development of the application example described in Section 8.2 for basic support of C#.

CSharp_XMLRPC_Writer Generates the XML-RPC adapter for the client in C#. The adapter implements a body to post an event to the server for each event specified for the virtual input device.

The package "toolkit.server"

The package contains five classes to generate the code for the single server instance from the model of a virtual input device.

JavaEventListenerWriter Specifies the Java interface of a dependant on status updates from a virtual input device. The generated source code defines a single performing method for each event specified for the virtual input device.

JavaDeviceImplWriter Generates a software realisation of a virtual input device. The generated class implements the Java interface representing the virtual input device. It is added to the handler mappings of the XML-RPC adapter of the server, and manages and informs the observers

JavaEventProcessorWriter Generates the skeleton of a processor class. The generated source code contains a default method body for all methods specified by the Java interface of dependants.

JavaEventsWriter Generates the object for input events to be passed with any status update notification.

JavaSingleXmlRpcServerWriter Generates the XML-RPC adapter for the server in JavaSE. The adapter adds a handler entry to map the name of a virtual input device to the instance of the class `VirtualInputDevice_Impl`.

The package "gui"

This package contains the classes for implementation of the graphical user interface using Java-Swing. It contains eight classes, most of which use several inner classes to implement event-adapters for recognising the user interaction. The tools and the their usage are described in more detail in the next section.

7.6 Working with the Toolkit

The toolkit is a compilation of five different tools, each supporting a single step in the system engineering process to build a distributed client-/server application: Modelling of the interaction, creating code, building and testing prototypes, and deployment of a final solution. This section explains each tool and exemplifies a solution for remotely controlling a movie player application. The entry point to work on virtual input devices is the graphical view on the model.

7.6.1 The Modelling Tool

The modelling tool provides a graphical interface for defining the semantics of intended user input, i.e. the events and their parameters to be posted to target service(s). The user of the toolkit works on the model of one virtual input device at a time, which the user creates new or loads from the persistent storage. The window displays the graphical representation of the model of the current virtual input device. The model is organised in hierarchical order (refer to Figure 7.4), each box can be selected by clicking with the mouse on it:

1. The single top box is the virtual input device.
2. The associated events appear as boxes in the central line.
3. The parameters associated with each event are in the boxes on the bottom of the screen.

Example: The interaction designer defines the controls of a remote movie controller without explicitly creating links to input hardware or interaction style. The movie controller provides features like load a movie, start playing, stop playing, and turning on/off loops in playing the file. The model of a virtual remote movie controller is displayed (see Figure 7.4). *

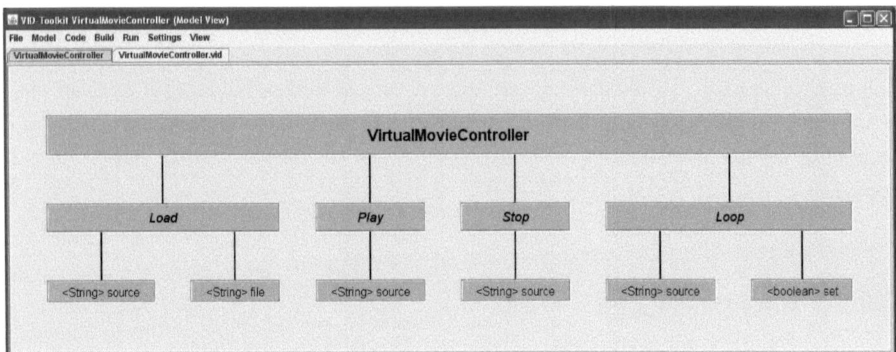

Figure 7.4: The model of a virtual movie controller

7.6.1.1 Creating Virtual Input Devices

For creating new models of virtual input devices from a template, the toolkit provides one feature that is activated from the '*Model*'-menu:

- *'New VID'* - This feature is used to create a new model of a virtual input device from the template of a minimal model

7.6.1.2 Modification of Virtual Input Devices

The semantic modeller modifies the model by changing the name of the virtual input device, adding, removing, or renaming events, and adding, removing, or changing parameter names and types.

To modify the model of a virtual input device, the toolkit provides three features that are activated from the '*Model*'-menu:

- *'Change Device Name'* - This feature is used to change the name of the virtual input device currently under modification.
- *'Add Event'* - This feature is used to add a new event to the model of the virtual input device.
- *'Remove Event'* - This feature is used to remove the selected event from the model of the virtual input device.

Example: To add the function 'FastForward' *to the model of a virtual movie controller, the user of the toolkit clicks on the top box representing the virtual input device to select the object, and uses the* 'Add Event'*-feature of the toolkit. The new function will appear in the model (see Figure 7.5).*∗

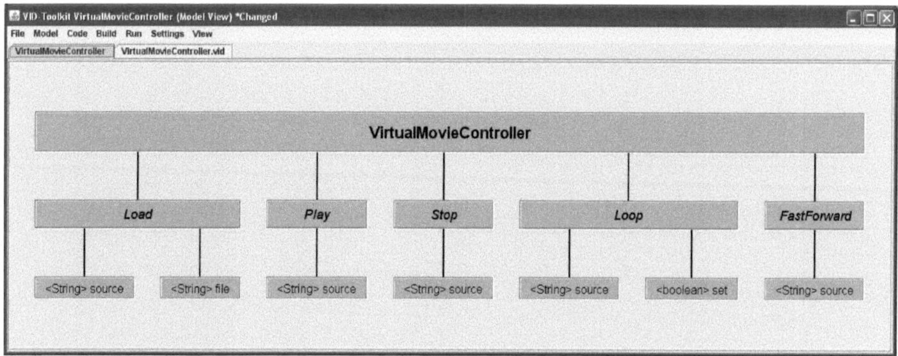

Figure 7.5: The event *'FastForward'* has been added to the model of a virtual movie controller

7.6.1.3 Modification of Events

To modify events, the toolkit provides three features that are activated from the *'Model'*-menu:

- *'Change Event Name'* - This feature is used to change the name of the selected event.
- *'Add Parameter'* - This feature is used to add a new parameter to the specification of the selected event.
- *'Remove Parameter'* - This feature is used to remove the selected parameter from the specification of the parent event.

Example: To add the parameter 'stepCount' *of type* 'int' *to the function* 'FastForward', *the user of the toolkit clicks on the of the box of the event to select the object, and uses the feature* 'Add Parameter' *of the toolkit. The new parameter will appear in the model (see Figure 7.6).* $*$

7.6.1.4 Modification of Parameters

To modify parameters, the toolkit provides two features that are activated from the *'Model'*-menu:

- *'Change Parameter Name'* - This feature is used to change the name of the selected parameter.
- *'Change Parameter Type'* - This feature is used to change the type of the selected parameter (cf. Section 5.5.3 for a list of valid parameter types, one of which is selected from a combo-box).

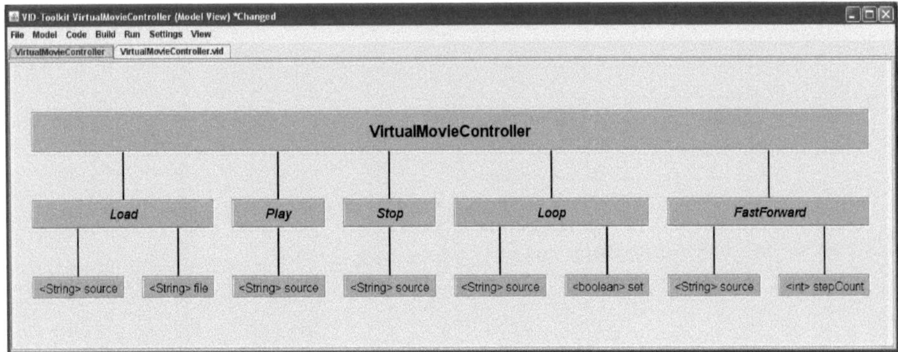

Figure 7.6: The parameter *'stepCount'* of type *'int'* has been added to the event *'FastForward'* of the model of a virtual movie controller

7.6.1.5 External Representation of Virtual Input Devices

The current model of a virtual input device is translated into XML for persistent storage. The XML representation can be updated using any external text or XML editor, and filed in into the toolkit afterwards.

For managing persistent storage of the models of virtual input devices the toolkit provides two features that are activated from the *'Model'*-menu:

- *'Load VID file'* - This feature is used to file in the model of virtual input device from the local file system.
- *'Save VID as'* - This feature is used to file out the model of a virtual input device to the local file system.

Example: The top section of the XML representation of the model of a virtual movie controller is shown in Figure 7.7. *

7.6.2 The Programming Tool

The programming tool[4] converts the current model of a virtual input device into Java source code. As a common basis for client and server, the model of the virtual input device is translated into a Java

[4]Because the tool does not provide real programming features, the reviewers were not satisfied with the name of this tool (refer to Section 9.3.2, in particular page 166). They proposed to use another name in future versions, like "Code Preview", to label its function more precisely. More favourable, the reviewers desired to be provided with real source code editing or a link to an external editor or development environment .

```
<?xml version="1.0" encoding="UTF-8"?>
<virtual_device>
	<device_name>VirtualMovieController</device_name>
	<events>
		<event>
			<event_name>Load</event_name>
			<parameters>
				<parameter>
					<parameter_name>source</parameter_name>
					<parameter_type>string</parameter_type>
				</parameter>
				<parameter>
					<parameter_name>file</parameter_name>
					<parameter_type>string</parameter_type>
				</parameter>
			</parameters>
		</event>
		<event>
```

Figure 7.7: The preview of the model of a virtual movie controller encoded in XML

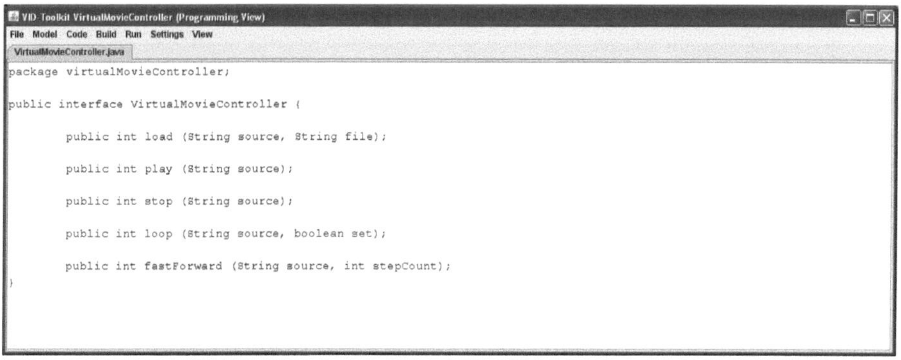

```
package virtualMovieController;

public interface VirtualMovieController {

	public int load (String source, String file);

	public int play (String source);

	public int stop (String source);

	public int loop (String source, boolean set);

	public int fastForward (String source, int stepCount);
}
```

Figure 7.8: The preview of the Java interface for the model of a virtual movie controller

interface. The user of the toolkit can additionally switch between the preview of a Java client (desktop client and mobile client) generating events, and a Java single server instance notifying registered observers about incoming events.

Example: The preview of the Java-interface generated from the model of a virtual movie controller is shown in Figure 7.8. ∗

The client code provides access to functions of posting events to remote receivers, which the developer can integrate into own solutions by accessing the methods from the library.

The server code provides implementation of a skeleton, from which a developer would overwrite the event-performing part in order to integrate own service logic.

7.6.2.1 Selecting Files for Preview

To preview the code generated from the model of the virtual input device, the toolkit provides five features that are activated from the '*Code*'-menu:

- '*Select All*' - This feature is used to preview all files for realising the model of the virtual input device in single tabs.
- '*Select Single Server*' - This feature is used to preview all files of the current skeleton of the single server in single tabs.
- '*Select Client (Java Desktop)*' - This feature is used to preview all files of the current stub of the Java desktop client in single tabs.
- '*Select Client (Java Mobile)*' - This feature is used to preview all files of the current stub of the Java mobile client in single tabs.
- '*Select None*' - This feature is used to remove all selections and preview no files.

Changes of the model (see section 7.6.1) will automatically update the source code displayed by the programming tool.

7.6.2.2 Exporting Code

To export the code of all files currently selected, the toolkit provides one feature that is activated from the '*Code*'-menu:

- '*Export Selection*' - This feature is used to export all selected files to the local file system.

Unlike the preview of the code, the source files are not automatically updated. All source files are generated on explicit request by the user. Changed source code due to updates of the model (see Section 7.6.1) will not be written to the local file system automatically.

7.6.3 The Building Tool

The building tool is used to compile the source code into executable byte code.

For building executable code derived from the current model of a virtual input device, the toolkit provides three features that are activated from the '*Build*'-menu:

- *'Build Java Server'* - This feature is used to build executable code for a default server instance using the skeleton of a single server instance.
- *'Build Java Client'* - This feature is used to build executable code for a default client instance using the stub of a Java desktop client.
- *'Build Java MIDlet'* - This feature is used to build executable code for a default client instance using the stub of a Java mobile client.

7.6.4 The Testing Tool

The testing tool is used to run the executable code generated by the building tool. It uses a standard Java-engine for starting server instance(s). For running Java mobile clients, it uses the emulator of Sun's Wireless Toolkit to run the MIDlet. The testing tool empowers the developer for quickly testing different versions of client user interfaces or service logic, and rapidly evaluation of the effect of modifications of the model.

For testing executable code derived from the model of a virtual input device, the toolkit provides four features that are activated from the '*Run*'-menu:

- *'Run Single Server'* - This feature is used to start a default server instance using the skeleton of a single server.
- *'Run System Queue Server'* - This feature is used to start a default server instance using the skeleton of a system queue proxy.
- *'Run Java Client'* - This feature is used to start a default client instance using the stub of a Java desktop client.
- *'Run Java MIDlet'* - This feature is used to start a default client instance using the stub of a Java mobile client.

7.6.4.1 Running the Java Single Server

When activated, the single server instance waits for incoming calls on port 5004 of the local host. When clients send events to that port, the server instance will invoke the performing method of the processor class. The user of the toolkit will find a default implementation of a processor labelled after the name of the virtual input device with the extension *"Processor"* in the source path. This implementation only generates a message on the console informing about the received event.

```
Event received: Load(
    source = virtualMovieController.client.desktop.Control_0
    file = file:///C:/Fun/Video.mpeg
).
Overwrite VirtualMovieControllerProcessor.performLoad to process the event.

Event received: Load(
    source = virtualMovieController.client.mobile.VirtualMovieControllerMIDlet
    file = file:///C:/Fun/Video.mpeg
).
Overwrite VirtualMovieControllerProcessor.performLoad to process the event.
```

Listing 7.1: Example of single server output

Example: The default output of a single server, which was triggered to activate the 'Load'*-event of a virtual movie controller, is shown in Listing 7.1. The server instance received two events for loading the file* 'file:///C:/Fun/Video.mpeg'*: The upper one from a desktop client, the lower one from a mobile client.* ∗

7.6.4.2 Running the System Queue Server

When activated, the shared server instance waits for incoming calls on port 5003 of the local host. When clients post events to this port, a realisation of a system queue proxy integrates the events into the local event queue of the operating system. By definition, the server instance can only process events that have a certain meaning to the operating system. The server instance therefore uses default specifications delivered with the toolkit for modelling of five virtual input devices:

Events simulating a remote keyboard:

- *VirtualKeyboardDevice* - Indicates that a key has been pressed or released. Submits the code of the key.
- *VirtualCharacterDevice* - Indicates that a character has been typed on the keyboard. Submits the ASCII-code of the typed character.
- *VirtualTextDevice* - Indicates that a series of characters has been typed. Submits the whole string.

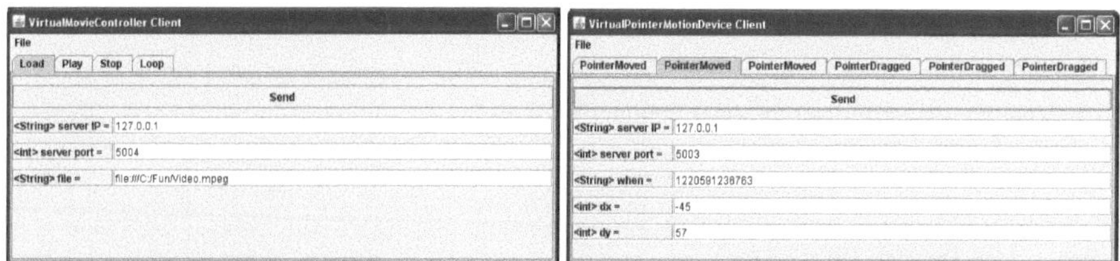

(a) Virtual movie controller (b) Virtual pointer motion device

Figure 7.9: The desktop clients

Events simulating a remote pointing device:

- *VirtualPointerMotionDevice* - Indicates that the position of the pointer device has been changed. Submits either absolute distances or abstract directions.
- *VirtualPointerSelectionDevice* - Indicates that one of the pointer actions has been invoked.

7.6.4.3 Running the Java Desktop Client

The default Java desktop client instance will appear on the screen inside a new window. On top of the window single tabs represent each event specified by the virtual input device. According to the specification of event-parameters, each tab contains different input fields for entering parameter values. After filling in the form, the user of the desktop client can activate the '*Send*' button on top of the panel to deliver the event to the server instance.

Example: Figure 7.9 displays the desktop client that has been used to trigger the first event listed in Listing 7.1 (left image), and the desktop client that triggers the mouse pointer to jump 45 pixels to the left and 57 pixels to the bottom (right image). ∗

7.6.4.4 Running the Java Mobile Client

The default Java mobile client instance will be emulated inside Sun's Wireless Toolkit, which appears on the screen. After launching the MIDlet in the emulator, the mobile client displays the list of events including the number of parameters required by the model of the virtual input device. The user of the mobile client selects the desired event and uses the '*Select*' option to browse to the next screen. After filling in the input fields for the parameter values, the user activates the '*Send*' option to submit the event to the server.

Example: Figure 7.10 displays the mobile client that has been used to trigger the second event listed in Listing 7.1 (left image), and the mobile client that triggers the mouse pointer to jump 45 pixels to the left and 57 pixels to the bottom (right image). ∗

7.6.5 The Deployment Tool

The aim of the deployment tool is to pack all binaries, libraries and scripts needed for deploying the solution. It is intended to serve as a basis for further developments, i.e. for overwriting and extending the auto-generated code.

For deployment of code derived from the current model of the virtual input device, the toolkit provides three features that are activated from the '*Deploy*'-menu:

- *'Deploy Single Server'* - This feature is used to deploy a library containing the default server instance using the skeleton of a single server, and scripts to launch the default server instance from the command line.
- *'Deploy Java Client'* - This feature is used to deploy a library containing the default client instance using the stub of a Java desktop client, and scripts to launch the default client instance from the command line.
- *'Deploy Java MIDlet'* - This feature is used to deploy a library containing the default client instance using the stub of a Java mobile client, the MIDlet descriptor of the default client instance, and scripts to launch the emulator from Sun's Wireless Toolkit and run the default client instance from the command line.

Deployment of the 'Java System Queue Server' is not implemented because it usually runs inside the toolkit without further updates.

7.7 Enhancing Generated Solutions

The toolkit provides the user with skeleton of services, stubs of non-mobile and mobile clients, and default implementations to test the client/server communication. Figure 7.2 on page 99 displays the components generated by the toolkit. The user of the toolkit attaches own code at the left side to connect the user interface implementation with the client stub, and at the right side of the image to derive the service implementation from the realisation of a default processor.

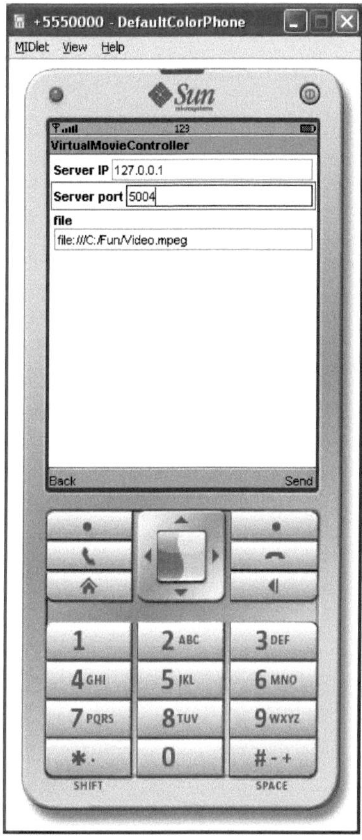

(a) Virtual movie controller

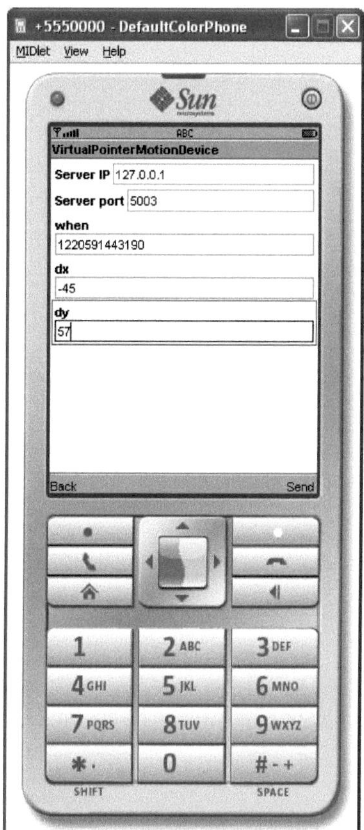

(b) Virtual pointer motion device

Figure 7.10: The mobile clients

It is recommended to finish the model of the virtual input devices before starting to integrate private code. The deploying tool creates the code-base of a software realisation of the virtual input device. The libraries of the code-base are intended to be added to the developer's class-path and the favourite development environment is used to invoke and/or overwrite the provided functionality.

The next two sub-sections illustrate the extension of the server skeleton, and the link with the client stubs for desktop and mobile use. The listings referred to from this section are available in Appendix A.

7.7.1 Extending the Java Server

The developer can integrate own service logic by implementing the interface named after the virtual input device with the extension *"Listener"*, and registering the implementation at a server instance. The skeleton created by the toolkit already contains a reference implementation named after the virtual input device with extension *"Processor"* of which the user of the toolkit can overwrite each of the event-processing methods with the desired application logic.

Extend the Java Single Server The processor already includes a main method to launch the service. As part of the generated source code, the user finds the single server instance named after the virtual input device with extension *"SingleXmlRpcServer"*.

> *Examples: Listing A.6 lists an example of an observer of a virtual input device. The corresponding auto-generated processor is listed in Listing A.8, which got extended by a service implementation in Listing A.9.* *

The recommended way for creating single server applications is to overwrite the generated processor class. The user of the toolkit can straightaway launch the service using the generated main-method.

Create a Shared Server The recommended way for creating shared server applications is to overwrite one processor class, and launch the service using the generated main-method. For each additional service, the user of the toolkit can implement the listener-interface manually and register the service in parallel to the first processor.

7.7.2 Extending the Java Desktop and Mobile Client

For the user interface, the user of the toolkit extends or replaces the generated GUI (desktop client) or MIDlet (mobile client) with own code. In both cases, the toolkit generates a class named after

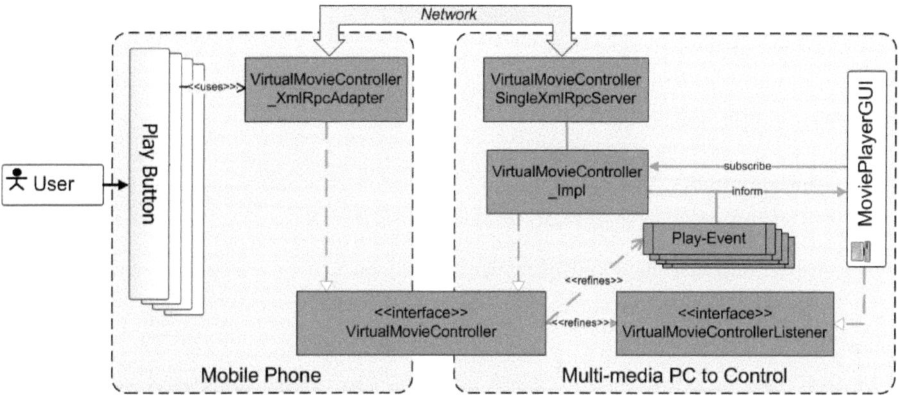

Figure 7.11: The class diagram and components auto-generated by the toolkit for the software realisation of a virtual movie controller

the virtual input device with extension "*_XmlRpcAdapter*" to communicate with the server. Because this class implements the Java-interface of the virtual input device, the user of the toolkit can deliver events by invoking the corresponding methods named after the events defined in the model of the virtual input device.

*Examples: Listing A.3 shows an example of a desktop user interface that delivers an event when the user clicks on the '*Send*' button. Listing A.4 shows an example of a mobile user interface that delivers an event when the user selects the '*Send*' option.* ∗

7.8 Wrapping-up the Media-Player Example

For demonstration purposes, the ambient media-player example has been realised in the course of an international project[5]. Figure 7.11 shows the class diagram of the system. The image uses orange colour to illustrate the components auto-generated by the toolkit from the model of the virtual movie controller, which was created in Section 7.6.1.

VirtualMovieController The software interface representing the virtual movie controller.

[5]Interactive Media with Personal Networked Devices (InterMedia). Funded by the European Commission (project No. 038419).

VirtualMovieControllerListener The specification of a component that depends on input events from the virtual movie controllers.

The other auto-generated components are:

VirtualMovieController_XmlRpcAdapter The adapter on the client side providing one single method for each event of the model of the virtual movie controller.

VirtualMovieControllerSingleXmlRpcServer The adapter waiting at a specific network port for incoming events, and informing the software implementation of the virtual movie controller about the events.

VirtualMovieController_Impl The software realisation of the virtual movie controller, which manages a list of services who asked for notification on controlling events.

Input Events The server side software realisation of the virtual movie controller creates instances according to each specified event.

The generated code is connected with two components: The user interface implementation and the movie player application.

UserInterface_Impl The realisation of the user interface in JavaMobile provides one menu entry for each of the defined events. It uses an instance of the XML-RPC adapter of the client to post events.

MoviePlayerGUI The graphical user interface of the player in JavaSE using Swing. It represents the consumer of the events. It implements the performing methods derived from the model of the virtual movie controller.

In this example, the media installation is running in the environment of the user. Figure 7.12 illustrates the movie player as a Java desktop application. The control panel on the bottom of the application is used to change the state of the movie player with a traditional mouse. It is registered at a single server instance generated with the toolkit to additionally receive remote control commands.

To demonstrate the integration with legacy code, a realisation of a short-cuts proxy was added to use the same input devices for remotely controlling the VLC-media player [@VLC, 2009b]. The realisation of the short-cuts proxy not only became dependent on the specific player application, it also cannot work on all operating systems without unification of the hot-keys [@VLC, 2009c][6].

[6]The instance running on Macintosh computers uses the Apple-key which is not available on other platforms

Figure 7.12: Screen-shot of a movie player application supporting remote controls

Finally, the player supports the realisation of the application interface proxy by disclosure of an API [@VLC, 2009a].

For remotely controlling the application from a distance, the movie player model has been created as exemplified in the course of this chapter. Extending the generated code, a small application has been developed to run on a Personal Digital Assistant (PDA) wirelessly delivering control commands to the player. A screen-shot from the remote control system running on a PDA is shown in the left image of Figure 7.13. In addition, a selection of the commands have also been integrated into the control panel in the sleeve of a jacket as illustrated in the right image of Figure 7.13. The jacket is described in more detail in [Righetti et al., 2008].

In a later version of the system, other input devices like a gesture recognition tool and a XBox-controller have been added for demonstration purposes. These devices have been adopted with very little effort from the realisation of the Interaction-Kiosk, which is subject of Chapter 8.

7.9 Summary

The design and implementation of the toolkit aimed at the provision of support for creating special purpose solutions. The source code of most components from the object-oriented architecture using

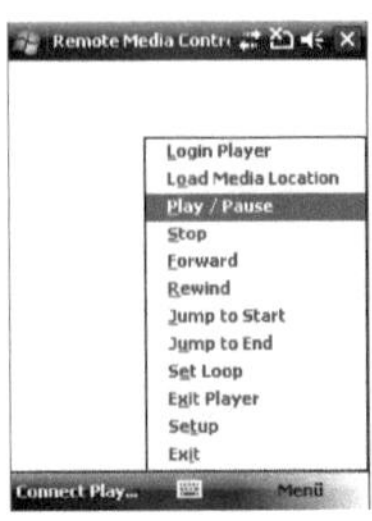

(a) On a mobile device

(b) In a sleeve of a jacket [Righetti et al., 2008]

Figure 7.13: Screen-shot of a remote movie player control

XML-RPC can be auto-generated. All tools for the metamorphose of the specification into executable programming code are delivered with the toolkit.

Always starting from modelling the semantics of a virtual input device, the approach step-wisely goes through the software development cycle, allowing to come back to the starting for updating the specification. Finishing the whole cycle, the developer benefits from using the source code for building the intended solution.

On the lowest level of abstraction, the code is dependent on the programming languages Java and Java Mobile, the network protocol TCP/IP, and the XML-RPC specification.

Chapter 8

An Application Example: The Interaction-Kiosk

The research work described in this thesis focuses on the support of developers for realising input methods for services of ambient computing environments. The concepts, software modules, and tools developed in the course of this thesis were applied to build an interactive system and connect it with a set of interaction devices offering buttons, movements, and gestures [Eisenhauer et al., 2008]. The development aimed at collecting feedback from a large range of potential users [Lorenz et al., 2009b] having the opportunity to select input devices regarding personal interest, task to be performed or situation.

This chapter shows end-users engaging such interaction tools and elaborates the benefits for software architects and software developers of using the software artefacts of this thesis to build them. The next section introduces the system presented to the public at the public trade fair CeBIT in March 2008, illustrates the design of a study and analyses the results.

8.1 Description of the Interaction-Kiosk

Similar to a kiosk of interaction styles, the *Interaction-Kiosk* comprises different input devices which provide a short-cut for the users to execute an activity in the application, which normally would be hard to achieve with traditional keyboard and mouse interaction from a distance. The system interprets the user intentions using a specific algorithm (gesture recognition, buttons mapping, etc.) and emulates mouse and keyboard events based on these interpretations. User interfaces were realised for a set of six input devices composed of mobile and handheld devices, game-controllers and gesture-recognition systems:

- Navigation buttons of an infra-red remote control (i.e. Microsoft's Remote Control for Windows XP Media Center Edition 2005)
- Dragging on the touch-sensitive display of a PDA
- Joystick and rocker switch of a XBox-controller

- Wii-controller
- Dance mat
- Camera-based gesture recognition with retro-reflective marker attached to a pen

Figure 8.1 shows the kiosk at CeBIT 2008, with the dance mat at the lower right corner and the other devices on the table below the large PacMan-screen (from left to right: PDA, pen with retro-reflective marker, Wii-controller, XBox-controller, and remote control).

The left picture of Figure 8.2 shows a user employing a stick for controlling the game. The infra-red camera mounted to the top of the display tracks the reflector surface attached to the end of the pen, which is passive and only reflecting the flash of the camera in the figure. The user is aiming with the pen in the air to make the PacMan move into the intended direction. The right image of Figure 8.2 shows another user who is doing similar gestures on the screen of the PDA. By dragging with the pen or the finger on the display, the user controls the PacMan as if drawing a line to the intended direction. The PDA transmits the derived control commands to the server using Wireless-LAN.

8.2 Realisation of the Interaction-Kiosk

The goal was to efficiently implement a prototype demonstrating the interoperability of the six user interfaces and the service.

8.2.1 Challenges

The challenge in realisation of a system like the Interaction-Kiosk is the heterogeneity in multiple aspects. The user interaction involves multiple interaction styles and modalities: The use of hardware buttons activated with fingers, hardware buttons activated by stepping on it, performing gestures on a touch-sensitive surface, and performing gestures in the air. The different ways of user interaction requires a detailed mapping of input expressions to unified control commands of the service.

The user interface implementations run on a heterogeneous set of physical input devices with the requirement to cope with different operating systems (i.e. Windows Mobile 6 and Windows XP), programming languages (i.e. JavaSE, JavaMobile, and C#), and communication technology (i.e. TCP/IP, Bluetooth, and USB). Beside these technical oriented constraints, the clients apply to three different categories[1]: A local client (i.e. the remote control), a mobile client (i.e. the PDA), and

[1]Five categories have been identified in Section 5.5.1.2: Local client, remote client, location-independent client, mobile client, and proxy client.

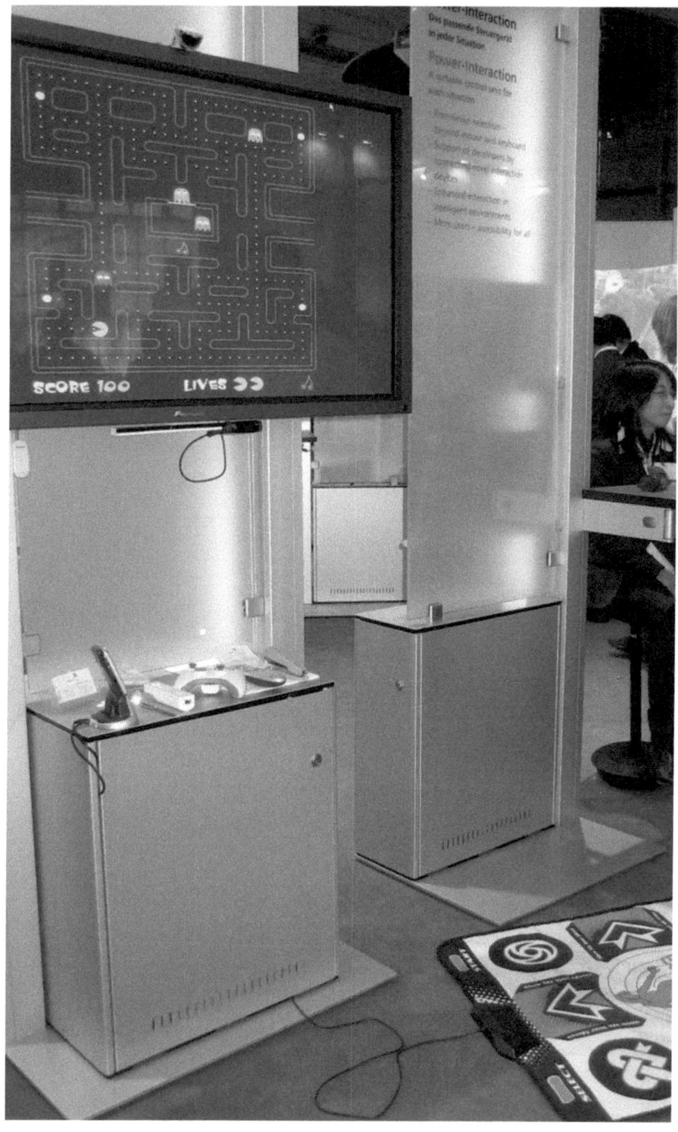

Figure 8.1: The Interaction-Kiosk at CeBIT 2008

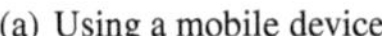

(a) Using a mobile device

(b) Performing gestures in the air

Figure 8.2: Examples of interacting with the PacMan-game

four local proxy clients forwarding the events from a recognition system to the service (i.e. the Wii-controller, the XBox-controller, the gesture tool, and the dance mat).

The realisation involved four persons with different expertise and programming skills (the author of this thesis and expert in JavaMobile and JavaSE, a junior researcher and expert in C#/.NET, a junior researcher without programming skills, and a student in computer science).

8.2.2 Architecture

The architectural design strictly followed the framework using virtual input devices explained in this thesis. The instantiation of the framework architecture with a virtual gamepad controller for delivery of control commands from a user interface to a PacMan-game is illustrated in Figure 8.3.

Because the PacMan-game reacts on keystrokes of the arrow-keys, the application of the virtual keyboard device in combination with a the system queue server is feasible (see Section 7.6.4.2). The *Keyboard-Adapter* of the the system queue server (see Section 5.5.1.3) integrates the incoming key events into the local event queue on the Game-PC. As the active application, the game receives and processes the key strokes.

The full system architecture is illustrated in Figure 8.3. The Java implementations of the server's and the mobile client's XML-RPC adapters (highlighted in orange colour in the image) were auto-generated with the aid of the toolkit, as described in Section 7.3. Because the realisation of the toolkit did not yet support C# at this time, the first programmer using this language was required to add a software realisation of the XML-RPC adapter for the client to the repository (highlighted in yellow). Because XML-RPC is well-supported for C#, the implementation did not require specific knowledge. The developer had to define an interface of two methods, use a factory method to get a

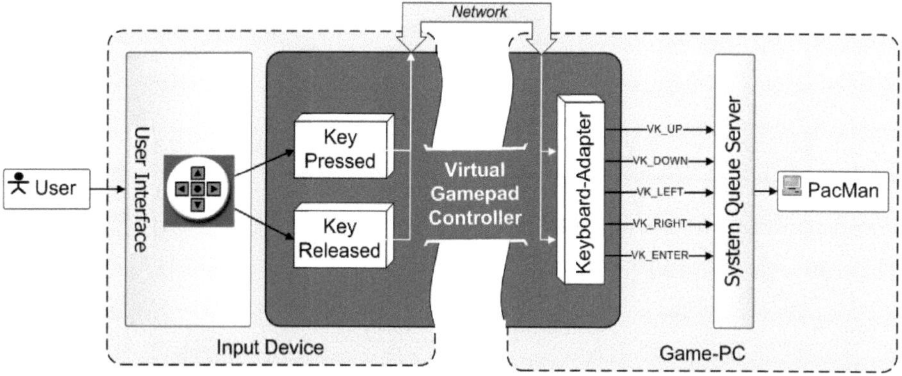

Figure 8.3: The virtual gamepad controller of the Interaction-Kiosk.

local representation of the server instance, and post messages by single method invocations. A tool to generate the adpater in C# was added to the toolkit based of the source code generated here.

Using this code-base, the realisation of the user interfaces only required to recognise user input expressions and convert the user input into the corresponding key event (highlighted in grey).

8.2.3 Realisation of Input Devices

XBox-Controller The realisation using C# is based on the XNA Framework [@XNA, 2008]. XNA provides direct access to the button-states via a "GamePadState"-object, which is frequently polled. When a button is pressed, a converter posts a message to the XML-RPC server to trigger the execution.

Remote Control The software driver of the remote control integrates actions from the four arrow-buttons into the operating system directly.

Dance Mat The vendor of the dance mat provides a software driver delivering a stream of mouse and keyboard shortcuts. The event stream is read by a converter who forwards the events to the XML-RPC server.

PDA A PDA with touch-sensitive display was used to run a mobile client written in JavaMobile (MIDlet). The MIDlet receives events from touching the display and dragging with finger or stick

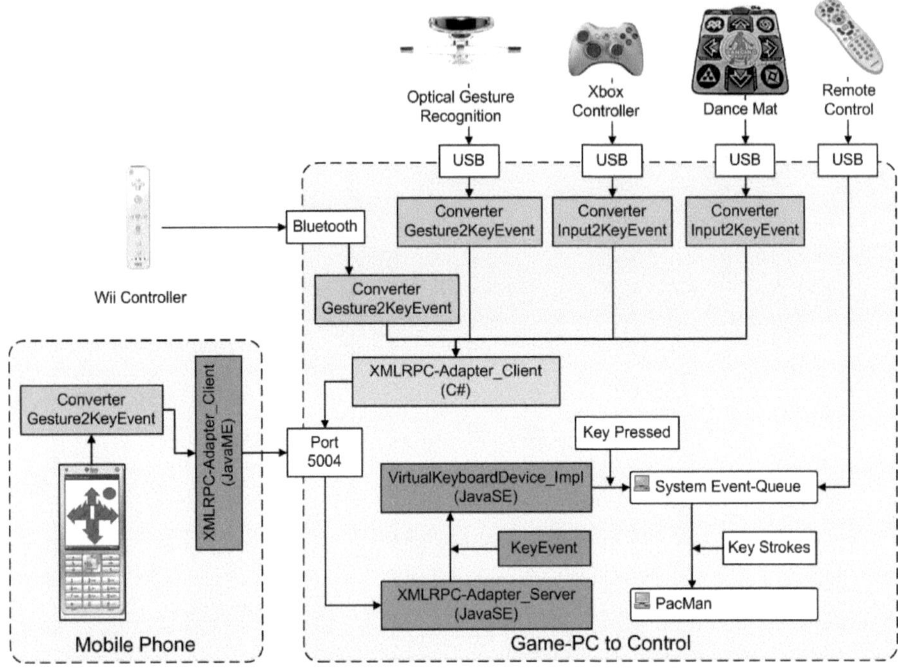

Figure 8.4: The system architecture of the Interaction-Kiosk

on the surface. The distance of x- and y-coordinates between the point of pressing down the stick on the surface and the point where the stick was released from it is calculated ($\triangle X = x_{end} - x_{start}$; $\triangle Y = y_{end} - y_{start}$). If $\triangle X$ is higher than $\triangle Y$ then a horizontal movement has been performed, otherwise a vertical movement has been performed. The direction is concluded from the sign of the distance value, i.e. a negative value indicates left/up movement, a positive value indicates right/down movement.

Wii-Controller The Wii-controller is a considerably affordable device providing different to map gestures to keyboard and mouse events. It delivers a 3D-acceleration vector of X-, Y- , and Z-axis. The recognising process is based on an extended approach of [Schlömer et al., 2008]. A K-Means algorithm is used with 14 cluster centres for clustering the acceleration data into discreet values (3D into 1D).

The recognising process first determines if the infra-red sensor of the Wii-controller detects IR emitters in range. Because the 2D calculation for gesture is much faster than relying on a 3D based gesture recognition using Hidden Markov Models (HMM), the algorithm secondly checks if IR lights are still in the range after move, and interprets the gesture based on IR lights position. Otherwise, the acceleration data is quantised into a sequence of discreet numbers and processed by the HMM machine with its probability matrices (A, B, π) from the training process. Finally it returns the probability that this gesture is member of the corresponding gesture model.

Hand gestures A gesture is performed by moving towards the intended direction and return to an area close to the starting. The vendor of the infra-red camera provides an application that directly maps the reflected IR light into mouse movements. The mouse coordinates are polled in a frequency of 100ms. The algorithm detects a movement by identifying whether the differences between the current mouse position and the previous position exceeds a threshold. The value of the threshold depends on the screen resolution. The threshold of the returning movement is half the threshold of the effectuating movement.

If the difference of the last mouse pointer position and the current position is more than the threshold, then the algorithm assumes that the user was making one part of a gesture. The direction of the movement is derived from calculation of ΔX and ΔY of the coordinates, similar to the implementation of the gestures on the PDA:

8.3 End-User Study of the Interaction-Kiosk

For the demonstrator, the remote computer system was hidden from the public and only the display was visible, where the PacMan game run in full screen mode. The user's task was to play the game with the chosen device, i.e. to control the small yellow icon moving to one of the four directions "Up", "Down", "Left" and "Right". On own decision, the user was able to select any other device at any time without interrupting the game. Potentially, all devices can be used in parallel to control the application. Because the game does not provide a multi-player mode, the number of active players was restricted to one.

8.3.1 Procedure

Users of the demonstrator were first provided with a general introduction to the research work. Because one cannot expect the user to have proper background knowledge, detailed explanation about the background of the project was provided. Additional help, assistance and feedback was provided during the game play if requested by the user. If necessary, the way to create specific control events was demonstrated, e.g. be performing the gestures.

8.3.2 Questionnaire

The users were interviewed after playing the game. A short questionnaire of seven mainly general items was used:

1. What devices did the user choose at the booth?
2. What devices was the user already familiar with?
3. What device was the first selection of the user and why?
4. What was the device the user scored highest with?
5. What was the personal rank list of the user?
6. Which devices were easy to handle?
7. What device could the user imagine to employ in daily life?

The full questionnaires in German and English version are attached to this thesis in Appendix C.4 and Appendix C.5.

8.3.3 Participants

Feedback from 42 persons of age between 9 and 52 years (average 24 years) was received. 12 persons were female, 29 male, one did not state personal sex. 35 persons owned a private mobile phone, only two persons did not (5 did not provide this information). About half the persons own a private game console (i.e. 20 persons, vs. 18 persons who do not, four persons did not answer this question). On average, each person used four different devices. Most people already knew the XBox-controller, remote control, and the Wii-controller. Only one quarter of the persons knew to use hand gestures in the air in order to operate a computer system (see yellow bars on Figure 8.5).

8.3.4 Results and Lessons Learned

The feedback from 42 users was used to identify seven lessons learned.

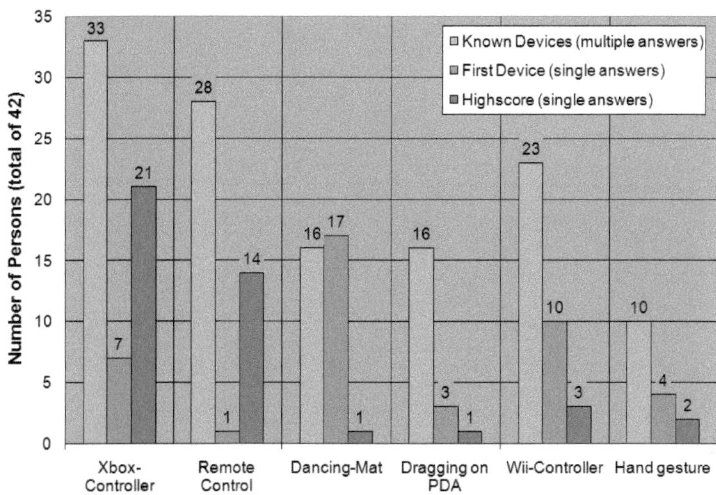

Figure 8.5: Comparison of devices known by the users, first chosen devices, and devices used for high-scoring of the Interaction-Kiosk

8.3.4.1 Selecting input devices

The green bars of Figure 8.5 show the number of first selections per device. Most users (17 out of 42) selected the dance mat first, 10 the Wii-controller, and seven the XBox-controller. Other devices rarely served as first choice.

Asked for the reason for selecting the particular device first, 24 out of 42 persons stated their interest in this device, in particular for the dance mat (10 of the 17 persons who selected the dance mat first stated their interest) and the Wii-controller (the same for 6 out of 10 persons). Nine persons selected the first device because they were already familiar with this device. In particular, the XBox-controller was selected mainly from users who knew the device already from playing games: It was selected first by seven persons, five of which stated “already familiar with”.

The left image of Figure 8.6 illustrates the top three devices served as the first choice. It shows a trend towards “was interested in” for dance mat and Wii-controller, whereas the area for the XBox-controller points towards “already familiar with” on a lower overall level. It seems that people either selected a new device out of curiosity, or a known device they are familiar with.

Lesson learned 1: Spontaneous interest is a trigger for selection of the first device.

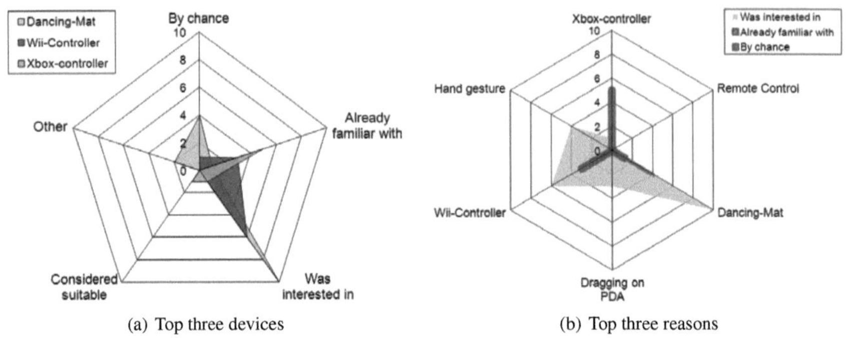

(a) Top three devices (b) Top three reasons

Figure 8.6: Analysis of the first selected devices

The overall interest was dedicated to the dance mat and gesture tools (hand gesture, Wii-controller, and dragging on PDA). When people stated "was interested in", they often choose the dance mat (10 out of 24). The right image of Figure 8.6 illustrates the devices selected first for the top three reasons. For the most often stated reason, "was interested in" (summary of 24 out of 42 persons), ten persons selected the dance mat, six the Wii-controller, four the hand gesture tool, three the PDA, and only one the XBox-controller. For the second most often stated reason, "already familiar with" (summary of 8 out of 42 persons), five selected the XBox-controller and three the Wii-controller.

Lesson learned 2: People are interested in innovative interaction styles and do not hesitate to try.

8.3.4.2 High-scoring

The high-scores were not explicitly traced for each person. The red bars of Figure 8.5 therefore represent the hard facts of some users who remembered the device, but might sometimes reflect the personal feeling of the user. The figure shows that the XBox-controller was the best input device to the PacMan-game. The similar interface of the remote control was second - this input style of four arrow keys reached more personal high scores than all other styles together. It is obvious, that the XBox-controller is pretty well designed for gaming.

Lesson learned 3: The applied device has impact on user performance. Some devices fit better for performing special tasks than others.

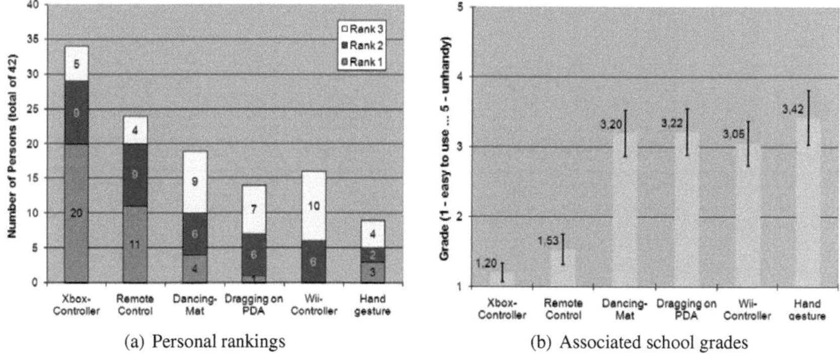

(a) Personal rankings

(b) Associated school grades

Figure 8.7: Analysis of personal ranks

8.3.4.3 Personal rankings

The distribution of personal rankings shows a similar image (see the left image of Figure 8.7). The XBox-controller was most often assigned with the highest rank. It got the same or more 1st rankings than any other device got ranked 1st or 2nd together. The dance mat, which was most often first choice but last place for personal high-scores, is far behind the top in the personal rankings. Though the first selection was driven by visual attraction and spontaneous interest, the rankings relate to the usefulness of the device for the task.

Lesson learned 4: After people satisfy curiosity and enthusiasm, they prefer useful input devices according to the task.

8.3.4.4 Ease of use

At the end, users were asked to assign school grades from 1 ("easy to use") to 5 ("unhandy") to each device. The right image of Figure 8.7 shows the mean of the answers and the 95% confidential interval. The mean separates two classes: the XBox-controller and the remote control with averages below 2, and all other devices with averages above 3. Even the worst grade for XBox-controller and remote control were lower than all other averages.

Lesson learned 5: The relevant indicator for the preferred device seems to be the easiness of using the input method.

8.3.4.5 Comments from the users

The observation revealed that all methods using gestures need intensive training. It was intuitively used by all users, but creating a specific event needs training of acceleration, speed, and length of movement. From only seven written comments provided by users, five were asking for improvements of the gesture tools, in particular the Wii-controller.

Lesson learned 6: Not only the interaction style needs to be intuitive, but the specific implementation of the interaction device needs to be carefully performed.

8.3.4.6 Observations

Some people took time, tried several times whereas other people only tried once and switched to another device. The main result is that people did not hesitate at all in interchanging devices. If a device seemed not to work well, it got replaced by another one. If the device was considered to be boring, another device was employed. Independent of age and sex, users interchanged devices in any order.

Lesson learned 7: It is a natural thing to interchange between devices for remotely controlling a computer application.

8.3.5 Summary

The study revealed that in the phase of "first contact" the users primarily showed considerable interest in devices tending to be unusual for the use in the specific situation of playing a game. Disregarding the shape and the intended usage of specific devices, most of the users satisfied their curiosity at first and started using uncommon means of interaction. During the second phase the users exchanged the devices with another in a natural way trying to find the one that meets best the requirements of their current situation. In this process it became apparent that the applied device significantly affects the performance of the users. The third phase entailed a type of consolidation, in which the users continued using input devices that allowed them to perform the task with the best possible result, i.e. reaching a new high-score. The key lesson learned from this study was that users are interested in selecting input devices according to their own preferences and performance of that device.

8.4 Software Measures

This section measures the benefits for software development of the Interaction-Kiosk on programming level. Two measures are used: A subjective measure and an objective measure.

8.4.1 Subjective Measurements

The subjective measurements address the soft facts. An indicator of the quality of the code-base and the toolkit is the level of expertise required to build a specific application. The subjective measures apply on design level supported by the description of the architecture of the framework, and on implementation level, which is supported by the code-base for the reference architecture described in section 6.4.1. This section therefore compares the level of expertise required to build an application with and without the support from the outcome of this thesis. It only identifies expertise introduced by the distribution of the user interface and the service logic. It does not address the expertise to realise a local user interface on the input device, nor the expertise to build the core of the services of ambient computing environments.

8.4.1.1 Architectural Design

The activity of system design creates a detailed description of the architecture of the system. The detailed description identifies all components of the system and their relationships. There is no general number explaining the effort to generate the description. The effort depends on complexity of the system, experience of the developers, quality of available specifications and documents, and communication inside the team.

Following the architectural design of the framework introduced in this thesis, six components were identified by the grey-box approach in section 5.6.2: Input event, encoder, network adapter for client and server, decoder, and subscribe-inform management. The effort for architectural design is reduced to identify and add the components for the core service logic and user interface components.

8.4.1.2 Defining the Software Interface

The design activity describes a distributed software architecture. The interface between the client components and the server is a key criteria for interoperability.

Without the artefacts developed by this thesis, the visibility and specification of the interface depends on the selected technology assessed in Section 6.3.

A design following the framework architecture uses a standard XML-RPC adapter. The interface is defined by the handler classes and the methods publicly available for remote invocation. The interface is visible in the Advanced Programming Interface (API) of the server implementation. It does not implement a unique software interface. Therefore the correct handler class and the exact method name must be provided when calling the executing method. Furthermore, all parameters must be added to a vector; the number of expected parameters and their types are not visible to the developer unless at the server's source code.

Using the modelling tool as explained in 7.6.1, the definition of the software interface is supported with a graphical tool. The interface is derived from the model of the virtual input device. In difference to using the standard XML-RPC adapter, the source code generated with the toolkit already implements the semantic interface of the virtual input device. The handler classes and method names are enclosed by the adapter at the client already; the expected parameters and their types are also visible to the developer in the method header. The software interface is therefore visible in three different representations: The graphical tree of the modelling tool, the unified representation of the virtual input device in XML, and the Java interface derived from the specification. In addition, realisations are readily available in the code-base.

8.4.1.3 Required Programming Skills

Server For the realisation of the server without the outcome of this thesis, the developer needs expertise in

- Networking: Create server-socket, accept connection requests, handle multiple channels, receive messages
- Multi-Threading: Do not block the application while waiting for data from a network socket
- Parsing: Decompose the message into its parts, get the meaning of the parts, and branch into processing paths

Using the artefacts developed in this thesis (i.e. the framework architecture, the toolkit and the code-base), the required expertise is reduced to understanding the observer mechanism in order to be able to register dependants at the software realisation of the observer interface (i.e. the server implementation of the framework's hot spots).

Client For the realisation of the client without the outcome of this thesis, the developer needs expertise in

- Networking: Open socket connection, write data
- Multi-Threading: Do not block an interactive application while sending data over a network

Using the artefacts developed in this thesis, the software developer of the client has only to invoke a single method of the software realisation of the semantic interface (i.e. the client implementation of the framework hot spots).

8.4.2 Objective Metric

Objective metrics measure the hard facts of the software. The objective measurements focus on the amount of extra-statements, which are pure overhead statements needed for event delivery only. The measures do not consider the code for the user interface implementation on the input device. The user interface is assumed to be available regardless of the fact of distributing the events over a network. The measures do also not consider code for consuming events by the service logic. The core implementation of the service logic is assumed to provide software methods available for consumption of the events.

This section identifies the total number of logic statements, that are coded as non-empty, non-comment lines of code (Logical Lines of Code, LoC [for example in Ludewig and Lichter, 2007]). The objective measures apply on the code level, which is supported by code-base and by the toolkit for auto-generating parts of solutions. This section therefore compares the lines of code needed to create the solution by hand, using the code-base following the white-box architecture, and using the toolkit. To assess the benefit of the software artefacts developed in this thesis, the size of programming code for realisation was analysed with a trial version of GeroneSoft's Code Counter Pro [@Gerone, 2009].

Figure 8.8 illustrates the reduction of the overhead to post the events in the Interaction-Kiosk application. The number of lines of code required to deliver incoming events to the processor is reduced by 69% by applying to the architecture, and is further reduced to 10% of the original size to derive a single server instance from the auto-generated code. If using the realisation of the system queue proxy, then no extra code needs to be implemented. The number of lines of code required at the client to post the events is reduced by one third by applying to the framework architecture. It is further reduced to 11% of the original size using the auto-generated code-base.

8.4.2.1 Server

From Scratch The Java-code for a server processing a single remote event is shown in Listing B.2. Without the aid of the toolkit, the developer needs 20 LoC for networking, multi-threading and

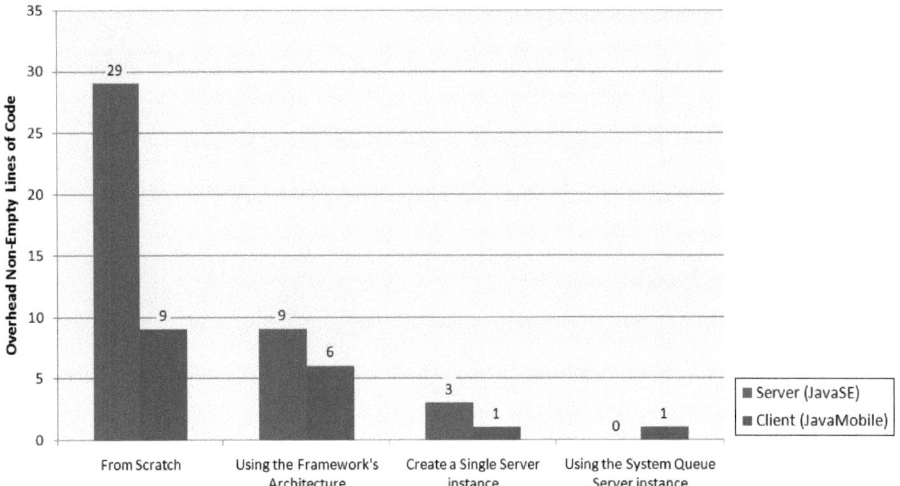

Figure 8.8: The overhead for system development

invocation of the event processor. The code for the server instance of the Interaction-Kiosk would require additional code to identify the processing branch for three more events, each requiring 3 additional LoC to identify the event from the list of accepted events (inside the construct of if-elseif-else). The code would then contain 29 LoC in addition to the implementation of the core service logic, excluding sending any response to the calling client. In particular, the number of LoC is a function of the size of the list of accepted events, which determines the number of LoC of the if-elseif-else construct to identify the processor to be called.

Developers might argument for optimisation, e.g. by not using an additional thread or by not closing the connection after performing the event. The former leads to a blocking server while waiting for input. This is usually not acceptable, because back-end tasks and rendering output for the user need to be performed continuously. The latter leads to a static connection between the server instance and one input device, if the server socket implementation does not accepts multiple connections on the same port in some programming languages.

Following the Framework Architecture Following the architectural design of the framework, i.e. creating an XML-RPC server and adding a mapping to the core service logic, then the developer needs 9 LoC similar to Listing B.5, including the return of an error code to the caller.

Using the Toolkit and the Skeleton With the aid of the outcome of this thesis, there is no implementation required for realisation of the server if using the realisation of the system queue proxy. If aiming at a dedicated single server instance extending the skeleton generated by the toolkit, then the developer needs 3 LoC in addition to the realisation of the core service logic to initialise the server instance, register the processor at the realisation of the observer interface and start the server instance listening on the port for incoming events. In particular, the number of LoC is completely independent of the number of events.

Code Size of the Server Implementation According to the output of GeroneSoft's Code Counter Pro, the server implementation uses the realisation of the system queue proxy, which was build of 1097 lines of code. The complete source code was generated with the toolkit and did not need any attention of the computer programmers.

8.4.2.2 Client

From Scratch The JavaMobile-code of a basic client is listed in Listing B.3. Without the toolkit, the developer needs 9 LoC for connection establishment, multi-threading, and event delivery, excluding any processing of response from the server. Developers might argument for optimisation, e.g. by not using an additional thread or by not closing the connection after sending the event. The former leads to a blocking user interface while waiting for network connection and sending data over the network. This is usually not acceptable, because the user interface is required to be responsive to the user and available for the next interaction step. The latter leads to a static connection between the input device and one service instance.

Following the Framework Architecture Following the architectural design of the framework, i.e. instantiating an XML-RPC adapter class and invoking its execution method, then the developer needs 6 LoC similar to Listing B.5.

Using the Toolkit and the Stub The source code of a solution based on the libraries generated with the toolkit is exemplified in Listing A.4. After deployment of the stub with the aid of the toolkit, the developer needs 6 LoC to initialise the adapter, set the connection, trigger the adapter to post the event, and to handle the response from the adapter in a new thread.

Code Size of the Client Implementation The client implementation of the Interaction-Kiosk integrates four C#-applications (i.e. the dance mat, the gesture recognition tool, the Wii-controller, and

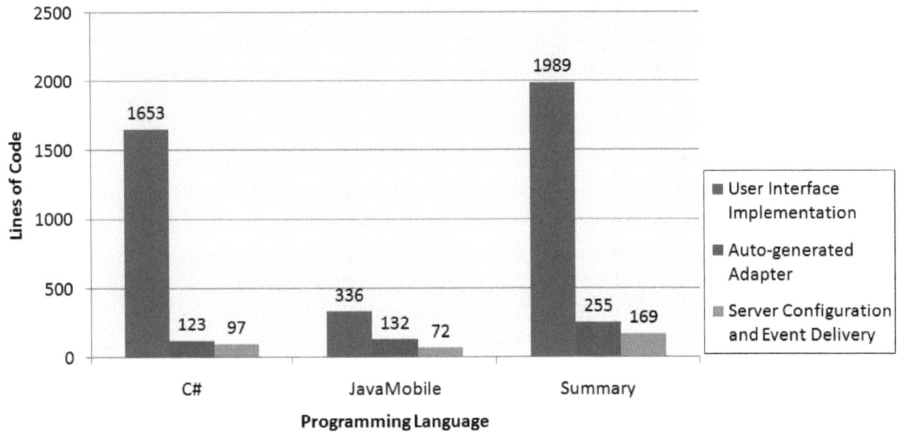

Figure 8.9: The distribution of Lines of Code for the five user interface realisations of the Interaction-Kiosk

the XBox-controller), one JavaMobile-application (i.e the MIDlet for dragging on the PDA). One input device did not require any implementation (i.e. the remote control).

According to the output of GeroneSoft's Code Counter Pro, the overall programming code consists of 1776 lines of C#-code and 468 line of JavaMobile-code (summary of 2244 lines of code). To cope with the distributed setting, 424 lines of code (18,68% of the overall size) were used for building client adapters, configuration of the server instance and posting the event to the remote processor. More than half the size of this code (i.e. 255 lines) realise client adapters that are auto-generated by the toolkit. Two professional computer programmers had to add only 169 lines of code (8,50% of the overall size) to configure the access to the server and deliver the events from five independent user interface realisations. Figure 8.9 illustrates the distribution of the code. For each programming language (C#-code, JavaMobile-code and the summary of both), the image illustrates the number of lines of code dedicated to the user interface implementation, the size of the auto-generated XML-RPC adapters, and the size of the code to be added by the programmer mainly to configure server access and to post the event.

8.4.3 Summary and Conclusions

The software measures identified the reduction of complexity of building a solution on the programming level. The subjective measurements of the expertise required to cope with the distributed setting emphasised the reduction of complexity on a conceptual level. The expertise in specific software constructs like multi-threading, parsing, and networking, is reduced if covered by the code-base developed in this thesis.

The objective measurements of the auto-generated code affirmed significantly improved efficiency of software development when using the toolkit. The use of the code-base directly leads to a lower size of programming code to be created by the developer.

8.5 Summary

This chapter described the development and user experiences of an application developed using the software artefacts of this thesis. The application example enables users to operate a simple PacMan game application from a distance. In order to achieve this task the users were allowed to take any device from the Interaction-Kiosk, which comprises a heterogeneous set of devices with different levels of familiarity to the users. The user study confirmed the interest of users in selecting input devices, and their capability to engage different devices if available.

The key challenge in realising the system was to implement interoperability of heterogeneous technology, interaction styles, and programming languages. The analysis of the software and the software development affirmed the benefits of using the artefacts developed in the course of this thesis. Applying the design of the framework architecture, the system designer focuses on the description of the components of the core service logic and the user interface components. The interface between the client application and the server is visible in the description and graphical representation of the virtual input device. The components implementing interoperability on code level are auto-generated by the toolkit. The effort compared with a realisation without the outcome of this thesis is substantially reduced.

Chapter 9

Technical Evaluation of the Framework and Toolkit

The previous chapter measured the benefits of the work considering subjective and objective software measures with an application example. It therefore looked at the code generated *with* the outcome of this work. This chapter more abstract describes the technical evaluation of the concepts, and the software evaluation of the tools available *to build* solutions.

Methods of software evaluation are applicable for examining the quality of any technical document resulting from the adapted life cycle of an interactive systems defined in Section 3.1, for example software design document, source code, use case description, business process definition, or test case specification. The technical document is referred to as the *software product*; the developer, designer, or other person who is in charge of the software product is denoted as its *author*. In general, the aim of the evaluation is to identify deviations of the results of the operation creating the software product from the set of requirements. The deviations are called *defects*:

Definition 9.1 (Defect).
A defect is an instance in which a requirement is not satisfied. [Fagan, 1986] ■

The next section introduces four methods for evaluating software products by using *walk-through*, *peer review*, *software inspection*, and *software audit*.

9.1 Methods of Software Evaluation

This section examines methods for evaluating the quality of the software products 'framework' and 'toolkit' developed in this thesis.

9.1.1 Software Walk-through

In software engineering, a walk-through is a static analysis technique in which

> "a designer or programmer leads members of the development team and other interested parties through a software product, and the participants ask questions and make comments about possible errors, violation of development standards, and other problems" [IEEE 1028, 1998, clause 3.8].

The major feature of a walk-through is its execution similar to a group lesson. The author presents an overview of the software product under examination, its purpose and design decisions. After the introduction, the author "walks through" the software product sequentially presenting the details. For each detail, the reviewers raise their specific items. No other software evaluation method provides room for the author to explain the software product, and its application, on this level of detail.

A walk-through also differs from other software evaluation methods in its objective of familiarisation. The walk-through is not only an approach for detecting anomalies by reviewers, but also for explaining the software product in great detail and train any person in the audience to use it. While the author presents details of the software product, the audience is educated in the details of the software product, the author's thoughts behind, and the process of its application.

9.1.2 Software (Peer) Review

Peer reviews refer to a type of software review in which a software product is examined by its author and one or more reviewers. Because the main objective is to evaluate the technical content and quality of the software product, the term *technical review* got widely accepted:

> "A systematic evaluation of a software product by a team of qualified personnel that examines the suitability of the software product for its intended use and identifies discrepancies from specification and standards. Technical reviews may also provide recommendations of alternatives and examination of various alternatives." [IEEE 1028, 1998, clause 3.7]

At the end of the review, a list of anomalies in the software product and recommendations of alternatives shall be documented in appropriate artefacts. The alternatives may be discussed at the meeting, in a separate meeting, or left to the author of the software product to be resolved.

The main differences from other software evaluation methods are its openness of the review team and the generation of recommendations for alternatives. The group of potential reviewers includes team members as well as external reviewers. The recommendations can be delivered to the management for planning correction, or they could be used by the team or the author internally. There is no mandatory use or requested commitment.

9.1.3 Software Inspection

In general, an inspection is seen as a special kind of software peer review: *"Inspection in software engineering refers to peer review of any work product by trained individuals who look for defects using a well defined process."* [@Wikipedia, 2008]. This general view is too shortsighted to distinguish between any method of group evaluation of a software product. More explicitly, an inspection is defined as

> "A visual examination of a software product to detect and identify software anomalies, including errors and deviations from standards and specification. Inspections are peer examinations led by impartial facilitators who are trained in inspection techniques. Determination of remedial or investigative action for an anomaly is a mandatory element of a software inspection, although the solutions should not be determined in the inspection meeting." [IEEE 1028, 1998, clause 3.3]

This definition reveals three major differences of a software inspection compared to other software evaluation methods:

- The inspection is moderated by an impartial person trained in inspection techniques.
- It is mandatory to determine actions for anomalies.
- The goal of the inspection is to reach a consensus of all inspectors on a software product and approve it for use in the project.

At the end of the inspection meeting, the list of anomalies is reviewed by the inspection team to ensure completeness and accuracy. This discussion substantiate all aspects of each anomaly. To bring an unambiguous closure to the inspection meeting, the inspection team rates each anomaly as one of "*Accept with no or minor rework*", "*Accept with rework verification*", or "*Re-inspect*".

9.1.4 Software-Audit

A software audit (or software audit review) is a type of software review conducted by independent auditors:

> "An independent examination of a software product, software process, or set of software processes to assess compliance with specifications, standards, contractual agreements, or other criteria" [IEEE 1028, 1998, clause 3.2].

Software audits are distinct from software peer reviews in that they are conducted by personnel external to, and independent of, the software development organisation. Software audits are concerned with compliance of products or processes, rather than with their technical content and quality.

9.1.5 Conclusions

The main attributes of the four methods for technical evaluation of software products are summarised in Table 9.1

The software products developed in this work available as subject to technical evaluation are

- The system architecture

  In this case the framework as "*a generic architecture of a solution*" (Definition 3.6).

- Tools for instantiation of the system architecture

  In this case the toolkit as "*a compilation of re-usable software, specification of interfaces and advice for developing software systems*" (Definition 3.7).

- Generated code

  In this case the code base available for creating software solutions.

The main objectives of the technical evaluation comprise the identification of anomalies in the design of the framework, the realisation of the toolkit and the documentation. It is not mandatory to reach a consensus on each software product. The main use of the results consists in improving the quality of the software products by the author, who takes the final decision on what recommendation is implemented.

Inspection and audit are considered too much focusing on process and organisational level, in particular representing a formal evaluation method requiring leaders trained in such methods. For examining software inspection, the IEEE 1028 [1998] proposes to have inspectors of different viewpoints (such as design, code, test; but also sponsor, safety, project management and hardware engineering). For evaluation of this work, most of the different viewpoints will not appear in a single review.

For evaluating programming code, i.e. the toolkit and the code generated with the toolkit, a walk-through seems adequate, because of its ability to find anomalies but work on alternatives in parallel. Peer reviews seem to be sufficient for evaluating concepts, the system architecture and documentation.

	Walk-through	**Peer Review**	**Inspection**	**Audit**
Input	A software product			A software product or software process(es)
Objectives	Find anomalies, examine alternatives, and provide a forum for learning	Examine suitability for its intended use, identify discrepancies from specification and standards	Find anomalies, errors, and deviations from standards and specification	Assess compliance with specification, standards, contracts and other criteria
Group	Interested parties	Group of qualified persons (internal or external)		Independent persons
Leader	The author	Qualified person	Trained facilitator	Auditor
Output	Recommendations to author and/or management		List of defects that must be removed by the team	List of discrepancies, responsibility of the audited organization

Table 9.1: Summary of software evaluation methods

9.2 Evaluation of the Framework

This section describes the technical evaluation of an intermediate state of the framework for open human-computer interaction with ambient computer systems.

9.2.1 Design of the Review

The review of the framework applies the general design of a technical review process according to section 9.1.2. From the formal approach defined by [IEEE 1028, 1998] this section specifies

The review input, i.e. the subject of the technical review, and a statement of objectives.

The review team, i.e. the persons responsible for conducting the review, the persons documenting anomalies, recommendations, or decisions made by the review team, and the persons actively participating in the review of the software product (reviewers).

The review procedure, i.e. planning the review, preparation, and examination.

The review output, i.e. the intended output from conducting the review.

9.2.1.1 Subject of the Technical Review

The software product being examined is the framework description.

9.2.1.2 Statement of Objectives

The objective of the technical review is to elaborate whether the framework is adequately designed and documented to provide a basis for the implementation of solutions for connecting user interfaces on remote input devices with services of ambient computing environments.

The review aims at determining to what degree the framework fulfils the following five requirements:

Requirement R1: The framework conforms to definitions, standards and guidelines applicable to the design of software architectures.

Requirement R2: The framework describes a complete architecture of a solution.

Requirement R3: The framework describes a valid architecture of a solution.

Requirement R4: The architecture of any other solution can be transformed into the framework without invalidation of the solution.

Requirement R5: The documentation of the framework is complete, clear, and helpful.

9.2.1.3 Review Team

The minimal review team is composed of a review leader, a recorder, and 3-6 reviewers.

The review leader is responsible for ensuring that the review is conducted in a structured manner, performing administrative tasks pertaining to the review, ensuring that all input is available in satisfactory quality, and ensuring that the reviewers are coming well prepared to the review meeting.

The review team is a set of 3-6 qualified persons. In general, the review team is any subset of the stakeholders identified in section 3.2, except end-users. Because the examined software product focuses on programming abstractions and design aspects of solutions, reviewers with strong interest and knowledge in performing design activities from the adapted life cycle of interactive systems (refer to Section 3.1) are preferred. The intended audience for the review are:

- Experts in human-computer interaction in ambient computing environments
- Interaction Designers using remote input devices
- Software Architects specifying distributed systems
- Software Developers building client/server components

The technical review is conducted by the author of the software product being examined. The author is responsible for designing the review and creating all preparation materials handed out to reviewers, creating material for assessment of the feedback from the reviewers. The author will participate in the review meeting and document all statements, comments, and recommendations of the reviewers (i.e. being the recorder). After the review meeting, the author is responsible for identifying anomalies, conclusions and correcting action items.

9.2.1.4 Review Procedure

The review is conducted in three phases: A preparation phase for the review team, a group meeting, and a phase of analysis and finding a consensus on the conclusions and action items. As a preparation of the review, the participants are provided with the statement of objectives of the review, including the list of requirements, and the preparation material. A time-line for preparing the review, and a schedule for the review meeting are announced.

Preparation The reviewers are provided with access to the design description of the framework and its intended use. For preparation, the reviewers are asked to perform four steps in the following order:

1. Please prepare a scenario for using a remote input device to control a service.
2. Please sketch an architecture of a solution for your scenario.
3. Please read the provided framework documentation.
4. Please try to match your solution onto the framework.

Review Meeting At the beginning of the review meeting, the author of the software product being examined presents a short introduction to the subject of the review. Each reviewer has the opportunity to ask questions for understanding the subject. The review leader then asks one after the other for statements, rates, open issues, and comments. Wherever necessary, the review leader asks for details. If other reviewers share similar views, or have contradictory opinions, the review leader opens a group discussion on specific issues. The author answers any technical question from the reviewers. Additionally, the author records each of the reviewers' statements.

Filling in the Review Forms After the meeting, a questionnaire consisting of 19 items is handed out to the reviewers. The reviewers fill in the form rating each item on a scale from 1 (*"strongly agree"*) to 7 (*"strongly disagree"*). Furthermore, the questionnaire enable the reviewers to freely state any comment.

Review Output After submission of all review forms, the author analyses all rates and comments from the reviewers. The author concludes the defects of the subject of the review where requirements might not be fulfilled to satisfactory extend. The author is responsible to prioritise the items on the list, create the correction plan, and perform correcting actions.

9.2.2 The Technical Review of the Framework

The technical review was performed with a group from the software development organisation.

The software product to be examined was an initial description of the framework's elaboration in an intermediate state. Prior to the review meeting, the reviewers were asked to assess the framework on the basis of the document "Elaboration of a framework for open human-computer interaction with ambient services" [Lorenz et al., 2008]. The full document is attached to this thesis in Appendix C.1.

The time-line for preparing the review was set to about 60 minutes.

9.2.2.1 Review Team

Six people participated in the review: A review leader, a recorder, and four reviewers. The review was lead by a senior researcher and developer who is familiar with the topics of this thesis. The author of the description of the framework was responsible for recording all statements during the review meeting.

The reviewers were internal personnel from the department "Information in Context" of Fraunhofer FIT. The reviewers were not involved in the development of the framework at all. Two reviewers are professional software developers, one is a psychologist and business information technologist, and one is a student in computer science. Three reviewers are male, one female.

The reviewers needed between 60 and 90 minutes for preparation.

9.2.2.2 Questionnaire

For formal assessing the reviewers statements and comments, the author of the description of the framework adopted the "*Computer System Usability Questionnaire*" (CSUQ) of Lewis [1995]. The CSUQ is used rather than the PSSUQ (see Section 9.3.2.2) when the usability study is in a non-laboratory setting, in this case a paper-based fictive realisation of a scenario. It consists of 19 items and four rules to calculate scores for overall agreement ("*OVERALL*"), system usage ("*SYSUSE*"), quality of documentation and information about the system ("*INFOQUAL*"), and quality of the user interface of the system ("*INTERQUAL*"). The score for OVERALL and SYSUSE remain unchanged.

Because the framework does not provide a user interface, the score INTERQUAL was removed. The item about organisation of information on the system screen was also removed, because the framework does not come with any screen at all. For the same reason, the items for error messages of the system and recovery from mistakes where removed from the questionnaire. The score for INFOQUAL therefore consists of only four items.

To assess the quality of the framework design, six new items replace the removed items from the original questionnaire. The six new items build the score "*SYSDESIGN*" in this work.

The full questionnaire is added to this thesis in Appendix C.2. The four scores are calculated according to the following scheme:

OVERALL Average the responses to item 1 through 19

SYSDESIGN Average the responses to item 1 through 6

Score	Items	Mean	Std. Deviation	Std. Error
OVERALL	Q1-Q19	3,17	0,928	0,464
SYSDESIGN	Q1-Q6	2,79	0,854	0,427
SYSUSE	Q7-Q14	3,19	1,092	0,546
INFOQUAL	Q15-Q18	4,00	1,275	0,637

Table 9.2: Results of the CSUQ of the framework evaluation

SYSUSE Average the responses to item 7 through 14[1]

INFOQUAL Average the responses to item 15 through 18

9.2.2.3 Results

This section summarises the rates and comments from the reviewers. Because of the relative low number of reviewers, any statistical analysis of the results are not expressive. The response from the reviewers, in particular their comments, are used as indicators of discrepancies to be addressed in the further development.

This section uses quantitative measurements by analysing the reviewers' ratings, and qualitative assessment by analysing reviewers' comments. It uses italic style in double quotes to distinguishing specific reviewers' ratings from the text, e.g. "*4*". The same format is applied for specific reviewers' comments, e.g. "*I would like to comment on this.*" The five requirements from section 9.2.1.2 are addressed using the character 'R' and the requirement number, e.g. R5. Specific items of the questionnaire are labelled with the letter 'Q' and the item number in the questionnaire.

The Scores The CSUQ scores are listed in Table 9.2. The lines of the table list the four scores, the associated items, and the the descriptive statistics (mean, standard error, and standard deviation) of responses from the reviewers. Figure 9.1 illustrates the mean and the 95% confidence interval (95% CI[2]). A lower value indicates a higher agreement with the statements due to the anchors used in the 7-point scales. The 95% confidence interval illustrates the range of the scores of 95% of the reviewers assuming a normal distribution.

All scores are on or below the median of "*4*". The overall score is 3,17 with a 95% confidence interval of 2,261 to 4,079. The best score is assigned with SYSDESIGN with a 95% confidence interval of 1,953 to 3,627, followed by SYSUSE with a 95% confidence interval of 2,120 to 4,260. For theses

[1]Equal to average the responses of item 1 through item 8 in [Lewis, 1995].

[2]$95\%CI = Mean \pm 1.96 \bullet StdErr$

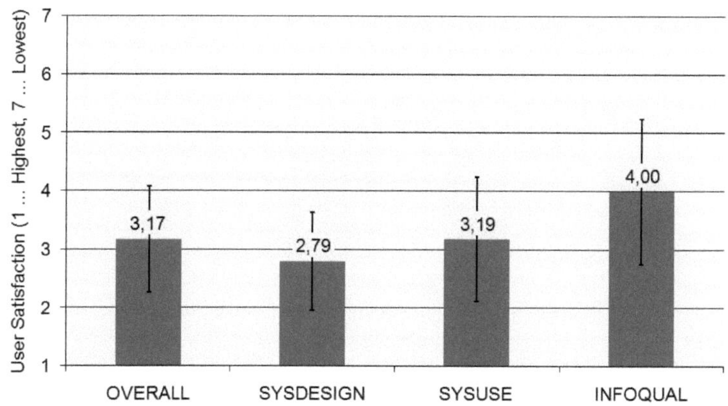

Figure 9.1: Results from evaluating the framework (mean and 95% CI)

scores, 95% of the reviewers in a normal distribution would assign scores below or close to the median of "*4*". The worst score was assigned with INFOQUAL with a 95% confidence interval of 2,751 to 5,249. For this score it is open if 95% of the reviewers would tend to be satisfied or not. Additional evaluation would be needed to clarify this.

Reviewers' Ratings On the positive side, the reviewers were satisfied with the framework, its components and information flow. Three of four reviewers agreed that the framework covers all required components (item Q1[3]). All reviewers agreed that the framework is free of overhead components (fifty-fifty between "*strongly agree*" and "2" for item Q2[4] with the best average of 1,50).

As shown by Table 9.2, INFOQUAL reaches the worst score. Figure 9.2 therefore illustrates the mean values and 95% confidence interval of all items of INFOQUAL. This score covers the only two items with a mean satisfactory level higher than the median of "*4*" (Q15[5] and Q16[6]). In fact, no reviewer rated item Q16 better than the median; the same holds true for item Q15 except one rate of "*3*".

The design of the data transmission was left undecided, because one reviewer "*strongly agreed*", two reviewers rated "*3*", and one reviewer "*strongly disagreed*" to item Q4[7]. One reviewer explicitly mentioned a missing communication channel back to the input device.

[3]Q1: "*The framework covers all components required for the intended use.*"

[4]Q2: "*The framework is free of overhead components.*"

[5]Q15: "*The information (such as on-line help, on-screen messages and other documentation) provided with the framework is clear.*"

[6]Q16: "*It is easy to find the information I need.*"

[7]Q4: "*All data transmission between components over a network is defined.*"

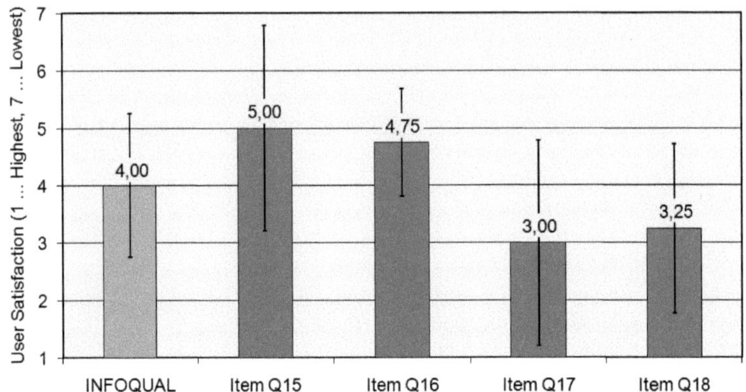

Figure 9.2: Results from evaluating INFOQUAL of the framework (mean and 95% CI)

Three reviewers criticised that the framework lacks completeness regarding functions and capabilities they expected it to have (rates "*4*", "*5*", and "*6*", one outlier with "***strongly agree***" to item Q5[8] with an average on the the median of "*4*").

All questions and the average ratings of all reviewers for each item are attached to this thesis in Table C.1.

Fulfilment of Requirements To assess fulfilment of the requirements R1-R5, Table 9.3 lists the five requirements, associated items from the questionnaire, and the descriptive statistics (mean, standard error, and standard deviation). Figure 9.3 illustrates the mean and the 95% Confidence Interval (95% CI).

In summary, all combined averages from the reviewers' ratings for the five requirements are on or below the median of "*4*". The table reveals that fulfilment of requirement R5[9] reaches the lowest level of satisfaction.

The analysis of the comments from the reviewers revealed that the "usability" features of the framework were not satisfactory implemented because of the weak documentation: The reviewers were not able to efficiently use the framework because of missing detailed information about the framework and its internal composition.

[8]Q5: *"The framework has all the functions and capabilities I expect it to have."*
[9]R5: *"The documentation of the framework is complete, clear, and helpful."*

	Requirement	Items	Mean	Std. Deviation	Std. Error
R1	The framework conforms to definitions, standards and guidelines applicable to the design of software architectures.	Q6, Q19	2,13	0,750	0,375
R2	The framework describes a complete architecture of a solution.	Q1, Q2, Q3	2,33	0,609	0,304
R3	The framework describes a valid architecture of a solution.	Q1, Q3, Q4, Q5	3,25	1,423	0,714
R4	The architecture of any other solution can be transformed into the framework without invalidation of the solution.	SYS-USE	3,19	1,092	0,546
R5	The documentation of the framework is complete, clear, and helpful.	INFO-QUAL	4,00	1,275	0,637

Table 9.3: Level of reviewers' satisfaction with each requirement to the framework

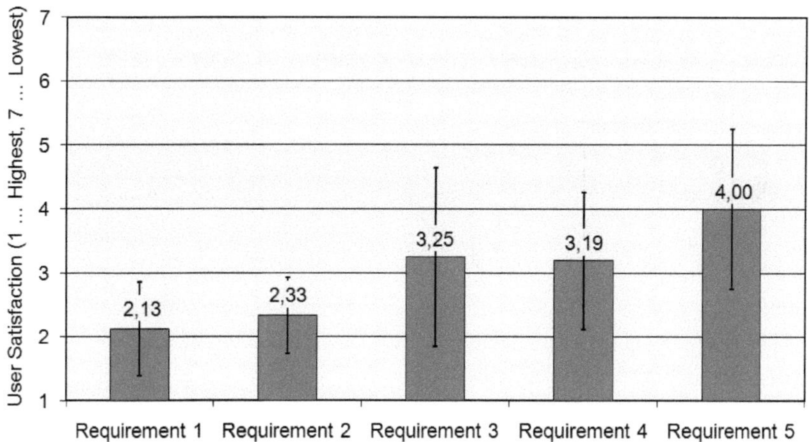

Figure 9.3: Results from evaluating the framework (mean and 95% CI)

Reviewers' Comments In general, the reviewers were able to match their solutions onto the architecture proposed by the framework. One of the reviewers elaborated a similar architecture only using different names for the components. Another reviewer would have needed a feedback channel towards the input device. However, the other reviewers explicitly agreed, that such a feedback channel is not necessarily part of the framework, mainly for two reasons:

- "*The Graphical User Interface is not necessarily running on the input device.*"
- "*You cannot generally assume that the input device is able to render feedback from the service.*"

In general, the detail level of the framework design description was considered too low. One reviewer commented on the whole framework design description: "*The Level of Detail is so low, I can hardly say anything*". Other negative comments address the framework documentation explicitly:

- "*Everything is missing, except one single image.*"
- "*The documentation is stingy.*"
- "*The document is too abstract.*"
- "*Though the document was on-line available, I would hardly call it on-line help or on-screen message.*"
- "*The work on preparing the review was more helpful than the documentation.*"

The question whether the framework matches Definition 3.6 on page 28 was "*strongly agreed*" by two reviewers, the others rated "*3*" and "*4*". The latter two reviewers put Definition 3.6 itself in question: "*I do not agree with the definition of 'framework'.*", and "*I consider a framework not only as an architecture but also as a toolkit. This is not reflected by the definition at all.*" In fact, the framework was seen as too abstract to provide much support for software developers.

Regarding the usage of a framework, the reviewers provided inconsistent and sometimes contradictory statements. On one hand, the reviewers emphasised that a framework defines the architecture of a solution rather than provides software components:

- "*I was not looking for programming support. It addresses system design on an abstract level.*"
- "*I did not expect technical support. It is too early to request libraries.*"

On the other hand, the reviewers stated

- *"I would have expected to have some libraries where I simple invoke some methods."*
- *"I would like to use it like Eclipse[10]: I can put together some parts by simple mouse clicks, but I do also have the opportunity to integrate my code."*

One reviewers' comment "*What does it mean: Using the framework?*" triggered a discussion in which the reviewers elaborated what to expect from a framework and how to use it:

- *"The aim of the framework is to get some work done that I would have to accomplish myself otherwise."*
- *"The framework provides the events but does not implement the application logic."*
- *"I would like to define the application logic not spending any thoughts on event-handling."* - *"The other way around: I would like to specify the structure rather quickly, and then to go into details by hand."*
- *"The framework should lead through the whole development process, from the beginning to the end."*
- *"It can be useful for Rapid Prototyping as well as for product development."*

This general confusion on how to use a framework is the main reason why three reviewers could not rate the coverage of all expected functions and capabilities by the framework better than the median of "*4*".

9.2.3 Conclusions

In summary, the reviewers accepted the general purpose and overall design of the framework. A communication channel enabling the input device to receive feedback and/or acknowledgements from the service might be of interest for some applications. For other applications, such a communication channel would be difficult to implement, especially if the device offers no capabilities for rendering the feedback. As a conclusion, this work remains treating the input device according to its name as pure information source.

The Definition 3.6 was put in question by two reviewers; one of whom asked to better reflect toolkit properties in the definition. The main purpose of the framework is to define the abstract architecture

[10]An open source project aiming to provide a universal tool-suite for software development. See `http://www.eclipse.org/`

of solutions for a family of problems. This view is supported by other researchers cited in section 3.4.3. For delivering practical support for the implementation phase, another software artefact is used according to Definition 3.7. Both artefacts remain separated to accentuate the boundaries between the framework with focus on design reuse and programming abstraction, and the toolkit with focus on tool support and creation of the code-base. However, their close relation to each other was not clear in the examined document accessed by the reviewers.

The design description of the framework was not satisfactory in the examined version. The low quality of the documentation formed the main reason for misunderstandings among reviewers. The main purpose of the framework's development was distorted. Moreover, it remained unclear how to use a framework and on what level of abstraction. The reviewers' answers to technical questions were therefore inconclusive.

The scales for questions were missing an item for "*Not Applicable*". One of the reviewers rated many items with the median ("*4*") in order to indicate "*N/A*".

The analysis of the filled questionnaires revealed that requirement R2[11] and R3[12] are close to each other. Putting together the items for these requirements is expected to result in more explanatory power. In addition, the order of the items of the questionnaire could be re-arranged in order to form more adequate item groups.

Leading the review by a person other than the author of the software product being examined revealed the positive effect that all issues could approached in a rather neutral way without the author taking a merely defensive position. In contrast, the author in the role of the recorder and observer introduces the risk of selective perception preferential documenting positive feedback.

9.2.4 Framework Evolution

All derived action items are summarised in Table 9.4. All items regarding the framework are implemented in the course of development of this thesis.

The review examined an intermediate description of the framework providing too little detailed information about the framework and its design. In result of the review, Chapter 5 addresses the required update of the description of the framework. In addition, the thesis was restructured to illustrate different software partitioning schemes close together in Section 3.4.

The contradictory expectations on how to use a framework required detailed explanation. This issue is now addressed in Section 3.4.3.2 describing three methods for using frameworks. The relation

[11]R2: *"The framework describes a complete architecture of a solution."*
[12]R3: *"The framework describes a valid architecture of a solution."*

	Objection	Action Items
Framework	Use of a framework is generally unclear.	• Description of Black-Box, Grey-Box, and White-Box approaches added in Section 3.4.3.2. • Explanation of abstraction and complexity levels added to Section 3.3.
	Fuzzy distinction between framework and toolkit.	• Thesis restructured to differentiate design reuse from tool support. • Definition 3.6 remains unchanged.
	Design description of the framework is not satisfactory.	• Framework description completely reworked in Chapter 5.
Review	No neutral answer available for the items of the questionnaire.	• Add option "*N/A*".
	Requirements R2 and R3 closely related.	• Combine R2 and R3 to "*The framework describes a complete architecture of a valid solution.*" • Re-order items of the questionnaire accordingly.

Table 9.4: Objections from the review of the framework and correcting action items

between the framework and the toolkit described in Section 7.5 is further reflected by stepwise decreasing the level of abstraction from the specification of the framework to the white box framework, which finally defines the reference architecture of solutions generated with the toolkit.

To define the points where stakeholders using the framework integrate their code, descriptions of hot and frozen spots were added in result of the review. The semantic interface was added to the framework to disclosure the functions of the service to the client. The 'service interface' from the original design was renamed to 'observer interface' to reflect its function more precisely. It was furthermore moved into the virtual input device in order to enable registration of dependants on its internal flow of events.

The inconsistent statements about the abstraction level of the framework and its particular contribution required additional explanation. The different complexity levels, and approaches to reduce complexity by programming abstractions, tool support and code bases, was added to Section 3.3.

9.2.5 Open Action Items

All items of Table 9.4 regarding the review process are left open to be considered in future reviews. For subsequent evaluations, requirements R2 and R3 will be integrated into one single requirement: "*The framework describes a complete architecture of a valid solution.*" The order of items of the questionnaire will be updated according to the new structure of requirements. The scale for each item will be extended with a "*N/A*" option.

9.3 Evaluation of the Toolkit

This section describes the technical evaluation of the tool support for generating solutions for interaction with services of ambient computing environments.

9.3.1 Design of the Walk-through

The review of the toolkit applies to the general design of a software walk-through process according to section 9.1.1. From the formal approach defined by [IEEE 1028, 1998] this section specifies

The review input, i.e. the subject of the walk-through, and a statement of objectives.

The review team, i.e. the persons responsible for conducting the walk-through, the persons documenting anomalies, alternatives, or recommendations provided by the review team, and the persons actively participating in the walk-through the software product (reviewers).

The review procedure, i.e. planning the walk-through, preparation, and examination.

The review output, i.e. the intended output from conducting the walk-through.

9.3.1.1 Subject of the Walk-Through

The software product being examined is the toolkit. The toolkit consists of a set of software programs with graphical user interfaces, and a user's manual.

9.3.1.2 Statement of Objectives

The objective of the walk-through is to elaborate whether the toolkit is adequately designed, implemented, and documented to provide programming support to create executable software instances of the framework.

The walk-through aims at determining to what degree the toolkit fulfils the following three requirements:

Requirement 1 The toolkit creates valid solutions for interactive software systems using remote input devices.

Requirement 2 The toolkit fulfils all functions for a full development cycle.

Requirement 3 The toolkit fulfils all non-functional requirements, in particular regarding usability and documentation.

9.3.1.3 Review Team

The minimal review team consists of the author of the software product, a moderator, and 3-10 reviewers.

The moderator is responsible for ensuring that the walk-through is conducted in a structured manner, performing administrative tasks pertaining to the walk-through, ensuring that all input is available in satisfactory quality, and ensuring that the reviewers are coming well prepared to the walk-through meeting.

The review team is a set of 3-10 qualified persons. In general, the review team is any subset of the stakeholders identified in section 3.2, except end-users. Because the examined software product focuses on tool support and creation of code bases for solutions, reviewers with strong interest and knowledge in performing interaction design, implementation, integration and installation activities from the adapted life cycle of interactive systems (refer to Section 3.1) are preferred. The intended audience for the walk-through are:

- Experts in human-computer interaction in ambient computing environments
- System Providers of interactive services and/or user interface technology
- Interaction-Designers using remote input devices
- System-Designers of distributed interactive applications
- Software Developers building client/server components, user-interface components, and/or service logic

The walk-through is conducted by the author of the software product being examined. The author is responsible for designing the walk-through, providing access to software programs and documentation for preparation, and creating material for assessment of the feedback from the reviewers. The author will participate in the review meeting to present the software product and go through each detail stepwise. After the review meeting, the author is responsible for identifying anomalies, conclusions and correcting action items.

9.3.1.4 Walk-through Procedure

The walk-through is conducted in three phases: A preparation phase for the review team, a group meeting, and a phase of analysis and elaborating and action items. As a preparation of the walk-through, the participants are provided with the statement of objectives of the walk-through, including the list of requirements, and the preparation material. A time-line for preparing the review, and a schedule for the review meeting are announced.

Preparation The reviewers are provided with access to the software programs and the user manual. For preparation, the reviewers are asked to perform five steps in the following order:

1. Download and install the toolkit on your local computer system.

2. Open the User's Guide. Start the toolkit and go through the example of the virtual movie controller in Chapter 4 of the User's Guide.

3. Create a new model of a virtual input device and change the model until it fulfils a given set of requirements.

4. Test, whether your single server instance receives input sequences.

5. Deploy the mobile client on a Java-enabled mobile phone. Perform the tests from step 4 on the mobile input device.

Walk-through Meeting At the beginning of the walk-through meeting, the author of the software product presents a short introduction to the subject of the walk-through. Each reviewer has the opportunity to ask questions for understanding the subject. If the subject is clear to all participants, the author of the software products presents the details of each of the software tools in sequential order. The reviewers always have the opportunity to interrupt the presentation to asks questions, denote open issues, point to alternatives, and give comments. The author answers any technical question from the reviewers.

The moderator presides over the walk-through meeting and documents all statements, comments, and recommendations of the reviewers.

Filling in the Review Forms After the meeting, a questionnaire is handed out to the reviewers. The questionnaire consists of 19 item of which 18 are categorised according to the tools under examination. The reviewers fill in the form rating each item on a scale from 1 (*"strongly agree"*) to 7 (*"strongly disagree"*). For a neutral answer, the reviewers leave the field empty. Furthermore, the questionnaire enable the reviewers to freely state any comment.

Review Output After submission of all review forms, the author analyses all rates and comments from the reviewers. The author concludes the anomalies of the subject of the walk-through where requirements might not be fulfilled to satisfactory extend. The author is responsible to prioritise the items on the list, create the correction plan, and perform correcting actions.

9.3.2 The Walk-through the Toolkit

The walk-through was performed with a group from the software development organisation. The reviewers were provided with access to the web-page where the software programs, the documentation, and the preparation material for the walk-through was available for download. Because some reviewers refused to install the software on their private machines the author provided access to a public installation of all parts of the software product on a shared server.

Prior to the walk-through meeting, the reviewers were asked to get familiar with the intended use of the tools, and to assess the user manual from the web. The reviewers were also asked to go through the MoviePlayer-example used in the user manual and prepare a list of their objections. The time-line for preparing the walk-through was set to about 60 minutes.

9.3.2.1 Review Team

Ten people participated in the walk-through: The author, a moderator and recorder, and eight reviewers. The review was moderated by a senior researcher and developer who is familiar with the topics of this thesis. The moderator was also responsible for recording all statements during the walk-through meeting.

The reviewers were internal personnel from the department "Information in Context" of Fraunhofer FIT. The reviewers were not involved in the development of the software product at all. Four reviewers are professional software developers, one is a business information technologist, and three are students in computer science. Seven reviewers are male, one female.

9.3.2.2 Questionnaire

For formal assessing the reviewers statements and comments, the author of the software system under examination adopted the "*Post-Study System Usability Questionnaire*" (PSSUQ) of Lewis [1995]. The PSSUQ is used rather than the CSUQ (see Section 9.2.2.2) after participants have completed all the scenarios in a usability study. It consists of 19 items and four rules to calculate scores for overall agreement ("*OVERALL*"), system usage ("*SYSUSE*"), quality of documentation and information about the system ("*INFOQUAL*"), and quality of the user interface of the system ("*INTERQUAL*"). The 19 items of the questionnaire remain unchanged. The four scores are calculated according to Lewis' original work:

OVERALL Average the responses to item 1 through 19

SYSUSE Average the responses to item 1 through 8

INFOQUAL Average the responses to item 9 through 15

INTERQUAL Average the responses to item 16 through 18

Score	Items	Mean	Std. Deviation	Std. Error
OVERALL	Q1-Q19	2,64	0,410	0,167
SYSUSE	Q1-Q8	2,39	0,450	0,184
INFOQUAL	Q9-Q15	2,62	1,046	0,427
INTERQUAL	Q16-Q18	2,78	0,689	0,281

Table 9.5: PSSUQ scores assigned with category "Overall" of the toolkit evaluation

To receive distinguishable ratings for the five tools, the installation and overall rating, the adopted questionnaire provides categories of "Overall", "Installation", "Modelling", "Programming", "Building", "Testing", and "Deploying". The category "Overall" has the full list of 19 items; the score OVERALL is only calculated from this category. The other six categories consist of the items 1 to 18. The score OVERALL is therefore not available for these categories. To the utmost, the reviewers are enabled to provide 127 different ratings. The full questionnaire is added to this thesis in Appendix C.3.

9.3.2.3 Results

This section summarises the rates and comments from the reviewers. The response from the reviewers, in particular their comments, are used as indicators of discrepancies to be addressed in the further development.

Similar to the analysis of the framework evaluation, this section uses quantitative measurements by analysing the reviewers' ratings, and qualitative assessment by analysing reviewers' comments. It also employs the same format as Section 9.2.2.3 for distinguishing specific items and comments from the text (i.e. italic style in double quotes).

The Scores The PSSUQ scores assigned with the category "Overall" are listed in Table 9.5. The lines of the table list the four scores, the associated items, and the the descriptive statistics (mean, standard error, and standard deviation) of responses from the reviewers in category "Overall". Figure 9.4 illustrates the mean and the 95% confidence interval (95% CI) of this category. A lower mean value indicates a higher agreement with the statements due to the anchors used in the 7-point scales. The 95% confidence interval illustrates the range of the scores of 95% of the reviewers assuming a normal distribution.

All scores are below the median of "*4*". Taking the confidence interval into account, 95% of reviewers in a normal distribution would tend to be satisfied with the toolkit and assign scores below the median of "*4*". The overall score is 2,64 with a 95% confidence interval of 2,313 to 2,967.

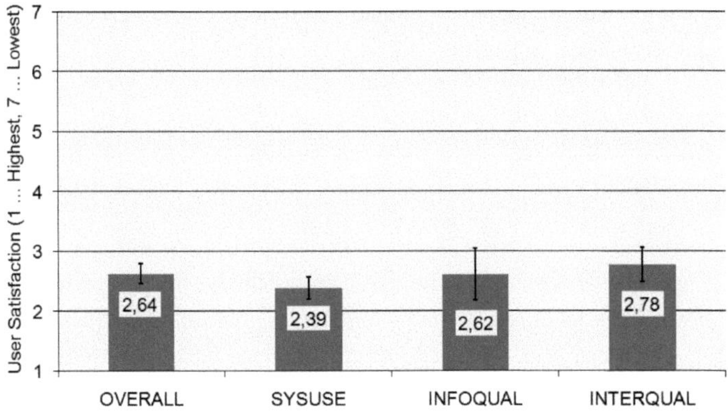

Figure 9.4: Results from evaluating the toolkit (mean and 95% CI of category "Overall")

Score	**Items**	**Installation**	**Modelling**	**Programming**	**Building**	**Testing**	**Deploying**
SYSUSE	Q1-Q8	3,01	2,33	3,43	2,53	2,29	2,49
INFOQUAL	Q9-Q15	2,83	3,15	3,26	3,15	2,35	2,44
INTERQUAL	Q16-Q18	2,94	2,93	3,05	2,50	2,18	2,43

Table 9.6: Results of the PSSUQ of the toolkit evaluation

The PSSUQ scores assigned with each tool are listed in Table 9.6. The lines of the table list the scores for SYSUSE, INFOQUAL, and INTERQUAL, the associated items, and the average of responses to each of the six tools. The best scores are assigned to INTERQUAL and SYSUSE of "Testing" (2,18 and 2,29), and SYSUSE of "Modelling" (2,33). The worst scores are assigned to SYSUSE and INFOQUAL of "Programming" (3,43 and 3,26), and to INFOQUAL of "Modelling" and "Building" (3,15 each).

Figure 9.5 illustrates the PSSUQ scores for each tool. It shows the scores for SYSUSE, INFOQUAL, and INTERQUAL as boxes from left to right. From the technical aspects, "Testing" and "Deploying" are rated best on a similar level with scores below 2,50; "Programming" is behind all others with all scores higher than 3,00. In particular, it has the worst score for each of SYSUSE, INFOQUAL, and INTERQUAL.

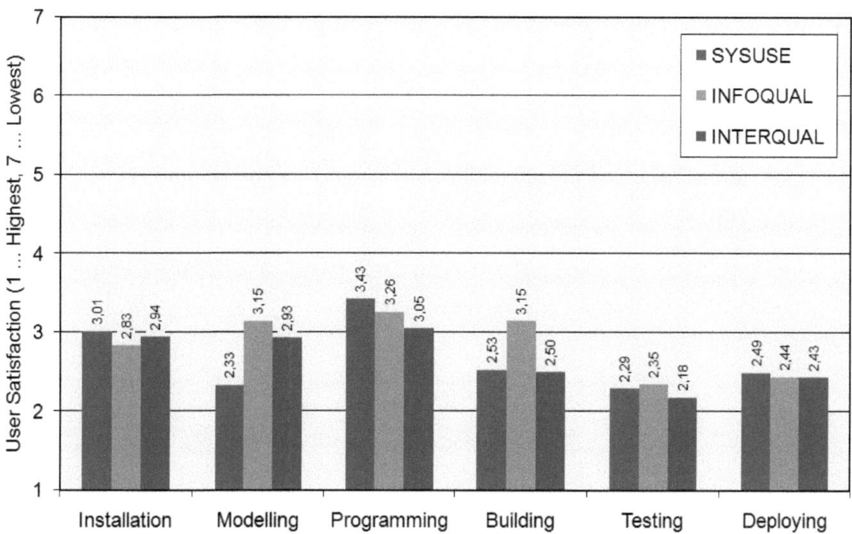

Figure 9.5: PSSUQ-scores to each category of the toolkit evaluation

Reviewers' Ratings Except one item (Q9[13]), all items are rated below the median of "*4*" in this category. The best rated items are Q7[14] (average of 1,33), Q13[15] and Q15[16] (both with an average of 2,00); the worst rated items are Q9 (average of 5,00), Q17[17] (average of 3,40), and Q8[18] (average of 3,33). The best rated item (i.e. Q7) was rated best in 5 out of 7 categories ("Overall", "Modelling", "Programming", "Building", and "Deploying"). For the other extreme, item Q9 is ranked worst for 6 out of 7 categories; only for category "Programming" it was ranked 17th out of 18.

All reviewer ratings combined for the OVERALL-score are attached to this thesis in Table C.2.

Fulfilment of Requirements To assess fulfilment of the requirements R1-R3, Table 9.7 lists the requirements, associated items from the category "Overall" to each requirement, and the descriptive statistics (mean, standard error, and standard deviation). Figure 9.6 illustrates the mean and the 95% Confidence Interval (95% CI). In summary, all combined averages from the reviewers' ratings for the

[13] *"The system gives error messages that clearly tell me how to fix problems."*
[14] *"It was easy to learn to use this system."*
[15] *"The information provided with the system is easy to understand."*
[16] *"The organisation of information on the system screens is clear."*
[17] *"I like using the interface of this system."*
[18] *"I believe I became productive quickly using this system."*

	Requirement	Items	Mean	Std. Deviation	Std. Error
R1	The Toolkit creates valid solutions for interactive software systems using remote input devices.	Q3, Q18, Q19	2,92	0,346	0,141
R2	The Toolkit fulfils all functions for a full development cycle.	SYSUSE	2,39	0,450	0,184
R3	The Toolkit fulfils all non-functional requirements, in particular regarding usability and documentation.	INTERQUAL and INFOQUAL	2,76	0,617	0,252

Table 9.7: Level of reviewers' satisfaction with each requirement to the toolkit

three requirements are on a similar level well below the median of "*4*". The Figure shows that all requirements are fulfilled to satisfactory extend.

Reviewers' Comments General comments addressing issues of using frameworks and their relations to toolkits emerged similar to the comments from the framework evaluation. Some reviewers treat frameworks as pure overhead without much support for the development phase. In parallel, the "*use of toolkits usually makes only sense for special purposes.*" At least, reviewers agreed that "*the examined toolkit delivers all features I require*" for this purpose. One reviewers stated that the "*overall idea is nice and it indeed show the solution that greatly easy developer's work.*" Reviewers also stated that the interface is "*simple and easy to understand*", "*a little bit ugly, and the information for all the sub menu is not shown completely.*"

Feature Requests Most of the comments address missing features. In general, the reviewers were missing context menus and shortcuts in all tools, a wizard guiding the installation step-by-step, and a direct deploy and launch of the application on a mobile device for testing. In addition, help support is requested ("*I am used to press F1 to show help*") for all screens.

The worst score was calculated for SYSUSE of "Programming" in Table 9.6. The comments reveal that the reviewers were not satisfied with the approach of only presenting the auto-generated code inside the toolkit, and save and import it in the preferred coding editor for manipulation. In conflict with the design decision to walk back to modelling to perform changes, the reviewers were missing an editing function to update the code manually: "*A programmer cannot change the code flexible without modelling it first*" in the current approach. This approach only works "*if there is no changes need to*

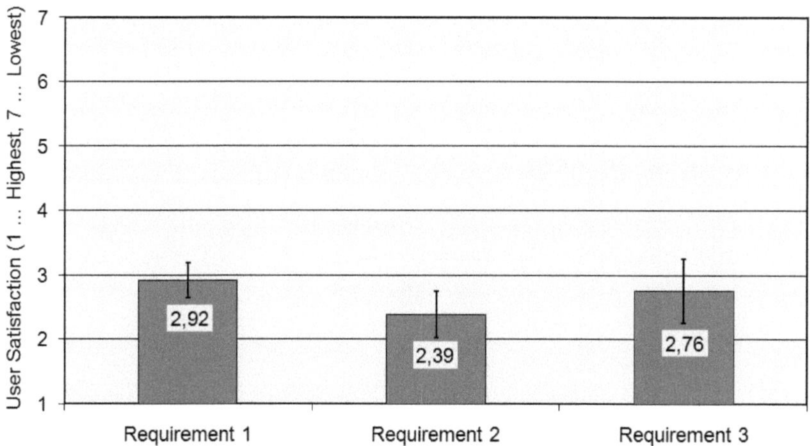

Figure 9.6: Results from evaluating the toolkit (mean and 95% CI)

be done after the source code is edited; otherwise copy-paste is a headache!". Another reviewer also refused using copy-paste of source code because "*copy-paste to other editor might result in inconsistencies of the source codes.* [...] *The model that was designed is not valid anymore because the source that has been edited cannot be imported back to the tool*". A comfortable solution is to"*use an external text editor that support code completion / intellisense to reduce coding mistakes.*" Last but not least, reviewers "*need to write comments to the semantic model that are transferred to the source code as well.*" This would ease to find the appropriate position where to enter own programming code, and it would support documentation of the generated code, e.g. by using JavaDoc.

Error Handling and Recovery from Errors The worst single rates were assigned with the item Q9 from the questionnaire. This item examines the quality of error messages of the system telling how to fix problems, which got mostly negative comments like

- "*I do not remember any error message.*"
- "*The only recovery from mistake was the renaming option in "Modelling".*"
- "*No information for the error in "Modelling".*"

In particular for "Modelling", two reviewers reported problems to recover from mistakes. One reviewer removed the (mandatory) source parameter from the model of a virtual input device by mistake, another reviewer used an underscore in the label of an event. In both cases, the "Modelling" tool accepted the changes without any error message; but working with the derived code was not possible in subsequent development activities.

Incorrect code can be identified using the "Building" tool, but "*the error line number is useless.*" because the "Programming" tool lacks line numbering. As a consequence, "*it will be hard for people to count the line themselves when the code is long.*"

Another comment addresses the configuration of the system, because "*there is no clear error message when Java path or WTK*[19] *path was not right configured.*"

Development Cycle The development cycle described in Section 7.1 proposes to have a sequential order of modelling, code generation, building, testing and deploying. In this approach, developers only have the opportunity to return to modelling for correcting errors or change of the behaviour. First of all all, this development cycle was seen to be unusual: "*the develop cycle starting from the model whenever to create or to modify is little bit change the normal way for developing.*"

The development cycle had provoked a lot of controversy in the course of the walk-through meeting. On the one hand, "*developers use code for their thinking process and thus, the paralleling of all steps is a very good approach. Developers need different views on the same thing.*" On the other hand, the image itself was not helpful because it is missing an entry point, the input and output of each activity is not clear, and the meaning of the lines between the bubbles is not explained.

The relationship between the activities of the development cycle, and the tools, could be strengthened by setting a sequence of using one tool after the other according to the transitions defined in Figure 7.1. This approach was not acceptable for the reviewers: "*Step-by-step approach (with a sequence of "next"-buttons) is not a good approach, since it restricts the way of using the framework in the developer's own development approach.*" The better approach was identified to have a "*Process bar / Map would be good to see how much need to be done to reach the goal.*"

Walk-through The reviewers found it difficult to distinguish between completing the work "quickly", "effectively", and "efficiently"; They commented that these three questions are going into the same direction. Furthermore, one reviewer mentioned that Q11 and Q13 (about the information to be clear vs. easy to understand) are almost the same.

They had no other comments regarding the walk-through.

[19]The compulsory Sun's Wireless Toolkit to compile and run JavaMobile-code [@Sun, 2008]

9.3.3 Conclusions

In summary, the reviewers accepted the intended process for the development of interactive systems. The guidance through the process can be strengthened by visualisation of the current position in the overall process. Mandatory stepwise processing from one activity to the next was refused by the reviewers. Going through the process in a prescribed order of activities was seen as being to restrictive. The reviewers want to retain control on the selection of the order of activities.

All tools have a clear position in the process. The reviewers agreed on the aim of the tools, their position in the process, and their usefulness. The "Programming" tool was associated with the lowest level of satisfaction in all categories. In particular, the reviewers questioned the effectiveness of this tool. In fact, "Programming" only provides code review with no chance to edit the code. Though the reviewers approved the process to change the model instead of the derived source code, software developers require sufficient coding functions to make changes directly. The model should be re-imported from the code reflecting changes automatically.

From the evaluated aspects, the quality of the documentation and information about the system were associated with the lowest level of satisfaction. The reviewers particularly criticised the quality of error messages, error handling, and recovery from errors. In fact, reviewers did not see any sensible error handling. Sensible error handling in combination with improved help features need to be added to all tools. The addition of other features like context-menus and short-cuts would further improve the efficiency of development.

The difference between "quickly", "efficiently", and "effectively" is not always clear from the items of the questionnaire.

9.3.4 Action Items

This section lists the action items to improve the toolkit. All items listed below are left open to be considered by future development of the toolkit; the code of the toolkit remained unchanged after the walk-through.

The guidance through the process needs to be improved by a visual element. A progress bar will be implemented at the bottom of the window. The progress bar will show the five items of "Semantic Modelling", "Code Generation", "Building Executable Code", Testing", and "Deployment" in sequential order. According to the current tool, the position in the overall process will be highlighted.

A feature for editing the code will be added to the "Programming" tool. By activating a menu item, short-cut, or button, the developer can load the current source file into the preferred code editor. The editor to be used will be specified in an additional line of the settings. Whenever the toolkit regains the focus, it parses the source files and updates the model. The "Programming" tool remains a code preview only; line numbers will be added to the preview to support identification of the line of errors.

To improve error messages, the toolkit will be extended with a dialogue window for error messages. A syntax check will be added to the "Modelling" tool, detecting if the model is an instance of the specification for virtual input devices of Section 5.5.3. The syntax check will also be performed when parsing source file.

To make development more comfortable, all items from the menu are made available in context menus, too. Short-cuts will be associated to specific activities, like switching to a specific screen, or activating a specific activity.A single button for deploy-launch on specific target devices, in particular mobile devices, will be added. Rudimentary help will be associated to activation of "F1". The help will show the aim of the tool currently used. For "Modelling", the help will also show the EBNF-notation which the model is required to fulfil. Because the model is encoded in XML, the developer can add XML-comments to the file. In the current version, the files are overwritten by the "Modelling" tool, potentially removing the comments. The tool will support comments on the model of the virtual input device. The comments are automatically transferred into Java documentation by the "Programming" tool.

Regarding the walk-through, the only action item address the items Q3-Q5 of the questionnaire. The items in question are required to assess different user aspects: Speed of task completion, achievement of the goals, and economical use of the tools. The items remain unchanged in content. The text of the items will be extended to provide deeper insight into the terms.

All derived action items are summarised in Table 9.8. All items are left open to be considered in future versions of the toolkit.

9.4 Summary

The basic concept developed in the course of this thesis was evaluated in a technical review. The reviewers accepted the general purpose and overall design of the framework elaborated in this thesis. The reviewers were able to match own solutions onto the architecture proposed by the framework. They explicitly agreed that a feedback channel towards the input device is not necessarily part of the framework. It would be difficult to implement, especially if the input device offers no capabilities for rendering the feedback. In conclusion, the input device remained treated according to its name as pure information source.

	Objection	Action Items
Toolkit	Improve guidance through the development process.	• Use progress bar.
	No editing option for source code.	• Use an external editor. • Parse source code whenever the toolkit regains the user focus.
	Weak error messages.	• Add error dialogue. • Add syntax check for "Modelling" and parsing source files. • Add line numbers to "Programming".
	Missing features.	• Add context-menus. • Add short-cuts to specific activities. • Add help screen associated with activating "F1".
Walk-through	Vague difference between "quickly", "effectively", and "effectively".	• Keep the items. • Add explanation, like "less time in development", "achievement of intended results", and "economical use".

Table 9.8: Objections from the walk-through the toolkit and correcting action items

The review of the tools supporting the development on programming level agreed on the aim of the tool support, the set of tools and their position in the overall development process, and their usefulness. Usability aspects of quality of error messages, recovering from errors, and documentation were assigned with the lowest level of satisfaction. The toolkit also misses some features in particular for editing programming code.

Chapter 10

Summary and Future Work

We stand at the border of the transition from local interaction with a computer system to location-independent remote interaction with systems available in the environment of the user. Current architectures, mechanism and features of user interface technology need to be adapted according to the shifts in computer usage. The thesis examined a fundamental understanding of the structure of interactive systems in ambient computing environments. Illustrating different levels of complexity established an understanding of the support for the stakeholders. Three artefacts were developed in the course of the thesis to reduce complexity on three levels: Programming abstractions (framework), tool support (toolkit), and full access to programming code (code-base of shared technology and reference implementations). Interoperation across devices was addressed at physical, conceptual, and software level.

10.1 Contributions

In the course of this thesis, a *framework* for human-computer interaction with ambient computer systems was designed. It delivers the *generic architecture* and defines the interplay between the components for the family of interactive systems with remote input devices. Recurrent functions are implemented in *libraries* of common technology. To support implementation of systems based on the framework, the *toolkit* delivers artefacts for specification, (automatic) code generation, and other aids for system development.

On the highest level of abstraction, the framework approach supports separating the user interface from the application logic, the application hardware and physical constraints. The definition of virtual input devices enables the specification of event exchange without constraints regarding shape, location and modality of the implementing user interface.

Further decreasing the level of abstraction, the designed software architecture manages the physical distribution of components, independent of hardware and software. It covers the complexity of network management, connection establishment, and information exchange between client and server.

Using XML-RPC is a de-facto standard, requires low resources, and is well supported for many programming languages. The generated solutions do not rely on any proprietary infrastructure on the service host.

On the lowest level of abstraction, the code for Java using XML-RPC over TCP/IP can be used directly. Using standard technology from distributed system development enabled for auto-generating source code from the models of virtual input devices. The design and implementation of the toolkit provides support for creating special purpose solutions. All tools for the design of the model and its metamorphosis into executable programming code are delivered with the toolkit.

The general purpose and overall design of the framework as main part of thesis was agreed in a technical review. The reviewers were able to match own solutions onto the architecture proposed by the framework. The subjective measurements of the expertise required to cope with the distributed setting emphasised the reduction of complexity on a conceptual level.

The review of the tools supporting the development on programming level agreed on the aim of the tool support, the set of tools and their position in the overall development process, and their usefulness. The objective measurements of the auto-generated code affirmed significantly improved efficiency of software development when using the toolkit.

The report on the Interaction-Kiosk described a study on how users select an interaction device for the control of a simple PacMan game application from a distance. In order to achieve this task the users were allowed to take any device from a heterogeneous set of devices with different interaction styles.

10.2 Future Work

The general items of future work address building more applications with the artefacts developed in the course of this thesis, and performing more exhaustive evaluations of the framework design, toolkit usability, and applications.

The practical use of the framework needs to be further explored in field tests of designing real world applications. The practical use of the different views on the framework needs to be further explored in evaluation of bringing the design to software architectures. The contribution to standards for software architectures would provide a high-level basis for design and development of solutions, which is likely to interoperate with systems produced by other vendors.

Usability aspects were assigned with lower levels of satisfaction in the review the toolkit. Some features are still missing in the current implementation. A visible path through the process would provide guidance for the developer. The use of short-cuts and context menu associated to specific activities would support more comfortable use for development. To improve documentation of the solution, developers required to add comments to the model, which are automatically transferred into code documentation. The toolkit needs improvements in error handling, including error messages presented to the user, error prevention, and recovering from errors.

Higher integration with existing IDEs would further increase efficiency. Developers using for example Eclipse would benefit from the creation of plug-ins for the tools to modify virtual input devices inside the IDE. The developer would benefit from constantly using the same environment, icons, short-cuts etc, and from not switching between incompatible tools.

The repository of libraries, required SDKs, documentation, and reference implementations for several programming languages to adopt stubs and skeletons for different programming languages needs be further extended. The repository should provide open access for sharing reference implementation between a community of developers.

Appendix A

Virtual Example Device

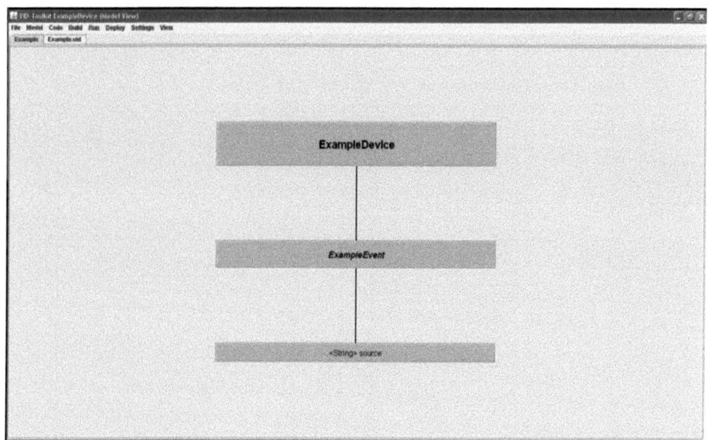

Figure A.1: The model of an example device

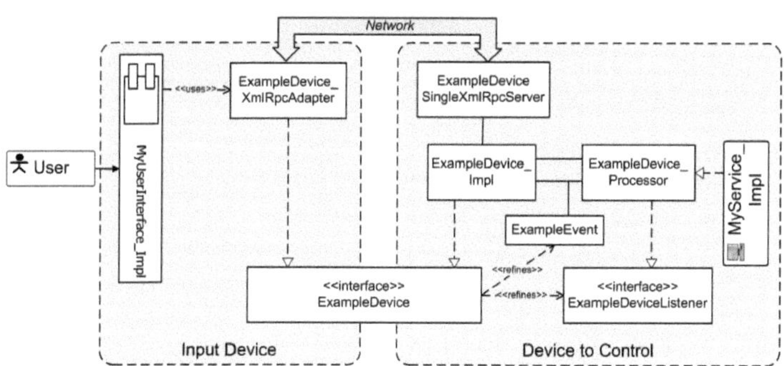

Figure A.2: The class diagram of the example device

```
<?xml version="1.0" encoding="UTF-8"?>
<virtual_device>
   <device_name>ExampleDevice</device_name>
   <events>
      <event>
         <event_name>ExampleEvent</event_name>
         <parameters>
            <parameter>
               <parameter_name>source</parameter_name>
               <parameter_type>string</parameter_type>
            </parameter>
         </parameters>
      </event>
   </events>
</virtual_device>
```

Listing A.1: The XML representation of the ExampleDevice

```
package exampleDevice;

public interface ExampleDevice {
   public int exampleEvent (String source);
}
```

Listing A.2: The Java representation of the ExampleDevice

```
package exampleDevice.client.desktop;

import javax.swing.*;

public class MyUserInterface_Impl extends JFrame {
   private final JButton sendButton = new JButton("Send");

   public MyUserInterface () {

      // create the user interface here

      sendButton.addActionListener(new ActionListener () {
         public void actionPerformed(ActionEvent e) {

            // do not block the GUI
            new Thread () {
               public void run() {

                  // set busy
                  sendButton.setEnabled(false);

                  // init XMLRPC adapter
                  ExampleDevice_XmlRpcAdapter adapter = new
                     ExampleDevice_XmlRpcAdapter ();

                  // set target IP and port
                  theAdapter.setConnection (SERVER_IP, SERVER_PORT);

                  // deliver event
                  if (adapter.exampleEvent("Desktop User Interface")) {
                     // handle error
                  }

                  // set idle
                  sendButton.setEnabled(true);
               }
            }.start();
         }
      });
   }
}
```

Listing A.3: Example of a desktop user interface

```
package exampleDevice.client.mobile;

import javax.microedition.lcdui.*;

public class MyUserInterface_Impl extends Form implements CommandListener {

   private Command CMD_SEND = new Command ("Send", Command.OK, 1);

   // create the user interface here

   // deliver events
   public void commandAction(Command command, Displayable displayable) {
      if (command.getCommandType() == Command.OK) {

         // do not block the GUI
         new Thread () {
            public void run () {

               // init XMLRPC adapter
               ExampleDevice_XmlRpcAdapter adapter = new
                  ExampleDevice_XmlRpcAdapter ();

               // set target IP and port
               theXmlRpcAdapter.setConnection (SERVER_IP, SERVER_PORT));

               // deliver event
               if (adapter.exampleEvent("Mobile User Interface")) {
                  // handle error
               }
            }
         }.start();
      }
   }
}
```

Listing A.4: Example of a mobile user interface

```
package exampleDevice.server;

import java.util.EventObject;

public class ExampleEvent extends EventObject {
   public ExampleEvent (final String source) {
      super (source);
   }

   public String toString() {
      return "ExampleEvent(" + "\n\tsource = " + getSource() + "\n)";
   }
}
```

Listing A.5: The example event

```
package exampleDevice.server;

import java.util.EventListener;

public interface ExampleDeviceListener extends EventListener {
   public void performExampleEvent (ExampleEvent e);
}
```

Listing A.6: Example of the listener interface

```
package exampleDevice.server;

import exampleDevice.ExampleDevice;
import javax.swing.event.EventListenerList;
import java.util.EventListener;
import java.util.EventObject;

public class ExampleDeviceImpl implements ExampleDevice {

   protected static final EventListenerList eventListenerList = new
       EventListenerList();
   protected static ExampleDeviceSingleXmlRpcServer theServer = null;

   public static void addInputListener (final EventListener l) {
      if (theServer == null) {
         theServer = ExampleDeviceSingleXmlRpcServer.getInstance();
         theServer.addHandler("ExampleDevice", ExampleDeviceImpl.class);
      }

      eventListenerList.add(ExampleDeviceListener.class, (ExampleDeviceListener)
          l);
   }

   public static void removeInputListener (final EventListener l) {
      eventListenerList.remove(ExampleDeviceListener.class, (
          ExampleDeviceListener)l);

      if (eventListenerList.getListenerCount (ExampleDeviceListener.class) == 0
          && theServer != null) {
         theServer.removeHandler("ExampleDevice");
         theServer = null;
      }
   }
```

```
    public void notifyInputListeners(final EventObject evt) {

        if (evt instanceof ExampleEvent) {
            final Object[] listeners = eventListenerList.getListenerList();

            // Process the listeners last to first, notifying those that are
                interested in this event
            for (int i = listeners.length - 2; i >= 0; i -= 2) {
                try {
                    // deliver the event
                    ((ExampleDeviceListener) listeners[i + 1]).performExampleEvent((
                        ExampleEvent) evt);
                }
                catch (ClassCastException e) {
                    e.printStackTrace();
                }
            }
        }
    }

    /* This method is invoked by the instance of the
        ExampleDeviceSingleXmlRpcServer */
    public int exampleEvent (String source) {
        this.notifyInputListeners (
            new ExampleEvent (source)
        );

        return 0;
    }
}
```

Listing A.7: Example of a device implementation on the server

```
package exampleDevice.server;

public class ExampleDeviceProcessor implements ExampleDeviceListener {

   public ExampleDeviceProcessor () {
      // register as lister
      ExampleDeviceImpl.addInputListener (this);
   }

   public void performExampleEvent (ExampleEvent e) {
      System.err.println ("Event received: " + e.toString() + ".");
      System.err.println ("Overwrite ExampleDeviceProcessor.performExampleEvent
         to process the event.");
   }

   public static void main (String[] args) {
      new ExampleDeviceProcessor();

      if (args.length > 0) {
         for (int i = 0; i < args.length; i++) {
            if (args[i].trim ().equals ("-p")) {
               theServer.stop();
               System.setProperty("run_server_port", args[++i]);
            }
         }
      }
      theServer.start();
   }
}
```

Listing A.8: Example of a processor class

```
package exampleDevice.server;

public class MyService_Impl extends ExampleDeviceProcessor {
   public void performExampleEvent (ExampleEvent e) {
      // service logic here
   }
}
```

Listing A.9: Example of a service implementation

Appendix B

Listings for Assessment of Technology

```
public class MediaPlayer {
    ...
    public short playMedia(String fileLocator) {
        ... // Do something

        // inform caller about state of process
        return error_code;
    }
}
```

Listing B.1: The `playMedia`-method of the `MediaPlayer-service` in Java

```
// Create listening socket
Socket serverSocket = new ServerSocket(SERVER_PORT_NUMBER);

// Waiting for connection requests
final Socket boundSocket = serverSocket.accept();

// Open stream
BufferedReader in = new BufferedReader(new InputStreamReader(boundSocket.
    getInputStream()));

// Read message from stream
line = in.readLine();

// Parse message
String command = null;
String parameter = null;
StringTokenizer tokenizer = new StringTokenizer(line," ",false);
if (tokenizer.hasMoreTokens()) {
   command = tokenizer.nextToken();
   if (tokenizer.hasMoreTokens()) {
      parameter = tokenizer.nextToken();
   }
}

// Process the received command
if (command != null) {
   ...
   if (command.equalsIgnoreCase("play_media") {
      if(parameter != null) {
         // Invoke method
         playMedia(parameter);
      }
      else {
         new RuntimeException("Parameter missing");
      }
   }

   // else-if construct for processong other commands

   else {
      new RuntimeException ("Invalid command");
   }
   ...
}

// Close
in.close();
boundSocket.close();
listeningSocket.close();
```

Listing B.2: Server implementation waiting for remote command-messages

```java
new Thread () {
    public void run () {
        // Create Socket
        SocketConnection socket = (SocketConnection) Connector.open(
            "socket://" + SERVER_IP_STRING + ":" + SERVER_PORT_NUMBER);

        // Open Stream
        OutputStream out = socket.openOutputStream();

        // Create Message
        byte[] buffer = "play_media file:///myMovies/Movie.avi".getBytes();

        // Send message
        out.write(buffer);

        // Close
        out.close();
        socket.close();
    }
}.start ();
```

Listing B.3: Client implementation in JavaMobile for sending control messages

```xml
<?xml version="1.0"?>
<methodCall>
    <methodName>MediaPlayer.playMedia</methodName>
    <params>
        <param>
            <value><string>file:///myMovies/Movie.avi</string></value>
        </param>
    </params>
</methodCall>
```

Listing B.4: The method-call to play a media file encoded in XML

```java
// Use Apache's XMLRPC library
import org.apache.xmlrpc.webserver.WebServer;
import org.apache.xmlrpc.server.XmlRpcServer;
import org.apache.xmlrpc.server.PropertyHandlerMapping;
import org.apache.xmlrpc.server.XmlRpcServerConfigImpl;

// Create the webserver listening on the port
WebServer webServer = new WebServer(SERVER_PORT_NUMBER);

// Create the server
XmlRpcServer xmlRpcServer = webServer.getXmlRpcServer();

// Set the mapping to the server
PropertyHandlerMapping mapping = new PropertyHandlerMapping();
mapping.addHandler(MediaPlayer, MediaPlayer.class);
xmlRpcServer.setHandlerMapping(theHandlerMapping);

// configure the server
XmlRpcServerConfigImpl serverConfig = (XmlRpcServerConfigImpl) xmlRpcServer.
    getConfig();
serverConfig.setEnabledForExtensions(true);
serverConfig.setContentLengthOptional(false);

// Start listening for remote calls
webServer.start();
```

Listing B.5: Server implementation of the media player for the use of XML-RPC.

```java
// Use the kxmlrpc library
import org.kxmlrpc.XmlRpcClient;

new Thread () {
    public void run () {
        // Create an XmlRpc-client
        XmlRpcClient client = new XmlRpcClient(SERVER_IP_STRING,
            SERVER_PORT_NUMBER);

        // Create list of parameters
        Vector parameter = new Vector();
        parameter.addElement ("file:///myMovies/Movie.avi");

        // Invoke the procedure and handle result
        short error_code = client.excecute("MediaPlayer.playMedia", parameter);
    }
}.start ();
...
```

Listing B.6: Client implementation for the media player invoking a remote method using XML-RPC

```java
/**
 * MediaPlayer.java
 *
 * This file was auto-generated from WSDL
 * by the Apache Axis 1.4 Apr 22, 2006 (06:55:48 PDT) WSDL2Java emitter.
 */

package webservice;

public interface MediaPlayer extends java.rmi.Remote {
    public short playMedia(java.lang.String fileLocator) throws java.rmi.
        RemoteException;
}
```

Listing B.7: The interface generated with `WSDL2Java`

```java
/**
 * MediaPlayerSoapBindingImpl.java
 *
 * This file was auto-generated from WSDL
 * by the Apache Axis 1.4 Apr 22, 2006 (06:55:48 PDT) WSDL2Java emitter.
 */

package webservice;

public class MediaPlayerSoapBindingImpl implements webservice.MediaPlayer{
    public short playMedia(java.lang.String fileLocator) throws java.rmi.
        RemoteException {
        // Enter your application logic here
        return (short)-3;
    }
}
```

Listing B.8: The skeleton for the `MoviePlayer`-WebService

```java
import javax.xml.rpc.Stub;
import java.rmi.RemoteException;

MediaPlayer_Stub service = new MediaPlayer_Stub();
short result = service.playMedia("file:///myMovies/Movie.avi");
```

Listing B.9: The remote invocation of the `MoviePlayer`-WebService

```
<?xml version="1.0" encoding="UTF-8"?>
<wsdl:definitions targetNamespace="urn:webservice" xmlns:apachesoap="http://xml.
    apache.org/xml-soap" xmlns:impl="urn:webservice" xmlns:intf="urn:webservice"
    xmlns:wsdl="http://schemas.xmlsoap.org/wsdl/" xmlns:wsdlsoap="http://schemas.
    xmlsoap.org/wsdl/soap/" xmlns:xsd="http://www.w3.org/2001/XMLSchema">
<!--WSDL created by Apache Axis version: 1.4 Built on Apr 22, 2006 (06:55:48 PDT
    )-->
   <wsdl:types>
   <schema elementFormDefault="qualified" targetNamespace="urn:webservice" xmlns
      ="http://www.w3.org/2001/XMLSchema">
   <element name="fileLocator" type="xsd:string"/>
   <element name="playMovieReturn" type="xsd:short"/>
   </schema></wsdl:types>
   <wsdl:message name="playMovieResponse">
      <wsdl:part element="impl:playMovieReturn" name="playMovieReturn"/></
          wsdl:message>
   <wsdl:message name="playMovieRequest">
      <wsdl:part element="impl:fileLocator" name="fileLocator"/>
   </wsdl:message>
   <wsdl:portType name="MoviePlayer">
     <wsdl:operation name="playMovie" parameterOrder="fileLocator">
         <wsdl:input message="impl:playMovieRequest" name="playMovieRequest"/>
         <wsdl:output message="impl:playMovieResponse" name="playMovieResponse"/
            >
     </wsdl:operation></wsdl:portType>
   <wsdl:binding name="MoviePlayerSoapBinding" type="impl:MoviePlayer">
      <wsdlsoap:binding style="document" transport="http://schemas.xmlsoap.org/
          soap/http"/>
      <wsdl:operation name="playMovie">
         <wsdlsoap:operation soapAction=""/>
         <wsdl:input name="playMovieRequest">
            <wsdlsoap:body use="literal"/>
         </wsdl:input>
         <wsdl:output name="playMovieResponse">
            <wsdlsoap:body use="literal"/>
         </wsdl:output>
      </wsdl:operation>
   </wsdl:binding>
   <wsdl:service name="MoviePlayerService">
      <wsdl:port binding="impl:MoviePlayerSoapBinding" name="MoviePlayer">
         <wsdlsoap:address location="http://localhost:8080/axis/MoviePlayer"/>
      </wsdl:port></wsdl:service>
</wsdl:definitions>
```

Listing B.10: The WSDL-file of MoviePlayer-Service

Appendix C

Review Material

C.1 Examined Document of the Review of the Framework

Andreas Lorenz, Markus Eisenhauer and Andreas Zimmermann. Elaborating a Framework for Open Human Computer Interaction with Ambient Services. *4th International Workshop on Pervasive Mobile Interaction Devices*, Sydney, Australia, 2008.

Elaborating a Framework for Open Human Computer Interaction with Ambient Services

Andreas Lorenz, Markus Eisenhauer, Andreas Zimmermann
Fraunhofer Institute for Applied Information Technology
Schloss Birlinghoven
53754 St. Augustin, Germany
{andreas.lorenz, markus.eisenhauer, andreas.zimmermann}@fit.fraunhofer.de

ABSTRACT

In a world of ambient services, the technology disappears into the surroundings until only the user interface remains perceivable by users. Most preferably, the interface to interact with an ambient service is separated from the device hosting the services, e.g. the user interface is running on a mobile device and connected with the devices in the environment. In our work we will define a framework enabling different ambient services to work together with different input devices and vice versa. The goal is to enable the user to employ the device that fits best to the current situation, personal capabilities and gusto. In particular the use of devices the user is already familiar with should be transferred to additional or new services.

1. INTRODUCTION

In an ambient intelligence world, devices work together to support people in carrying out their daily activities in an easy, natural way using information and intelligence that is hidden in the network connecting these devices. The technology disappears into the surroundings until only the user interface remains perceivable by users. Key terms describing ambient services are

- Embedded hardware integrated in the environment (smart devices, sensors, interaction devices),
- Seamless mobile/fixed communication and computing infrastructure (interoperability, wired and wireless networks) and
- Personalized human-computer interfaces.

In opposition to the desktop paradigm, in which a single user consciously engages a single device for a specialized purpose, someone interacting with ambient services engages several computational devices and systems simultaneously. In this work we will describe technologies to enable any device to be an interaction device for interacting with ambient services. Because we address a wide range of computing devices (mobile devices like mobile phone, Pocket-PC, voice recording devices, gesture-based interaction device like Wii-Controller, and other) we use the term *input device* for the device the user has at hand.

In this paper we will elaborate a framework that abstracts from concrete input devices. The paper covers the whole process from identifying the needs and requirements, definition of the terms and components to the specification of the framework.

1.1 Scenario

Burkhard, a business man always interested in the newest technology, went to his favorite media store to get the newest home cinema equipment. He has to listen to a long introduction from the shop assistant, because there are so many options; at the end, Burkhard has the choice between another remote control or just a Compact-Disc with software for any Java-equipped mobile device. Because his wife is already tired of the zoo of remote controls on the coffee table in the living room, Burkhard takes the CD and installs a small piece of software at his pen-enabled PDA, which enables the device to be the remote control of the home-cinema equipment. For his wife, he installs the same software on her mobile phone - because her device does not support a pen, she uses another version that is using the joystick instead of the touch-sensitive screen. With the software, everybody is able to elect the best device and the favorite input style. The input is automatically translated to control commands and sent to the environmental device, which reacts accordingly. From now, it will be an important feature of any new electronic product to work together with Burkhard's smartphone as control device, too.

The scenario illustrates the vision of replacing hardware remote controls with software applications to be installed on any existing device. Other scenario would envision high integration of different input modalities with one and the same service, for example to have a haptic remote user interface for one user and in parallel a speech control for another user with visual acuity. Both envisions the selection of any modality by the user without the need to change the service.

2. PROBLEM DESCRIPTION

One limiting factor for market penetration of ambient services is the dependency between services and required interaction devices and methods. In private environments, e.g. at home, it combines purchasing a new product with the accompanied requirement to learn operating a new device and a new interaction method. In foreign environments, private devices are completely useless because they are not able to interact with the environment. The provision of special purpose devices by the vendor has proven to be one of the most limiting factor for acceptance of public ambient services.

What device is used is defined by the vendor of the service - regardless on the capabilities of the user, her devices already available and the task currently performed. For remote interaction with a service this pre-selection of the input device(s) becomes obsolete. *Example: A Movie-Player is running on a PC with TV-output. For starting the play-*

Andreas Lorenz, Markus Eisenhauer and Andreas Zimmermann. Elaborating a Framework for Open Human Computer Interaction with Ambient Services. *4th International Workshop on Pervasive Mobile Interaction Devices*, Sydney, Australia, 2008.

back, the player understands clicking on the "Play"-Button with the mouse, entering "Ctrl-P" with a keyboard or saying "Play" into the microphone.

The interaction could be improved if the user is in position of decision-maker, mainly because of four reasons:

1. The service usually does not care about the physical device the user employed. The source can be any device that is able to deliver the input to the service.

   Example: To invoke the "play"-method it is equal to the Movie-Player if the user employed the mouse, the keyboard or the microphone to express the input.

2. The service usually does not care about the input modality the user has chosen. The user can select any style that can be transformed one-to-one into the right format.

   Example: To invoke the "play"-method it is equal to the Movie-Player if the user has pressed "Ctrl-P", clicked on the "Play"-button or spoke the command.

3. The input devices usually work independent of the performing services, in particular they do not care about the behavior of the service.

   Example: Whenever the user pressed "Ctrl-P", clicked on the button, or spoke "Play" neither of the keyboard, the mouse or the microphone cares about whether the movie starts playing or not. Either knows nothing about movies.

4. **The user cares about the device, the modality and the behavior of the service** depending on

   - Situation

     Example: In front of the PC, the user might take the mouse; sitting on the couch, the user might employ a spoken command.

   - Task

     Example: For starting the playback, the user might employ the speech recognition - for browsing the file system searching a movie, the user might switch to the mouse.

   - Preferences

     Example: The user might find it strange to chat with a computer system and prefer to use mouse or keyboard if possible.

   - Capabilities

     Example: A physical impaired user might not be able to operate a mouse but capable of speech.

With our work we address service developers who want to enable users employ any device as input device, and interaction developers who want to enable input devices to work together with environmental services. We will empower distributing input events from any source to any service currently enabled without loosing it's meaning to the service. The remote access is illustrated in Figure 1.

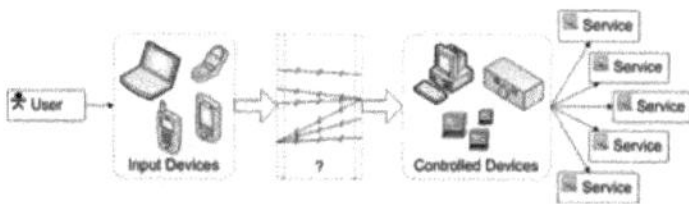

Figure 1: Transmission of user input from any remote device to service(s).

2.1 Requirements

The first step is to enable services to receive and consume input from devices a user already knows. The way to create desired input with the device, its meaning to the service, and the expected reaction from the service must be clear to the user. To be attractive to a wide range of users, the solution should work on different devices and in different environments. The communication of the device with the service must be wireless in order to be usable from any location.

The more developers are able to integrate their solutions, the more solutions will be available for selection. Usually, services from different vendors do not speak the same language. For integration we need to have a common way to express meaning of input events and a unique process for the exchange. The interface of the service should be consistent with available standards as much as possible. All specifications need to be well defined, first-class documented, easy to understand (here: "easy" from the perspective of a software-developer) and as low resource consuming as possible in order to be acceptable by developers. The implementation on both the input device and the service should be independent from operating systems and programming language as much as possible.

2.2 Goal

The goal of this work is to enable input devices to deliver user input to ambient services. The input device offers any kind of user interface meaningful to the selected ambient service(s). The input device transfers this information to the service which reacts in its specific way.

2.3 Research Statement

One-to-one semantic correspondence between remote input device and processing service is key to open Human-Computer Interaction with interactive ambient services with the user's choice of input devices.

3. RELATED WORK

System capabilities of ambient services are limited if the user is not equipped with a specific input device to have a channel for explicit input or controlling the behavior. To overcome limitations, the user could be equipped with a service-related device. The hand-out of devices from a vendor of the service boosts costs, requires the user to be willing to pick it up and requires trust into the user to bring it back at the end of the stay. The use of any private device is not possible today because they do usually not speak the language of the environment, not even in private settings.

The zoo of remote controls in home environments indicates high relevance of expressing input to remote devices. Excluding (wireless) mouse and keyboard input, the type

Andreas Lorenz, Markus Eisenhauer and Andreas Zimmermann. Elaborating a Framework for Open Human Computer Interaction with Ambient Services. *4th International Workshop on Pervasive Mobile Interaction Devices*, Sydney, Australia, 2008.

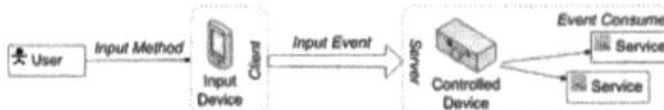

Figure 2: The Technical Components

of remote input can be categorized with rapidly decreasing percentage of use: Action events like On/Off, Up/Down, Play/Stop are present at almost all remote controls; Numbers and short texts are sometimes used, for example to operate the phone, switch TV-channels, or name movie recordings; hardly any use of longer text and pointer controls.

Iftode *et al* [5] identified the need for a simple, universal solution to control different applications in the environment of the user, which end-users are likely to accept easily. The input device should be programmable and support dynamic software extension for interaction with additional ambient services. For controlling the service, many approaches allow users to design their own remote control by creating new graphical interfaces that are downloaded to the input device after compilation. Beside these haptic input capabilities it is also possible to use speech recorded by a mobile device to control a remote system. Using for instance the Personal Universal Controller [8] a user can speak a command through which this is executed by the system. The focus is on automatic creation of the user interface from a description language.

Research in projects like IBM's "Universal Information Appliance" (UIA, [3]) or XWeb [9] results in the definition of a set of incompatible description languages like MoDAL (the XML-based language used by UIA) and UIML [1], where the programmer provides a specification (model) of the application, the display and the user. The concrete user interface is thus decoupled from the application, but only valid for a specific one. Though they are often based on similar components, they cannot be applied to another ambient service.

The iStuff Mobile architecture [2] is a platform combining (physical) sensor enhanced mobile phones and interactive spaces. The platform uses an Event-Heap [6] for distributing events of a specific type with specific fields. The mobile phone is then capable of sensing (local) user activity (e.g. key pressed) that are posted as (iStuff-)events on the heap.

3.1 Summary

Transferring events to any ambient service generally capable of performing the input but not able to correctly understand that particular type and content is useless. For development of GUI-based desktop applications there exist already common techniques and events that have a clear meaning to any application. For example, independent events like mouse-clicks can be delivered to any service; the mouse or the mouse-button itself does not know about the meaning to the application. The mouse could be replaced with any other physical device; if it fires correct mouse-events, the application will understand.

4. TERMS AND DEFINITIONS

For our work we identified the following components. Figure 2 illustrates their places in the overall process.

Input Device. The mobile device the user engages to control the ambient service. The type and shape of the device is not defined per se. On the remote device there is a client application running as the counterpart of the user-interaction.
Examples: Mobile phone, laptop, microphone, traditional computer systems.

Controlled Device. A computing device that is available in the current environment of the user.
Examples: Small items providing information (sensors), output devices (displays, speakers), traditional computer systems.

Ambient Service. An interactive application (short *service*) running on any controlled device. The user *consciously interacts* with the service in order to get information, adjust settings or control the behavior.
Examples: Small services providing information to the user (like the temperature), electronically actuate output devices (like playing an audio file at a speaker installation in a room), GUI-based applications on embedded devices (like showing a movie on the TV).

Client. The role of the information provider in the client/-server approach. In our case, the client is the *application running on the input device*, receiving input from the user and delivering the input in a feasible manner to the event-consumer.
Examples: Networked application with graphical components, audio/voice-recognition systems, camera-based input, gesture recognition applications.

Server. The role of an information receiver in the client/-server approach. In our case, the server is the *application running on the controlled device* providing any number of services.
Examples: Networked application with or without local user-interface, TCP/IP-Socket listener, Web-Server.

Input Method. An abstract definition of *a way to express input by the user*, including the modality used with the input device. The potential meaning, interpretation and reaction depends on the service implementation.
Examples: Common GUI-based methods (for example clicking a certain button), voice commands (like spoken word "up"), gestures (like "Thumb up") or any other method. The examples could be interpreted to increase the volume by an audio player, but other services could implement their own interpretation (for example to move the cursor upwards).

Input Event. The event delivered by the client to the server, containing the type of the event and other event-specific data.
Examples: Button-pressed events, key-typed events, or mouse-move events. The events include additional information like the character assigned with a pressed key or the position where a mouse click occurred.

Event Consumer. A set of any number (including zero) of ambient services processing an event in their defined manner. If the set is empty, no service is able to make use of the information; the event is ignored.

Andreas Lorenz, Markus Eisenhauer and Andreas Zimmermann. Elaborating a Framework for Open Human Computer Interaction with Ambient Services. *4th International Workshop on Pervasive Mobile Interaction Devices*, Sydney, Australia, 2008.

5. DESIGN OF A FRAMEWORK

A software framework is an abstract design for a category of software systems. It defines a set of cooperating components, and the control flow in the system [7]. Some definitions implicitly require an object-oriented software design, defining a framework as an *"architecture of class hierarchies"* [10]. This might exclude efficient implementations based on other paradigms and get in the way of mixing up different software-designs for implementing specific components or operations. Because we are focusing on a *design* of solution(s), we will use the following definition of a framework:

Framework. A Framework is a generic architecture of a solution for a set of similar problems.

In computer science, the used term *architecture* is defined as the *"fundamental organization of a system embodied in its components, their relationships to each other, and to the environment, and the principles guiding its design and evolution"* [4].

In traditional (Graphical) User Interfaces (GUI), the user has access to application dependent graphic components. The user employs a mouse or keyboard in order to deliver input to the service. Most programming languages offer components to support the development of user interfaces, together with back-end-mechanisms for performing user input (for example event-listener mechanism). In this case, the service provides a performing method that is associated to input events occurring on the control component.

For the definition of our architecture, we abstract from the GUI-based control flow by defining a *Virtual Input Device*. It has the same attributes and behavior like any other device running a user interface except that it's shape is not defined; in particular, it does not necessarily provide any graphical representation. The only visible knowledge is a precise specification of input event(s) it delivers on the user's request. Potentially in parallel to existing graphical items, the developer registers listeners to the events for performing the input stream coming from virtual input devices.

The derived abstract system architecture is illustrated in Figure 3. The information flow to transfer an input event occurring on an input device to an ambient service consists of six steps to be performed: (1) Triggered by the user interaction, the client on the input device receives an input event from the local resources. (2) The input event is translated into a common representation. (3) The event is sent from the input device to the controlled device. (4) The input event is unpacked from its representation. (5) The input event is delivered to the target service(s). (6) The target service(s) consume the event. In this flow, the virtual input device covers the steps (2)-(5). For implementation we will use standard web-service technology defining input-adapters as web-services that are remotely executed over the network.

6. BENEFITS

The virtual input device covers the complexity of delivering input events from the client to the server. On the client side, the local event is handed over to a specific component as if the component was a local event consumer ("fire-and-forget"). On the server side, there is no difference between traditional event handlers and listeners to virtual input devices, which supports the integration between the two and transferring developer skills to the new setting. Because the *meaning* of an input event becomes independent from its representation, the creation of an input event is not bound to any static process: it is open to the developer, the capabilities of the device and the abilities of the user to employ any physical device and select the appropriate input method.

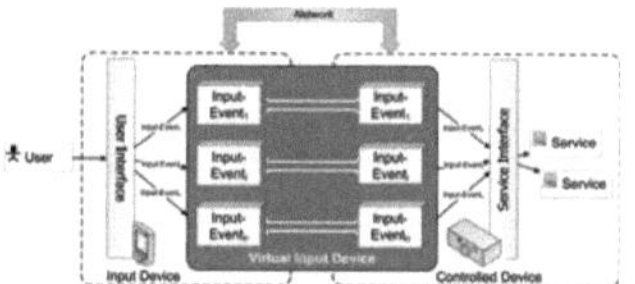

Figure 3: The abstract system architecture

7. REFERENCES

[1] M. Abrams, C. Phanouriou, A. Batongbacal, S. Williams, and J. Shuster. UIML: An appliance-independent XML user interface language. In *International World Wide Web Conference*, Toronto, Canada, 1999.

[2] R. Ballagas, F. Memon, R. Reiners, and J. Borchers. iStuff Mobile: Rapidly prototyping new mobile phone interfaces for ubiquitous computing. In *SIGCHI Conference on Human Factors in Computing Systems*, pages 1107–1116, San Jose, CA, 2007. ACM Press.

[3] K. Eustice, T. Lehman, A. Morales, M. Munson, S. Edlund, and M. Guillen. A universal information appliance. *IBM Systems Journal*, 38(4):575–601, 1999.

[4] IEEE. Systems and software engineering - recommended practice for architectural description of software-intensive systems. *ISO/IEC 42010 IEEE Std 1471-2000*, pages c1–24, July 2007.

[5] L. Iftode, C. Borcea, N. Ravi, P. Kang, and P. Zhou. Smart phone: An embedded system for universal interactions. In *IEEE Intl. Workshop on Future Trends of Distributed Computing Systems*, 2004.

[6] B. Johanson and A. Fox. The event heap: A coordination infrastructure for interactive workspaces. In *IEEE Workshop on Mobile Computing Systems and Applications*, page 83. IEEE, 2002.

[7] J. Ludewig and H. Lichter. *Software Engineering*. dpunkt.verlag, Heidelberg, 2007.

[8] J. Nichols, B. A. Myers, M. Higgins, J. Hughes, T. K. Harris, R. Rosenfeld, and M. Pignol. Generating remote control interfaces for complex appliances. In *ACM symposium on User interface software and technology*, Paris, France, 2002. ACM Press.

[9] D. Olsen, S. Jefferies, T. Nielsen, W. Moyes, and P. Fredrickson. Cross-modal interaction using xweb. In *Annual ACM Symposium on User Interface Software and Technology*, pages 191–200. ACM Press, 2000.

[10] H. Züllighoven. *Object-Oriented Construction Handbook*. dpunkt.verlag, Heidelberg, 2005.

C.2 Questionnaire for the Review of the Framework

Questionnaire for Technical Review of a Framework for Open Human-Computer Interaction with Ambient Services

Objectives of the technical review

The objective of the technical review is to elaborate whether the framework is adequately designed to fulfill the following requirements:

1. The framework conforms to definitions, standards and guidelines applicable to the design of software architectures.
2. The framework describes a complete architecture.
3. The framework describes a valid architecture of a solution.
4. The architecture of any other solution can be transformed into the framework without invalidation of the solution.
5. The documentation of the framework is complete, clear, and helpful.

Intended Audience

* Experts in human-computer interaction in ambient computing environments
* Interaction Designers using remote input devices
* Software Architects specifying distributed systems
* Software Developers building client/server components

Procedure

1. Planning
2. Preparation
3. On-line collection of reviewers' statements
4. Acknowledgement on list of defects

Preparation

For preparation please perform four steps in the given order.
Please prepare notes and have them with you at the review-meeting.

1. Please prepare a scenario for using a remote input device to control a service. Keep it simple.

   > What is your service / application?
   > What is your input device?

   > What are the control commands you need to interchange between the input device and the controlled device?

   > How does the user create the control commands with the input device?
   > How does the service react?

2. Please sketch a solution for your scenario.

   > Identify your components on the input device.
   > Identify your components on the controlled device.
   > Identify the information flow between the components.
   > Identify information transmitted over a network, if any.

3. Please read the document "Elaboration of a framework for open human-computer interaction with ambient services."

   You can download it from

http://www.fit.fraunhofer.de/projects/mobiles-wissen/power-interaction/mobile-experience/lorenz-framework-permid.pdf

4. Please try to match your solution onto the framework.

   > Match your components to components in the framework
   > Match your information flow to flow of information among components of the framework

Note: Though not explicitely required you might want to send your preparation material to the author.

Questions

*** Framework Design ***

1. The framework covers all components required for the intended use.

STRONGLY AGREE 1 2 3 4 5 6 7 STRONGLY DISAGREE

Your Rate:
Comments:

2. The framework is free of overhead components.

STRONGLY AGREE 1 2 3 4 5 6 7 STRONGLY DISAGREE

Your Rate:
Comments:

3. All information flow between components is clearly defined.

STRONGLY AGREE 1 2 3 4 5 6 7 STRONGLY DISAGREE

Your Rate:
Comments:

4. All data transmission between components over a network is defined.

STRONGLY AGREE 1 2 3 4 5 6 7 STRONGLY DISAGREE

Your Rate:
Comments:

5. The framework has all the functions and capabilities I expect it to have.

STRONGLY AGREE 1 2 3 4 5 6 7 STRONGLY DISAGREE

Your Rate:
Comments:

6. The framework matches the following definition:

   "A Framework is a generic architecture of a solution for a set of similar problems."

   where an architecture is

   "The fundamental organization of a system embodied in its components, their relationships to each other, and to the environment, and the principles guiding its design and evolution."

STRONGLY AGREE 1 2 3 4 5 6 7 STRONGLY DISAGREE

Your Rate:
Comments:

*** Framework Application ***

7. Overall, I am satisfied with how easy it is to use the framework.

STRONGLY AGREE 1 2 3 4 5 6 7 STRONGLY DISAGREE

Your Rate:
Comments:

8. It was simple to use the framework.

STRONGLY AGREE 1 2 3 4 5 6 7 STRONGLY DISAGREE

Your Rate:
Comments:

9. I could effectively complete the tasks and scenarios using the framework.

STRONGLY AGREE 1 2 3 4 5 6 7 STRONGLY DISAGREE

Your Rate:
Comments:

10. I was able to complete the tasks and scenarios quickly using the framework.

STRONGLY AGREE 1 2 3 4 5 6 7 STRONGLY DISAGREE

Your Rate:
Comments:

11. I was able to efficiently complete the tasks and scenarios using the framework.

STRONGLY AGREE 1 2 3 4 5 6 7 STRONGLY DISAGREE

Your Rate:
Comments:

12. I felt comfortable using the framework.

STRONGLY AGREE 1 2 3 4 5 6 7 STRONGLY DISAGREE

Your Rate:
Comments:

13. I believe I could become productive quickly using the framework.

STRONGLY AGREE 1 2 3 4 5 6 7 STRONGLY DISAGREE

Your Rate:
Comments:

14. It was easy to learn to use the framework.

STRONGLY AGREE 1 2 3 4 5 6 7 STRONGLY DISAGREE

Your Rate:
Comments:

*** Framework Documentation ***

15. The information (such as on-line help, on-screen messages and other documentation) provided with the framework is clear.

STRONGLY AGREE 1 2 3 4 5 6 7 STRONGLY DISAGREE

Your Rate:
Comments:

16. It is easy to find the information I need.

STRONGLY AGREE 1 2 3 4 5 6 7 STRONGLY DISAGREE

Your Rate:
Comments:

17. The information provided with the framework is easy to understand.

STRONGLY AGREE 1 2 3 4 5 6 7 STRONGLY DISAGREE

Your Rate:
Comments:

18. The information was effective in helping me complete the tasks and scenarios.

STRONGLY AGREE 1 2 3 4 5 6 7 STRONGLY DISAGREE

Your Rate:
Comments:

*** Summary ***

19. Overall, I am satisfied with the framework.

STRONGLY AGREE 1 2 3 4 5 6 7 STRONGLY DISAGREE

Your Rate:
Comments:

Thank you very much!

References
Questions are adopted from:
Lewis, James R. (1995): IBM Computer Usability Satisfaction Questionnaires: Psychometric Evaluation and Instructions for Use. In: International Journal of Human-Computer Interaction, 7(1):57-78

Score			Question	Average rating
OVERALL	SYSDESIGN	Q1	The framework covers all components required for the intended use.	2,50
		Q2	The framework is free of overhead components.	1,50
		Q3	All information flow between components is clearly defined.	3,00
		Q4	All data transmission between components over a network is defined.	3,50
		Q5	The framework has all the functions and capabilities I expect it to have.	4,00
		Q6	The framework matches the definition.	2,25
	SYSUSE	Q7	Overall, I am satisfied with how easy it is to use the framework.	3,25
		Q8	It was simple to use the framework.	3,50
		Q9	I could effectively complete the tasks and scenarios using the framework.	2,75
		Q10	I was able to complete the tasks and scenarios quickly using the framework.	3,75
		Q11	I was able to efficiently complete the tasks and scenarios using the framework.	3,25
		Q12	I felt comfortable using the framework.	3,25
		Q13	I believe I could become productive quickly using the framework.	2,25
		Q14	It was easy to learn to use the framework.	3,50
	INFOQUAL	Q15	The information (such as on-line help, on-screen messages and other documentation) provided with the framework is clear.	5,00
		Q16	It is easy to find the information I need.	4,75
		Q17	The information provided with the framework is easy to understand.	3,00
		Q18	The information was effective in helping me complete the tasks and scenarios.	3,25
		Q19	Overall, I am satisfied with the framework.	2,00

Table C.1: Reviewer ratings to the framework evaluation

C.3 Questionnaire for the Toolkit Walk-Through

Questionnaire for Technical Review of a Toolkit for Open Human-Computer Interaction with Ambient Services

Objectives of the technical rewiew

The objective of the technical review is to elaborate whether the toolkit is adequately build to fulfil the functionnal and non-functional requirements. The review shall accomplish to determine:

1. The Toolkit creates valid solutions for interactive software systems using remote input devices.
2. The Toolkit fulfils all functions for a full development cycle.
3. The Toolkit fulfils all non-functional requirements, in particular regarding usability and documentation.

Intended Audience

* Experts in human-computer interaction in ambient computing environments
* System Providers of interactive services and/or user interface technology
* Interaction-Designers using remote input devices
* System-Designers of distributed interactive applications
* Software Developers building client/server components, user-interface components, and/or service logic

Preparation

1. Download and install the Toolkit on your local computer system.

   See
   http://www.fit.fraunhofer.de/projects/mobiles-wissen/power-interaction/mobile-experience en.html
   for system requirements, download and installation guidelines.

2. Open the User's Guide.
   Start the Toolkit and go through the example of the VirtualMovieController in Chapter 4.
   > Open the model.
   > Add the "FastForward" event and the "stepCount"-Parameter
   > Review the code of the "VirtualMovieControllerProcessor.java"
   > Review the code of the "VirtualMovieControllerMIDlet.java"
   > Build the Single Server and the Java-mobile client
   > Run the Single Server
   > Run the MIDlet
   > Send a "FastForward"-event with a stepCount of 5 using the MIDlet.
   > Check the output of the Single Server

3. Create a new VirtualInputDevice. Let us call it "VirtualAlarmControl".
   It defines the remote control of an alarm system of the house.
   Change the model until it fulfils the following functional requirments
   > The device is able to send single numbers to a remote service.
   > The device is able to arm the alarm system.
   > The device is able to disarm the alarm system.
   > The device is able to submit the activation code.

4. Test, whether your Single Server receives the following input sequence:
   > Arm the alarm system.
   > Trigger to disarm the alarm system.
   > Enter the code.
   > Submit the code.

5. Deploy the mobile client on Java-enabled mobile phone. Perform the tests (see 4.) on the mobile input device.

Questions

What is your expertise?

[ ] Expert in human-computer interaction

[ ] Expert in ambient computing environments

[ ] System Provider of interactive services

[ ] System Provider of user interface technology

[ ] Interaction-Designer using remote input devices

[ ] System-Designer of distributed interactive applications

[ ] Software Developer of client/server applications

[ ] Software Developer of user-interfaces

[ ] Software Developer of service logic

Wich of the tools did you use?

[ ] Modeling

[ ] Programming

[ ] Building

[ ] Testing

[ ] Deploying

For the next 19 items please enter one number of 1 ... 7 into your cell(s). Leave it empty if not applicable.

1. Overall, I am satisfied with how easy it is to use this system.

STRONGLY AGREE 1 2 3 4 5 6 7 STRONGLY DISAGREE

```
+----------------------------------------------------------------+
| Your Rates                                                     |
+----------------------------------------------------------------+
|Overall|Installation|Modeling|Programming|Building|Testing|Deploying|
+-------+------------+--------+-----------+--------+-------+---------+
|       |            |        |           |        |       |         |
+-------+------------+--------+-----------+--------+-------+---------+
```

Your Comments:

...

2. It is simple to use this system.

STRONGLY AGREE 1 2 3 4 5 6 7 STRONGLY DISAGREE

```
+-----------------------------------------------------------------+
| Your Rates                                                      |
+-----------------------------------------------------------------+
|Overall|Installation|Modeling|Programming|Building|Testing|Deploying|
+-------+------------+--------+-----------+--------+-------+---------+
|       |            |        |           |        |       |         |
+-------+------------+--------+-----------+--------+-------+---------+

  Your Comments:

  ...


3. I can effectively complete my work using this system.

STRONGLY AGREE    1    2    3    4    5    6    7    STRONGLY DISAGREE

+-----------------------------------------------------------------+
| Your Rates                                                      |
+-----------------------------------------------------------------+
|Overall|Installation|Modeling|Programming|Building|Testing|Deploying|
+-------+------------+--------+-----------+--------+-------+---------+
|       |            |        |           |        |       |         |
+-------+------------+--------+-----------+--------+-------+---------+

  Your Comments:

  ...


4. I am able to complete my work quickly using this system.

STRONGLY AGREE    1    2    3    4    5    6    7    STRONGLY DISAGREE

+-----------------------------------------------------------------+
| Your Rates                                                      |
+-----------------------------------------------------------------+
|Overall|Installation|Modeling|Programming|Building|Testing|Deploying|
+-------+------------+--------+-----------+--------+-------+---------+
|       |            |        |           |        |       |         |
+-------+------------+--------+-----------+--------+-------+---------+

  Your Comments:

  ...


5. I am able to efficiently complete my work using this system.

STRONGLY AGREE    1    2    3    4    5    6    7    STRONGLY DISAGREE

+-----------------------------------------------------------------+
| Your Rates                                                      |
+-----------------------------------------------------------------+
|Overall|Installation|Modeling|Programming|Building|Testing|Deploying|
+-------+------------+--------+-----------+--------+-------+---------+
|       |            |        |           |        |       |         |
+-------+------------+--------+-----------+--------+-------+---------+

  Your Comments:

  ...


6. I feel comfortable using this system.

STRONGLY AGREE    1    2    3    4    5    6    7    STRONGLY DISAGREE
```

Your Rates						
Overall	Installation	Modeling	Programming	Building	Testing	Deploying

Your Comments:

...

7. It was easy to learn to use this system.

STRONGLY AGREE 1 2 3 4 5 6 7 STRONGLY DISAGREE

Your Rates						
Overall	Installation	Modeling	Programming	Building	Testing	Deploying

Your Comments:

...

8. I believe I became productive quickly using this system.

STRONGLY AGREE 1 2 3 4 5 6 7 STRONGLY DISAGREE

Your Rates						
Overall	Installation	Modeling	Programming	Building	Testing	Deploying

Your Comments:

...

9. The system gives error messages that clearly tell me how to fix problems.

STRONGLY AGREE 1 2 3 4 5 6 7 STRONGLY DISAGREE

Your Rates						
Overall	Installation	Modeling	Programming	Building	Testing	Deploying

Your Comments:

...

10. Whenever I make a mistake using the system, I recover easily and quickly.

STRONGLY AGREE 1 2 3 4 5 6 7 STRONGLY DISAGREE

```
+-----------------------------------------------------------------+
| Your Rates                                                      |
+-----------------------------------------------------------------+
|Overall|Installation|Modeling|Programming|Building|Testing|Deploying|
+-------+------------+--------+-----------+--------+-------+---------+
|       |            |        |           |        |       |         |
+-------+------------+--------+-----------+--------+-------+---------+
```

Your Comments:

...

11. The information (such as on-line help, on-screen messages and other documentation) provided with this system is clear.

STRONGLY AGREE 1 2 3 4 5 6 7 STRONGLY DISAGREE

```
+-----------------------------------------------------------------+
| Your Rates                                                      |
+-----------------------------------------------------------------+
|Overall|Installation|Modeling|Programming|Building|Testing|Deploying|
+-------+------------+--------+-----------+--------+-------+---------+
|       |            |        |           |        |       |         |
+-------+------------+--------+-----------+--------+-------+---------+
```

Your Comments:

...

12. It is easy to find the information I need.

STRONGLY AGREE 1 2 3 4 5 6 7 STRONGLY DISAGREE

```
+-----------------------------------------------------------------+
| Your Rates                                                      |
+-----------------------------------------------------------------+
|Overall|Installation|Modeling|Programming|Building|Testing|Deploying|
+-------+------------+--------+-----------+--------+-------+---------+
|       |            |        |           |        |       |         |
+-------+------------+--------+-----------+--------+-------+---------+
```

Your Comments:

...

13. The information provided with the system is easy to understand.

STRONGLY AGREE 1 2 3 4 5 6 7 STRONGLY DISAGREE

```
+-----------------------------------------------------------------+
| Your Rates                                                      |
+-----------------------------------------------------------------+
|Overall|Installation|Modeling|Programming|Building|Testing|Deploying|
+-------+------------+--------+-----------+--------+-------+---------+
|       |            |        |           |        |       |         |
+-------+------------+--------+-----------+--------+-------+---------+
```

Your Comments:

...

14. The information is effective in helping me complete my work.

STRONGLY AGREE 1 2 3 4 5 6 7 STRONGLY DISAGREE

```
+--------------------------------------------------------------------+
| Your Rates                                                         |
+--------------------------------------------------------------------+
|Overall|Installation|Modeling|Programming|Building|Testing|Deploying|
+-------+------------+--------+-----------+--------+-------+---------+
|       |            |        |           |        |       |         |
+-------+------------+--------+-----------+--------+-------+---------+
```

Your Comments:

...

15. The organization of information on the system screens is clear.

STRONGLY AGREE 1 2 3 4 5 6 7 STRONGLY DISAGREE

```
+--------------------------------------------------------------------+
| Your Rates                                                         |
+--------------------------------------------------------------------+
|Overall|Installation|Modeling|Programming|Building|Testing|Deploying|
+-------+------------+--------+-----------+--------+-------+---------+
|       |            |        |           |        |       |         |
+-------+------------+--------+-----------+--------+-------+---------+
```

Your Comments:

...

Note: The interface includes those items that you use to interact with the system. For example, some components of the interface are the keyboard, the mouse, the screens (including their use of graphics and language).

16. The interface of this system is pleasant.

STRONGLY AGREE 1 2 3 4 5 6 7 STRONGLY DISAGREE

```
+--------------------------------------------------------------------+
| Your Rates                                                         |
+--------------------------------------------------------------------+
|Overall|Installation|Modeling|Programming|Building|Testing|Deploying|
+-------+------------+--------+-----------+--------+-------+---------+
|       |            |        |           |        |       |         |
+-------+------------+--------+-----------+--------+-------+---------+
```

Your Comments:

...

17. I like using the interface of this system.

STRONGLY AGREE 1 2 3 4 5 6 7 STRONGLY DISAGREE

```
+--------------------------------------------------------------------+
| Your Rates                                                         |
+--------------------------------------------------------------------+
|Overall|Installation|Modeling|Programming|Building|Testing|Deploying|
+-------+------------+--------+-----------+--------+-------+---------+
|       |            |        |           |        |       |         |
+-------+------------+--------+-----------+--------+-------+---------+
```

Your Comments:

...

```
18. This system has all the functions and capabilities I expect it to
    have.

STRONGLY AGREE    1    2    3    4    5    6    7    STRONGLY DISAGREE

+-------------------------------------------------------------------+
| Your Rates                                                        |
+-------------------------------------------------------------------+
|Overall|Installation|Modeling|Programming|Building|Testing|Deploying|
+-------+------------+--------+-----------+--------+-------+---------+
|       |            |        |           |        |       |         |
+-------+------------+--------+-----------+--------+-------+---------+

  Your Comments:

  ...


19. Overall, I am satisfied with this system.

STRONGLY AGREE    1    2    3    4    5    6    7    STRONGLY DISAGREE

Your Rate:
Comments:



Thank you very much!


References
The questionnaires are adopted from:
Lewis, James R. (1995): IBM Computer Usability Satisfaction
Questionnaires: Psychometric Evaluation and Instructions for Use.
In: International Journal of Human-Computer Interaction, 7(1):57-78
```

Score			Question	Average rating ("Overall")
OVERALL	SYSUSE	Q1	Overall, I am satisfied with how easy it is to use this system.	2,50
		Q2	It is simple to use this system	2,33
		Q3	I can effectively complete my work using this system.	2,20
		Q4	I am able to complete my work quickly using this system.	3,00
		Q5	I am able to efficiently complete my work using this system.	2,33
		Q6	I feel comfortable using this system.	2,60
		Q7	It was easy to learn to use this system.	1,33
		Q8	I believe I became productive quickly using this system.	3,33
	INFOQUAL	Q9	The system gives error messages that clearly tell me how to fix problems.	5,00
		Q10	Whenever I make a mistake using the system, I recover easily and quickly.	3,00
		Q11	The information (such as on-line help, on-screen messages and other documentation) provided with this system is clear.	2,80
		Q12	It is easy to find the information I need.	2,80
		Q13	The information provided with the system is easy to understand.	2,00
		Q14	The information is effective in helping me complete my work.	2,67
		Q15	The organization of information on the system screens is clear.	2,00
	INTER-QUAL	Q16	The interface of this system is pleasant.	2,33
		Q17	I like using the interface of this system.	3,40
		Q18	This system has all the functions and capabilities I expect it to have.	2,83
		Q19	Overall, I am satisfied with this system.	3,08

Table C.2: Reviewer ratings in category "Overall" of the toolkit evaluation

C.4 Questionnaire for CeBIT 2008 (German)

Fragebogen zum Interaktions-Kiosk (CeBIT 2008)

Datum: **Interview durchgeführt von:**

Frage 1: Welche der Eingabemöglichkeiten haben Sie heute an unserem Stand ausprobiert?

Fernbedienung	Stift und PDA-Display	Wii-Controller	XBox-Controller	Tanz-Matte	Geste mit der Hand
☐	☐	☐	☐	☐	☐

Frage 2: Welche der Eingabemöglichkeiten waren Ihnen bereits vorher bekannt?

Fernbedienung	Stift und PDA-Display	Wii-Controller	XBox-Controller	Tanz-Matte	Geste mit der Hand
☐	☐	☐	☐	☐	☐

Frage 3: Welches Gerät haben Sie als erstes ausgesucht?

Fernbedienung	PDA	Wii-Controller	XBox-Controller	Tanz-Matte	Geste mit der Hand
☐	☐	☐	☐	☐	☐

Ergänzung zu Frage 3: Warum haben Sie dieses ausgewählt?

Zufall	War mit vertraut	Wollte ich ausprobieren	Erschien mir geeignet	Sonstiges	
☐	☐	☐	☐	☐	...

Frage 4: Mit welchem Gerät haben Sie Ihre beste Punktzahl erreicht?

Fernbedienung	PDA	Wii-Controller	XBox-Controller	Tanz-Matte	Geste mit der Hand
☐	☐	☐	☐	☐	☐

Frage 5: Wie lautet Ihre persönliche Rangliste von Platz 1 (am besten gefallen) bis Platz 6 (am wenigsten gefallen)?

Fernbedienung	Stift und PDA-Display	Wii-Controller	XBox-Controller	Tanz-Matte	Geste mit der Hand
Platz: ...	Platz: ...	Platz: ...	Platz: ...	Platz: ...	Platz: ...

Frage 6: Wie bewerten Sie die Eingabemöglichkeiten auf einer Skala von 1 (Einfach) bis 5 (Umständlich)?

	Note 1 (Einfach)	*Note 2*	*Note 3 (Braucht Übung)*	*Note 4*	*Note 5 (Umständlich)*
Fernbedienung	☐	☐	☐	☐	☐
Stift und PDA-Display	☐	☐	☐	☐	☐
Wii-Controller	☐	☐	☐	☐	☐
XBox-Controller	☐	☐	☐	☐	☐
Tanz-Matte	☐	☐	☐	☐	☐
Geste mit der Hand	☐	☐	☐	☐	☐

Frage 7: Für welche Geräte könnten Sie sich einen Einsatz im Alltag vorstellen?

Fernbedienung	Stift und PDA-Display	Wii-Controller	XBox-Controller	Tanz-Matte	Geste mit der Hand
☐	☐	☐	☐	☐	☐

Freiwillige Angaben zur statistischen Auswertung.

Ihr Alter	Ihr Geschlecht	Ihr erlernter Beruf	Nutzen Sie regelmäßig ein Handy / PDA?	Besitzen Sie eine Spielkonsole?
...	☐ w / ☐ m	...	☐ ja / ☐ nein	☐ ja / ☐ nein

Haben Sie weitere Kommentare oder Anregungen?

...

C.5 Questionnaire for CeBIT 2008 (English)

Questionnaire for the Interaction-Kiosk (CeBIT 2008)

Date: **Interviewer:**

Question 1: With which input methods did you experiment today?

Remote control	Dragging on PDA	Wii-Controller	XBox-Controller	Dancing-Mat	Hand gesture
☐	☐	☐	☐	☐	☐

Question 2: Which input methods did you already know?

Remote control	Dragging on PDA	Wii-Controller	XBox-Controller	Dancing-Mat	Hand gesture
☐	☐	☐	☐	☐	☐

Question 3: Which device was your first selection?

Remote control	PDA	Wii-Controller	XBox-Controller	Dancing-Mat	Hand gesture
☐	☐	☐	☐	☐	☐

Follow up to Question 3: For what reason did you select it?

By chance	Already familiar with	Considered suitable	Was interested in	Other	
☐	☐	☐	☐	☐	...

Question 4: What was the device you scored highest with?

Remote control	PDA	Wii-Controller	XBox-Controller	Dancing-Mat	Hand gesture
☐	☐	☐	☐	☐	☐

Question 5: Please rank the devices according to your preference, beginning from first place (you liked most).

Remote control	Dragging on PDA	Wii-Controller	XBox-Controller	Dancing-Mat	Hand gesture
Rank: ...	Rank: ...	Rank: ...	Rank: ...	Rank: ...	Rank: ...

Question 6: Please indicate the ease of use for each device from 1 (easy to use) to 5 (unhandy).

	1 (Easy to use)	*2*	*3 (Needs training)*	*4*	*5 (Unhandy)*
Remote control	☐	☐	☐	☐	☐
Dragging on PDA	☐	☐	☐	☐	☐
Wii-Controller	☐	☐	☐	☐	☐
XBox-Controller	☐	☐	☐	☐	☐
Dancing-Mat	☐	☐	☐	☐	☐
Hand gesture	☐	☐	☐	☐	☐

Question 7: Which input method would you use for your applications?

Remote control	Dragging on PDA	Wii-Controller	XBox-Controller	Dancing-Mat	Hand gesture
☐	☐	☐	☐	☐	☐

Optional data for statistical evaluation only.

Age	Gender	Profession	Do you frequently use mobile phone / PDA?	Do you have a games console?
...	☐ f / ☐ m	...	☐ yes / ☐ no	☐ yes / ☐ no

Do you have any comments or suggestions?

...

Bibliography

Abrams, M., Phanouriou, C., Batongbacal, A., Williams, S., and Shuster, J. (1999). UIML: An appliance-independent XML user interface language. In *Eighth International World Wide Web Conference*, Toronto, Canada.

Ahmad, F. and Musilek, P. (2006). A keystroke and pointer control input interface for wearable computers. In *Fourth Annual IEEE International Conference on Pervasive Computing and Communications (PerCom 2006)*, pages 2–11.

Alonso, G. (2004). *Web Services - Concepts, Architectures and Applications*. Springer.

Anson, E. (1979). The semantics of graphical input. In *SIGGRAPH '79: Proceedings of the 6th annual conference on Computer graphics and interactive techniques*, pages 113–120, New York, NY, USA. ACM.

Anson, E. (1982). The device model of interaction. In *SIGGRAPH '82: Proceedings of the 9th annual conference on Computer graphics and interactive techniques*, pages 107–114, New York, NY, USA. ACM.

@Apache (last accessed December 2008a). Java2WSDL: Building WSDL from java. http://ws.apache.org/axis/java/user-guide.html#Java2WSDLBuildingWSDLFromJava.

@Apache (last accessed December 2008b). WSDL2Java: Building stubs, skeletons, and data types from WSDL. http://ws.apache.org/axis/java/user-guide.html#WSDL2JavaBuildingStubsSkeletonsAndDataTypesFromWSDL.

@Apache (last accessed October 2009). Apache XML-RPC. http://ws.apache.org/xmlrpc/.

Ballagas, R., Memon, F., Reiners, R., and Borchers, J. (2007). iStuff Mobile: Rapidly prototyping new mobile phone interfaces for ubiquitous computing. In *CHI '07: Proceedings of the SIGCHI Conference on Human Factors in Computing Systems*, pages 1107–1116, New York, NY, USA. ACM Press.

Ballagas, R., Ringel, M., Stone, M., and Borchers, J. (2003). istuff: a physical user interface toolkit for ubiquitous computing environments. In *CHI '03: Proceedings of the SIGCHI conference on Human factors in computing systems*, pages 537–544, New York, NY, USA. ACM.

Ballagas, R., Rohs, M., and Sheridan, J. (2005). Sweep and point & shoot: Phonecam-based interactions for large public displays. In *CHI '05: Proceedings of the SIGCHI Conference on Human Factors in Computing Systems*.

Ballagas, R., Rohs, M., Sheridan, J., and Borchers, J. (2006). The smart phone: A ubiquitous input device. *IEEE Pervasive Computing*, 5(1):70–77.

Ballagas, R., Rohs, M., Sheridan, J., and Borchers, J. (2008). The design space of ubiquitous mobile input. In Lumsden, J., editor, *Handbook of Research on User Interface Design and Evaluation for Mobile Technologies*. IGI Global, Hershey, PA, USA.

Barralon, N., Coutaz, J., and Lachenal, C. (2007). Coupling interaction resources and technical support. In Stephanidis, C., editor, *HCI (6)*, volume 4555 of *Lecture Notes in Computer Science*, pages 13–22. Springer.

Büchi, M. and Weck, W. (1997). A plea for grey-box components. Technical report, Turku Centre for Computer Science.

Büchi, M. and Weck, W. (1999). The greybox approach: When blackbox specifications hide too much. Technical report, Turku Centre for Computer Science.

Beringer, J. (2004). Reducing expertise tension. *Communications of the ACM*, 47(9):39–40.

Bharat, K. A. and Hudson, S. E. (1995). Supporting distributed, concurrent, one-way constraints in user interface applications. In *UIST '95: Proceedings of the 8th annual ACM symposium on User interface and software technology*, pages 121–132, New York, NY, USA. ACM.

Booch, G. (1991). *Object Oriented Design with Applications*. Benjamin/Cummings, Rewood City, CA.

Brinck, T. and Hill, R. D. (1993). Building shared graphical editors using the abstraction-link-view architecture. In *ECSCW'93: Proceedings of the third conference on European Conference on Computer-Supported Cooperative Work*, pages 311–324, Norwell, MA, USA. Kluwer Academic Publishers.

Calvary, G., Coutaz, J., and Nigay, L. (1997). From single-user architectural design to pac*: a generic software architecture model for cscw. In *CHI '97: Proceedings of the SIGCHI conference on Human factors in computing systems*, pages 242–249, New York, NY, USA. ACM.

Carmichael, A. (1999). Style guide for the design of interactive television services for elderly viewers. Technical report, Independent Television Commission, Kings Worthy Court, Winchester, UK.

Carriero, N. and Gelernter, D. (1989). Linda in context. *Communications of the ACM*, 32(4):444–458.

@COM (last accessed October 2009). Com: Component object model technologies. http://www.microsoft.com/com/default.mspx.

Coutaz, J. (1997). PAC-ing the architecture of your user interface. In Harrison, M. D. and Torres, J. C., editors, *DSV-IS*, pages 13–27. Springer.

Coutaz, J. (2006). Meta-user interfaces for ambient spaces. In Coninx, K., Luyten, K., and Schneider, K. A., editors, *TAMODIA*, volume 4385 of *Lecture Notes in Computer Science*, pages 1–15. Springer.

da Costa, C. A., Yamin, A. C., and Geyer, C. F. R. (2008). Toward a general software infrastructure for ubiquitous computing. *IEEE Pervasive Computing*, 7(1):64–73.

Davis, M. and Ellis, T. (1964). The RAND tablet: A man-machine graphical communication device. In *Proceedings of AFIP Fall Joint Computer Conference*, pages 325–331, Baltimore, Maryland. Spartan Books.

de Bruin, H. (2000). A grey-box approach to component composition. In *GCSE '99: Proceedings of the First International Symposium on Generative and Component-Based Software Engineering*, pages 195–209, London, UK. Springer-Verlag.

Dix, A., Finlay, J., Abowd, G. D., and Beale, R. (2004). *Human-computer interaction*. Prentice-Hall, 3rd edition.

Edmonds, E. (1982). The man-computer interface: A note on concepts and design. *International Journal of Man-Machine Studies*, 16(3):231–236.

Edmonds, E. (1992a). The emergence of the separable user interface. In [Edmonds, 1992b], pages 5–18.

Edmonds, E. (1992b). *The Separable User Interface*. Academic Press.

Eisenhauer, M., Lorenz, A., and Zimmermann, A. (2008). Interaction-kiosk for open human-computer interaction with pervasive services. In *Adjunct Proceedings of the 6th International Conference on Pervasive Computing*, pages 134–137. Österreichische Computer Gesellschaft.

Eisenhauer, M., Lorenz, A., Zimmermann, A., Duong, T., and James, F. (2005). Interaction by movement - one giant leap for natural interaction in mobile guides. In *Proceedings of the 4th Workshop on HCI in Mobile Guides*.

@Encarta (last accessed January 2008a). Encarta MSN: Architecture. http://encarta.msn.com/dictionary_/Architecture.html.

@Encarta (last accessed January 2008b). Encarta MSN dictionary. http://encarta.msn.com/encnet/features/dictionary/dictionaryhome.aspx.

@Encarta (last accessed January 2008c). Encarta MSN: Framework. http://encarta.msn.com/dictionary_/Framework.html.

@Encarta (last accessed January 2008d). Encarta MSN: Library. http://encarta.msn.com/dictionary_-/Library.html.

@Encarta (last accessed January 2008e). Encarta MSN: Toolkit. http://encarta.msn.com/dictionary_-/Toolkit.html.

English, W., Engelbart, D., and Berman, M. (1967). Display selection techniques for text manipulation. *Transactions of IEEE*, HFE-8:5–17.

Eustice, K., Lehman, T., Morales, A., Munson, M., Edlund, S., and Guillen, M. (1999). A universal information appliance. *IBM Systems Journal*, 38(4):575–601.

Fagan, M. E. (1986). Advances in software inspections. *IEEE Transactions on Software Engineering*, SE-12(7):744–751.

Fernández De Castro, C. (2008). The homemedia project, studying mobile interaction in ubiquitous home environments. Master's thesis, RWTH Aachen.

Fischer, G. (2002). Beyond "couch potatoes": From consumers to designers and active contributors. *First Monday*, 7(12).

Foley, J. D. and Wallace, V. L. (1974). The art of natural graphic man-machine conversation. *Proceedings of the IEEE*, 62(4):462–471.

Foley, J. D., Wallace, V. L., and Chan, P. (1984). The human factors of computer graphics interaction techniques. *IEEE Comput. Graph. Appl.*, 4(11):13–48.

Gamma, E., Helm, R., Johnson, R., and Vlissides, J. M. (1994). *Design Patterns: Elements of Reusable Object-Oriented Software*. Addison-Wesley Professional.

@Gerone (last accessed September 2009). Gerone soft: Code counter pro. http://www.geronesoft.com/.

Green, M. (1985). Report on dialogue specification tools. In [Pfaff, 1985], pages 9–20.

Greenberg, S. and Fitchett, C. (2001). Phidgets: easy development of physical interfaces through physical widgets. In *UIST '01: Proceedings of the 14th annual ACM symposium on User interface software and technology*, pages 209–218, New York, NY, USA. ACM.

Henderson, A. and Kyng, M. (1992). There's no place like home: continuing design in use. In Greenbaum, J. and Kyng, M., editors, *Design at work: cooperative design of computer systems*, pages 219–240. Lawrence Erlbaum Associates, Inc., Mahwah, NJ, USA.

Hill, R. D. (1992). The abstraction-link-view paradigm: using constraints to connect user interfaces to applications. In *CHI '92: Proceedings of the SIGCHI conference on Human factors in computing systems*, pages 335–342, New York, NY, USA. ACM.

Hill, R. D. (1993). The rendezvous constraint maintenance system. In *UIST '93: Proceedings of the 6th annual ACM symposium on User interface software and technology*, pages 225–234, New York, NY, USA. ACM.

Hill, R. D., Brinck, T., Rohall, S. L., Patterson, J. F., and Wilner, W. (1994). The rendezvous architecture and language for constructing multiuser applications. *ACM Trans. Comput.-Hum. Interact.*, 1(2):81–125.

Holleis, P. (2009). *Integrating Usability Models into Pervasive Application Development. Dissertation*. PhD thesis, LMU München: Fakultät für Mathematik, Informatik und Statistik.

Hong, J. I. and Landay, J. A. (2001). An infrastructure approach to context-aware computing. *Human-Computer Interaction*, 16(2-4):287–303.

Hurley, W. D. and Sibert, J. L. (1989). Modeling user interface-application interactions. *IEEE Software*, 06(1):71–77.

Hutchins, E., Hollan, J., and Norman, D. (1985). Direct manipulation interfaces. In Norman, D. A. and Draper, S. W., editors, *User centered system design*, pages 87–124. Lawrence Erlbaum Associates Inc, Hillsdale, NJ.

IEEE 1028 (4 Mar 1998). IEEE standard for software reviews. *IEEE Std 1028-1997*, pages –.

IEEE 1471 (July 15 2007). Systems and software engineering - recommended practice for architectural description of software-intensive systems. *ISO/IEC 42010 IEEE Std 1471-2000 First edition 2007-07-15*, pages c1–24.

IEEE 610 (10 Dec 1990). IEEE standard glossary of software engineering terminology. *IEEE Std 610.12-1990*, pages –.

Iftode, L., Borcea, C., Ravi, N., Kang, P., and Zhou, P. (2004). Smart phone: An embedded system for universal interactions. In *10th IEEE International Workshop on Future Trends of Distributed Computing Systems*.

ISO 14977 (1996). Information technology - syntactic metalanguage - extended bnf. *ISO/IEC 14977:1996*.

@JavaNCSS (last accessed August 2009). JavaNCSS - a source measurement suite for java. http://www.kclee.de/clemens/java/javancss/.

@JavaRMI (last accessed October 2009). Remote method invocation home. http://java.sun.com/javase/technologies/core/basic/rmi/index.jsp.

Jentsch, M. (2009). Spotlight - augmenting devices by pointing at them. In *Proceedings of the intl. InterMedia Summer School*, pages 109–115.

Jiang, H., Ofek, E., Moraveji, N., and Shi, Y. (2006). Direct pointer: direct manipulation for large-display interaction using handheld cameras. In *CHI '06: Proceedings of the SIGCHI Conference on Human Factors in Computing Systems*, pages 1107–1110. ACM Press.

Johanson, B. and Fox, A. (2002). The event heap: A coordination infrastructure for interactive workspaces. In *WMCSA '02: Proceedings of the Fourth IEEE Workshop on Mobile Computing Systems and Applications*, page 83, Washington, DC, USA. IEEE Computer Society.

Johanson, B., Fox, A., and Winograd, T. (2002). The interactive workspaces project: experiences with ubiquitous computing rooms. *Pervasive Computing, IEEE*, 1(2):67–74.

Johnson, R. E. and Foote, B. (1988). Designing reusable classes. *Journal of Object-Oriented Programming*, 1(2):22–35.

@JSR172 (last accessed May 2009). J2ME web services APIs (WSA), JSR 172. http://java.sun.com/products/wsa/.

Kapor, M. (1996). A software design manifesto. In [Winograd, 1996], pages 1–9.

Kendon, A. (1986). Current issues in the study of gestures. In Nespoulus, J., Peron, P., and Lecours, A. R., editors, *The Biological Foundations of Gestures: Motor and Semiotic Aspects*, pages 23–47. Lawrence Erlbaum Assoc.

Kindberg, T. and Fox, A. (2002). System software for ubiquitous computing. *IEEE Pervasive Computing*, 1(1):70–81.

Kjeldsen, R. (2006). Improvements in vision-based pointer control. In *Assets '06: Proceedings of the 8th international ACM SIGACCESS conference on Computers and accessibility*, pages 189–196, New York, NY, USA. ACM.

Koskela, T. and Väänänen-Vainio-Mattila, K. (2004). Evolution towards smart home environments: empirical evaluation of three user interfaces. *Personal Ubiquitous Computing*, 8(3-4):234–240.

Krasner, G. E. and Pope, S. T. (1988). A cookbook for using the model-view controller user interface paradigm in smalltalk-80. *J. Object Oriented Program.*, 1(3):26–49.

Lewis, J. (1995). IBM computer usability satisfaction questionnaires : psychometric evaluation and instructions for use. *International Journal of Human-Computer Interaction*, 7(1):57–78.

Lewis, T., Rosenstein, L., Pree, W., Weinand, A., Gamma, E., Calder, P., Andert, G., Vlissides, J., and Schmucker, K. (1995). Framework fundamentals. In Lewis, T., editor, *Object oriented application frameworks*, pages 27–44. Manning Publications Co., Greenwich, CT, USA.

Lichter, H. and Schneider, K. (1993). vis-a-vis: An object-oriented aplication framework for graphical design-tools. In Rix, J. and Schlechtendahl, E. G., editors, *Proceedings of the IFIP TC5/WG5.10 Working Conference on Interfaces in Industrial Systems for Production Engineering*, pages 43–57, Amsterdam, The Netherlands, The Netherlands. North-Holland Publishing Co.

Lieberman, H., Paterno, F., and Wulf, V., editors (2006). *End User Development*. Springer.

Lorenz, A., Eisenhauer, M., and Zimmermann, A. (2008). Elaborating a framework for open human computer interaction with ambient services. In *4th International Workshop on Pervasive Mobile Interaction Devices*, pages 171–174.

Lorenz, A., Fernandez de Castro, C., and Rukzio, E. (2009a). Using handheld devices for mobile interaction with displays in home environments. In *Proceedings of the 11th International Conference on Human-Computer Interaction with Mobile Devices and Services*, pages 133–142.

Lorenz, A., Pramudianto, F., and Zimmermann, A. (2009b). Lessons learned from open selection of input devices for a gaming application. In *Adjunct Proceedings of the 11th International Conference on Human-Computer Interaction with Mobile Devices and Services.*

Ludewig, J. and Lichter, H. (2007). *Software Engineering*. dpunkt.verlag, Heidelberg.

Lumsden, J. and Brewster, S. (2003). A paradigm shift: alternative interaction techniques for use with mobile & wearable devices. In *CASCON '03: Proceedings of the 2003 conference of the Centre for Advanced Studies on Collaborative research*, pages 197–210. IBM Press.

Marquardt, N. and Greenberg, S. (2007). Distributed physical interfaces with shared phidgets. In *TEI '07: Proceedings of the 1st international conference on Tangible and embedded interaction*, pages 13–20, New York, NY, USA. ACM.

Moggridge, B. (2006). *Designing Interactions*. MIT Press.

Moran, T. P. (1980). A framework for studying human-computer interaction. In Guedij, R., ten Hagen, P., Hopgood, F., Tucker, H., and Duce, D., editors, *Methodology of Interaction*, pages 293–301. North-Holland, Amsterdam.

Mørch, A. (1997). Three levels of end-user tailoring: customization, integration, and extension. In Kyng, M. and Mathiassen, L., editors, *Computers and design in context*, pages 51–76. MIT Press, Cambridge, MA, USA.

Myers, B. A. (2002). Mobile devices for control. In *Mobile HCI '02: Proceedings of the 4th International Symposium on Mobile Human-Computer Interaction*, pages 1–8, London, UK. Springer-Verlag.

Newman, W. (1968a). A system for interactive graphical programming. In *Proceedings of AFIP Spring Joint Computer Conference*, volume 32, pages 47–54.

Newman, W. M. (1968b). A graphical technique for numerical input. *The Computer Journal*, 11(1):63–64.

Nichols, J. (2001). Using handhelds as controls for everyday appliances: A paper prototype study. In *CHI '01: Extended Abstracts of the SIGCHI Conference on Human Factors in Computing Systems*, pages 443–444.

Nichols, J. and Myers, B. A. (2003). Studying the use of handhelds to control smart appliances. In *ICDCSW '03: Proceedings of the 23rd International Conference on Distributed Computing Systems*, page 274, Washington, DC, USA. IEEE Computer Society.

Nichols, J., Myers, B. A., Higgins, M., Hughes, J., Harris, T. K., Rosenfeld, R., and Pignol, M. (2002). Generating remote control interfaces for complex appliances. In *15th annual ACM symposium on User interface software and technology*, Paris, France. ACM Press.

Nielsen, J. (1993). Noncommand user interfaces. *Communications of the ACM*, 36(4):83–99.

Niemelä, E. and Latvakoski, J. (2004). Survey of requirements and solutions for ubiquitous software. In *MUM '04: Proceedings of the 3rd international conference on Mobile and ubiquitous multimedia*, pages 71–78, New York, NY, USA. ACM.

@ODLIS (last accessed January 2008). Online dictionary for library and information science: Toolkit. http://lu.com/odlis/odlis_t.cfm#toolkit.

Oh, J.-Y. and Stuerzlinger, W. (2002). Laser pointers as collaborative pointing devices. In *Proceedings of Graphics Interface'02*.

Olsen, D. R. (1992). *User Interface Management Systems: Models and Algorithms*. Morgan Kaufmann.

Olsen, D. R. (2007). Evaluating user interface systems research. In *UIST '07: Proceedings of the 20th annual ACM symposium on User interface software and technology*, pages 251–258, New York, NY, USA. ACM Press.

Olsen, D. R., Jefferies, S., Nielsen, T., Moyes, W., and Fredrickson, P. (2000). Cross-modal interaction using xweb. In *13th Annual ACM Symposium on User Interface Software and Technology*, pages 191–200. ACM Press.

Olsen, D. R. and Nielsen, T. (2001). Laser pointer interaction. In *CHI '01: Proceedings of the SIGCHI Conference on Human Factors in Computing Systems*.

@OMG (2002). Common object request broker architecture (CORBA), v3.0. http://www.omg.org/technology/documents/formal/corba_2.htm.

@OMG (last accessed July 2009). Orb basics. http://www.omg.org/gettingstarted/orb_basics.htm.

Orfali, R., Harkey, D., and Edwards, J. (1996). *The Essential Distributed Objects Survival Guide*. Wiley.

Orfali, R., Harkey, D., and Edwards, J. (1999). *Client/Server Survival Guide*. Wiley, third edition.

Oviatt, S. (2000). Multimodal interface research: A science without borders. In *Proceedings of the 6. International Conference on Spoken Language Processing*.

Pfaff, G. E. (1985). *User Interface Management Systems*. Springer-Verlag New York, Inc.

Ponnekanti, S., Lee, B., Fox, A., Hanrahan, P., and Winograd, T. (2001). Icrafter: A service framework for ubiquitous computing environments. In Abowd, G. D., Brumitt, B., and Shafer, S. A., editors, *Proceedings of the 3rd international conference on Ubiquitous Computing*, volume 2201 of *Lecture Notes in Computer Science*, pages 56–75. Springer.

Pree, W. (1997). *Komponentenbasierte Softwareentwicklung mit Frameworks*. dpunkt.verlag, Heidelberg.

Pree, W. and Sikora, H. (1997). Design patterns for object-oriented software development. In *Proceedings of the 19th International Conference on Software Engineering*, pages 663–664.

Reenskaug, T. (1995). *Working with Objects - The OOram Software Engineering Method*. Manning Publications Co.

Reiners, R. (2009). Discovering the ubiquitous world - the ubilens approach. In *Proceedings of the intl. InterMedia Summer School*, pages 92–99.

Reiners, R., Jentsch, M., and Prause, C. (2009). Interaction metaphors for the exploration of ubiquitous environments. In *Proceedings of the 5th intl. conference on ICT that makes the difference - The future of Ambient Intelligence and ICT for Security*. to appear.

Righetti, X., Peternier, A., Hopmann, M., and Thalmann, D. (2008). Design and Implementation of a wearable, context-aware MR framework for the Chloe@University application. In *13th IEEE International Conference on Emerging Technologies and Factory Automation*, pages 1362–1369.

Roduner, C., Langheinrich, M., Floerkemeier, C., and Schwarzentrub, B. (2007). Operating appliances with mobile phones - strengths and limits of a universal interaction device. In *5th International Conference on Pervasive Computing*, pages 198–215, Toronto, Canada. LNCS, Springer, Berlin-Heidelberg.

Roman, M. (2003). *An Application Framework for Active Space Applications*. PhD thesis, University of Illinois at Urbana-Champaign.

Roman, M. and Campbell, R. H. (2000). Gaia: enabling active spaces. In *ACM SIGOPS European Workshop*, pages 229–234. ACM.

Roman, M., Hess, C. K., Ranganathan, A., Madhavarapu, P., Borthakur, B., Viswanathan, P., Cerqueira, R., Campbell, R. H., and Mickunas, M. D. (2001). Gaiaos: An infrastructure for active spaces. Technical report, University of Illinois at Urbana-Champaign, Champaign, IL, USA.

Rosenthal, D. S. H., Michener, J. C., Pfaff, G., Kessener, R., and Sabin, M. (1982). The detailed semantics of graphics input devices. *SIGGRAPH Computer Graphics*, 16(3):33–38.

Rosson, M. B. and Carroll, J. M. (2001). *Usability engineering: scenario-based development of human computer interaction*. Morgan Kaufmann, Redwood City, CA.

Ruh, W., Herron, T., and Klinker, P. (2000). *IIOP Complete: Understanding CORBA and Middleware Interoperability*. Addison-Wesley.

Rukzio, E. (2006). *Physical Mobile Interactions: Mobile Devices as Pervasive Mediators for Interactions with the Real World*. PhD thesis, Faculty of Mathematics, Computer Science and Statistics, University of Munich.

Rukzio, E., Broll, G., and Wetzstein, S. (2008). The physical mobile interaction framework (PMIF). Technical Report LMU-MI-2008-2, Department of Computer Science, University of Munich.

Rukzio, E., Wetzstein, S., and Schmidt, A. (2005). A framework for mobile interactions with the physical world. In *Proceedings of Wireless Personal Mulitmedia Communication*.

Santos, A. L., Lopes, A., and Koskimies, K. (2007). Framework specialization aspects. In *AOSD '07: Proceedings of the 6th international conference on Aspect-oriented software development*, pages 14–24, New York, NY, USA. ACM.

Satyanarayanan, M. (2002). A catalyst for mobile and ubiquitous computing. *IEEE Pervasive Computing*, 1(1):2–5.

Schlömer, T., Poppinga, B., Henze, N., and Boll, S. (2008). Gesture recognition with a wii controller. In *Proceedings of the 2nd international conference on Tangible and embedded interaction (TEI 2008)*, pages 11–14, New York, NY, USA. ACM.

Shneiderman, B. (1983). Direct manipulation: A step beyond programming languages. *Computer*, 16(8):57–69.

Sibert, J., Belliardi, R., and Kamran, A. (1985). Some thoughts on the interface between user interface management systems and application software. In [Pfaff, 1985], pages 183–192.

Smith, G. C. (2006). What is interactiondesign? In [Moggridge, 2006].

Snell, J., MacLeod, K., and Kulchenko, P. (2001). *Programming Web Applications with SOAP*. O'Reilly.

Sommerville, I. (2007). *Software Engineering*. Addison Wesley, 8th edition.

Srinivasan, R. (1995). Rpc: Remote procedure call protocol specification version 2. RFC 1831. http://www.rfc-archive.org/getrfc.php?rfc=1831.

Stokoe, W. (1960). Sign language structure: An outline of the visual communication systems of the american deaf. *Studies in Linguistics, occasional papers*, 8.

@Sun (last accessed December 2008). Sun java wireless toolkit for CLDC. http://java.sun.com/products/sjwtoolkit/index.jsp.

Szekely, P. A. (1987). *Separating the user interface from the functionality of application programs*. PhD thesis, Carnegie Mellon University, Pittsburgh, PA, USA.

Tandler, P. (2001). Software infrastructure for ubiquitous computing environments: Supporting synchronous collaboration with heterogeneous devices. In *Proceedings of the 3rd international conference on Ubiquitous Computing*, pages 96–115.

Tandler, P. (2004). The beach application model and software framework for synchronous collaboration in ubiquitous computing environments. *J. Syst. Softw.*, 69(3):267–296.

Thomas, J. J. and Hamlin, G. (1983). Graphical input interaction technique (GIIT). *SIGGRAPH Computer Graphics*, 17(1):5–30.

@UDDI (last accessed March 2008). Universal description, discovery and integration of web services. http://www.uddi.org.

Ulmer, B. and Ishii, H. (2000). Emerging frameworks for tangible user interfaces. *IBM Systems Journal*, 39(3/4).

Vinoski, S. (1997). CORBA: Integrating diverse applications within distributed heterogeneous environments. *IEEE Communications Magazine*, 14(2).

@VLC (last accessed October 2009a). Mediacontrolapi. http://wiki.videolan.org/MediaControlAPI.

@VLC (last accessed October 2009b). VLC media player - open-source multimedia framework and player. http://www.videolan.org/vlc/.

@VLC (last accessed October 2009c). VLC play howto - basic use. http://wiki.videolan.org/Documentation:Play_HowTo/Basic_Use#Hotkeys.

@W3C (2000). W3C: Simple object access protocol (soap) 1.1. http://www.w3.org/TR/2000/NOTE-SOAP-20000508/.

@W3C (2001). Web services description language (WSDL) 1.1. http://www.w3.org/TR/wsdl.

@W3C (2007). Web services description language (WSDL) version 2.0 part 1: Core language. http://www.w3.org/TR/wsdl20/.

@W3C (last accessed December 2008). Extensible markup language (XML). http://www.xmlrpc.org/.

Wallace, V. L. (1976). The semantics of graphic input devices. *SIGGRAPH Computer Graphics*, 10(1):61–65.

Weiser, M. (1991). The computer for the twenty-first century. *Scientific American*, pages 94–104.

Weiser, M. (1994). The world is not a desktop. *Interactions*, pages 7–8.

White, J. E. (1976). A high-level framework for network-based resource sharing. RFC 707. http://www.rfc-archive.org/getrfc.php?rfc=707.

White, J. E. (1977). Elements of a distributed programming system. *Comput. Lang.*, 2(14):117–134.

@Wikipedia (last accessed July 2008). Wikipedia, the free encyclopedia: Software inspection. http://en.wikipedia.org/wiki/Software_inspection.

Winograd, T. (1996). *Bringing Design to Software*. Addison-Wesley.

Winograd, T. (1997). The design of interaction. In Denning, P. J. and Metcalfe, R. M., editors, *Beyond calculation: the next fifty years*, pages 149–161. Copernicus, New York, NY, USA.

Wu, Y. and Huang, T. (1999). Human hand modeling, analysis and animation in the context of hci. In *IEEE Intl. conf. Image Processing*.

Wulf, V. and Golombek, B. (2001). Direct activation: A concept to encourage tailoring activities. *Behaviour & Information Technology*, 20(4):249–263.

Wundt, W. (1973). *The language of gestures*. The Hague, Mouton.

@XML-RPC (last accessed March 2008). XML-RPC home page. http://www.xmlrpc.org/.

@XNA (last accessed October 2008). XNA developer center. http://msdn.microsoft.com/en-us/xna/default.aspx.

Zimmermann, A. (2007). *Context Management and Personalization: A Tool Suite for Context and User Aware Computing*. PhD thesis, Rheinisch-Westfälische Technischen Hochschule Aachen, Aachen, Germany.

Zimmermann, A. and Lorenz, A. (2008). LISTEN: a user-adaptive audio-augmented museum guide. *User Modeling and User-Adapted Interaction*, 18(5):389–416.

Index

Printed by Books on Demand GmbH, Norderstedt / Germany